FUNNY STORIES

by
JIMMY GOWNLEY

A Publication of Renaissance Press

Amelia Rules! Funny Stories

Dedicated with love to my parents,
James "Rock" Gownley
and
Anna Mae Gownley.
And to the memory of my grandmother,
Anna McAndrew.
I got somewhere with the books.

Portions of this book originally appeared in
Amelia Rules! comic books published by Renaissance Press

A Renaissance Press Book

Renaissance Press
PO Box 5060
Harrisburg, PA 17110

www.ameliarules.com

ISBN 978-0-9796052-0-8

First Renaissance Press edition 2007
10 9 8 7 6 5 4 3 2 1

Editor: Michael Cohen
Marketing and Promotion: Karen E. A. Gownley
Director of Publishing and Operations: Harold Buchholz
Brand Manager: Ben Haber

Printed in India

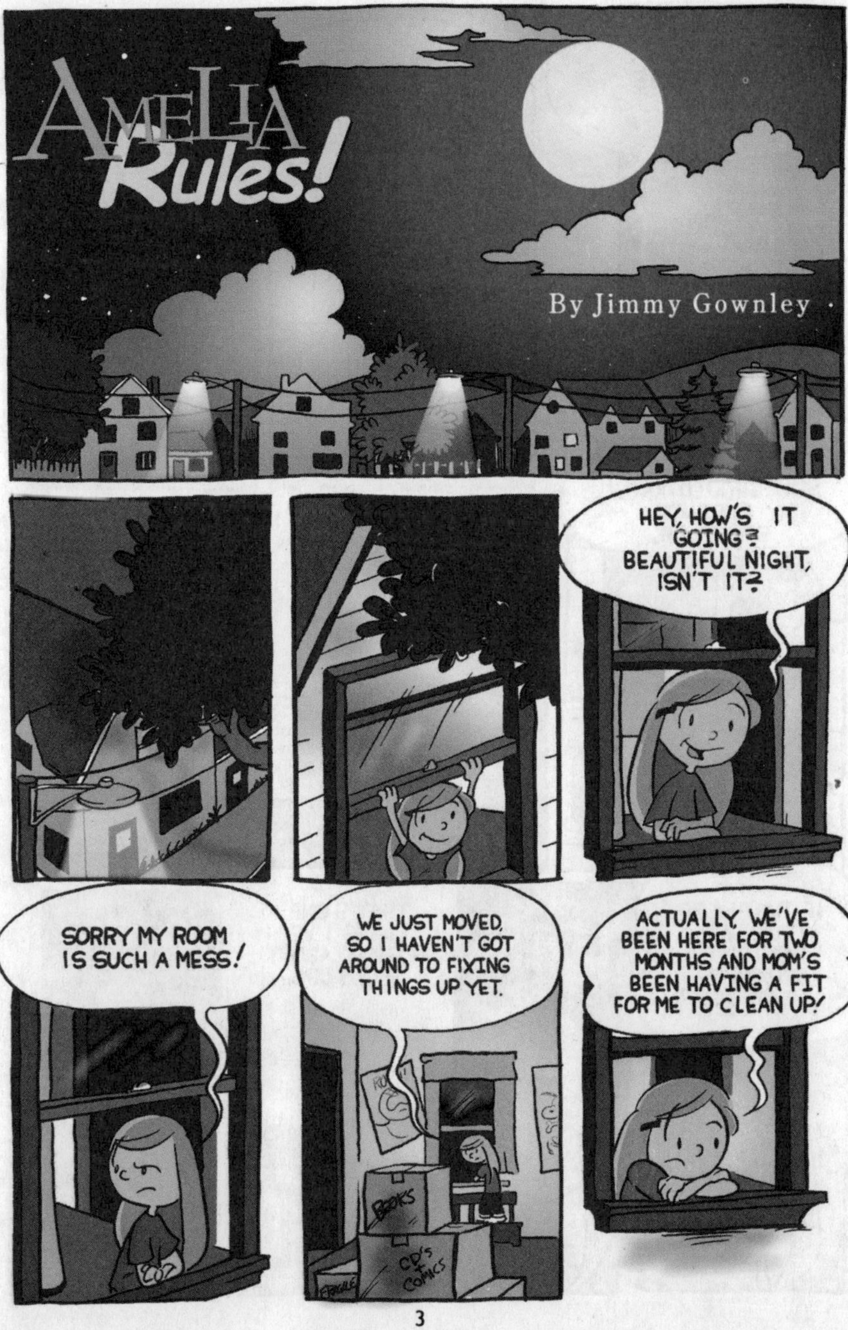
AMELIA Rules!
By Jimmy Gownley
HEY, HOW'S IT GOING? BEAUTIFUL NIGHT, ISN'T IT?
SORRY MY ROOM IS SUCH A MESS!
WE JUST MOVED, SO I HAVEN'T GOT AROUND TO FIXING THINGS UP YET.
BOOKS
CD'S + COMICS
ACTUALLY, WE'VE BEEN HERE FOR TWO MONTHS AND MOM'S BEEN HAVING A FIT FOR ME TO CLEAN UP!

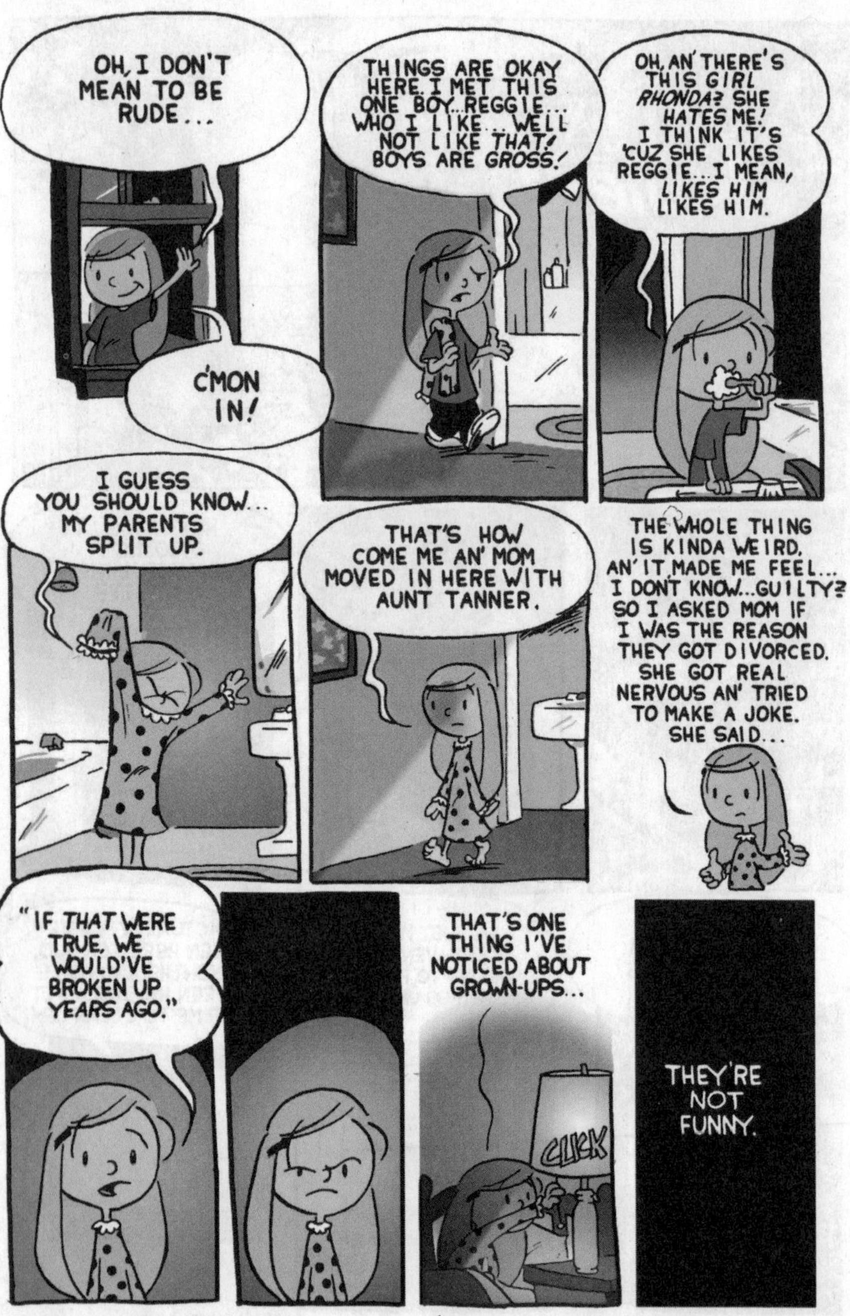
OH, I DON'T MEAN TO BE RUDE...
C'MON IN!
THINGS ARE OKAY HERE. I MET THIS ONE BOY...REGGIE... WHO I LIKE... WELL NOT LIKE THAT! BOYS ARE GROSS!
OH, AN' THERE'S THIS GIRL RHONDA? SHE HATES ME! I THINK IT'S 'CUZ SHE LIKES REGGIE...I MEAN, LIKES HIM LIKES HIM.
I GUESS YOU SHOULD KNOW... MY PARENTS SPLIT UP.
THAT'S HOW COME ME AN' MOM MOVED IN HERE WITH AUNT TANNER.
THE WHOLE THING IS KINDA WEIRD, AN' IT MADE ME FEEL... I DON'T KNOW...GUILTY? SO I ASKED MOM IF I WAS THE REASON THEY GOT DIVORCED. SHE GOT REAL NERVOUS AN' TRIED TO MAKE A JOKE. SHE SAID...
"IF THAT WERE TRUE, WE WOULD'VE BROKEN UP YEARS AGO."
THAT'S ONE THING I'VE NOTICED ABOUT GROWN-UPS...
CLICK
THEY'RE NOT FUNNY.

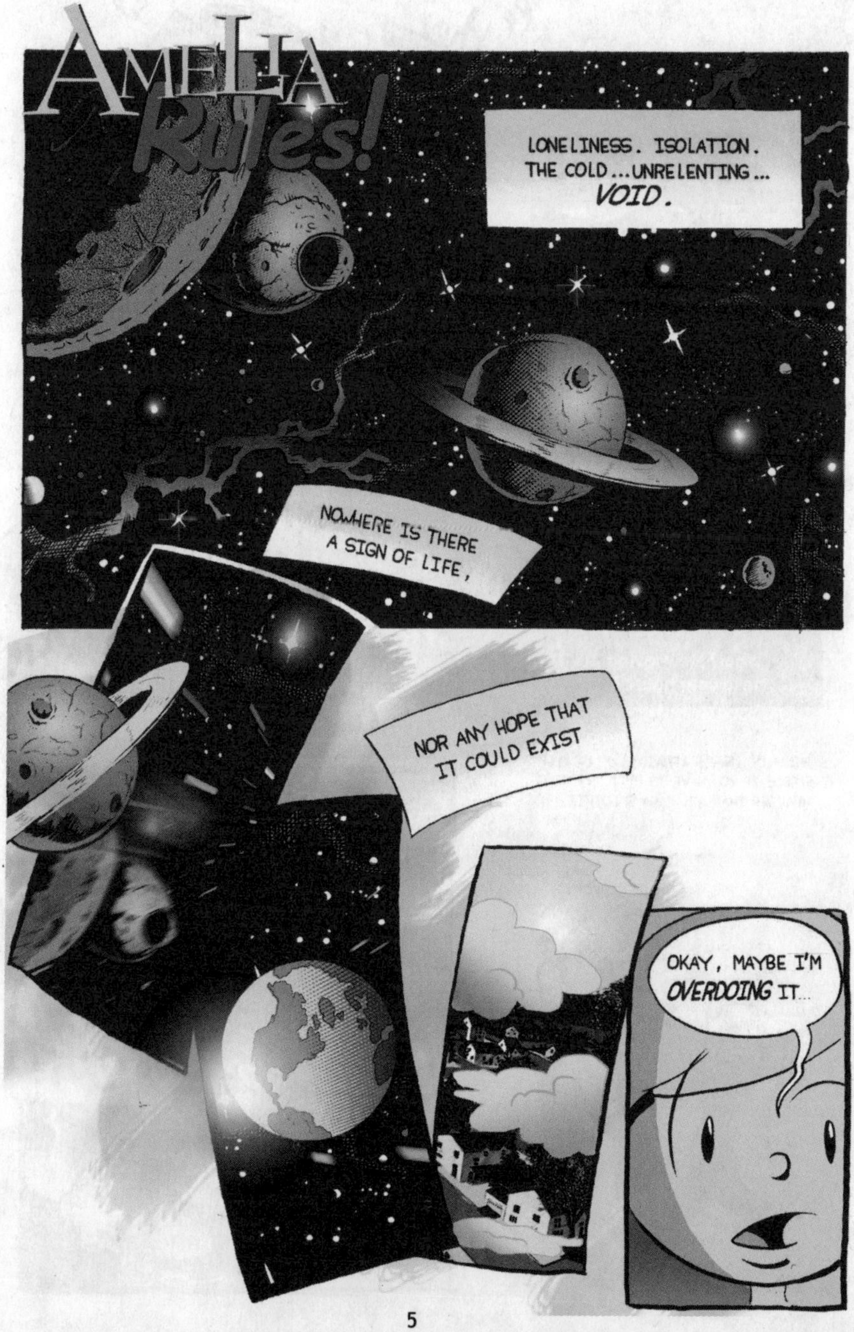
AMELIA Rules!
LONELINESS. ISOLATION. THE COLD... UNRELENTING... *VOID*.
NOWHERE IS THERE A SIGN OF LIFE,
NOR ANY HOPE THAT IT COULD EXIST
OKAY, MAYBE I'M *OVERDOING* IT...

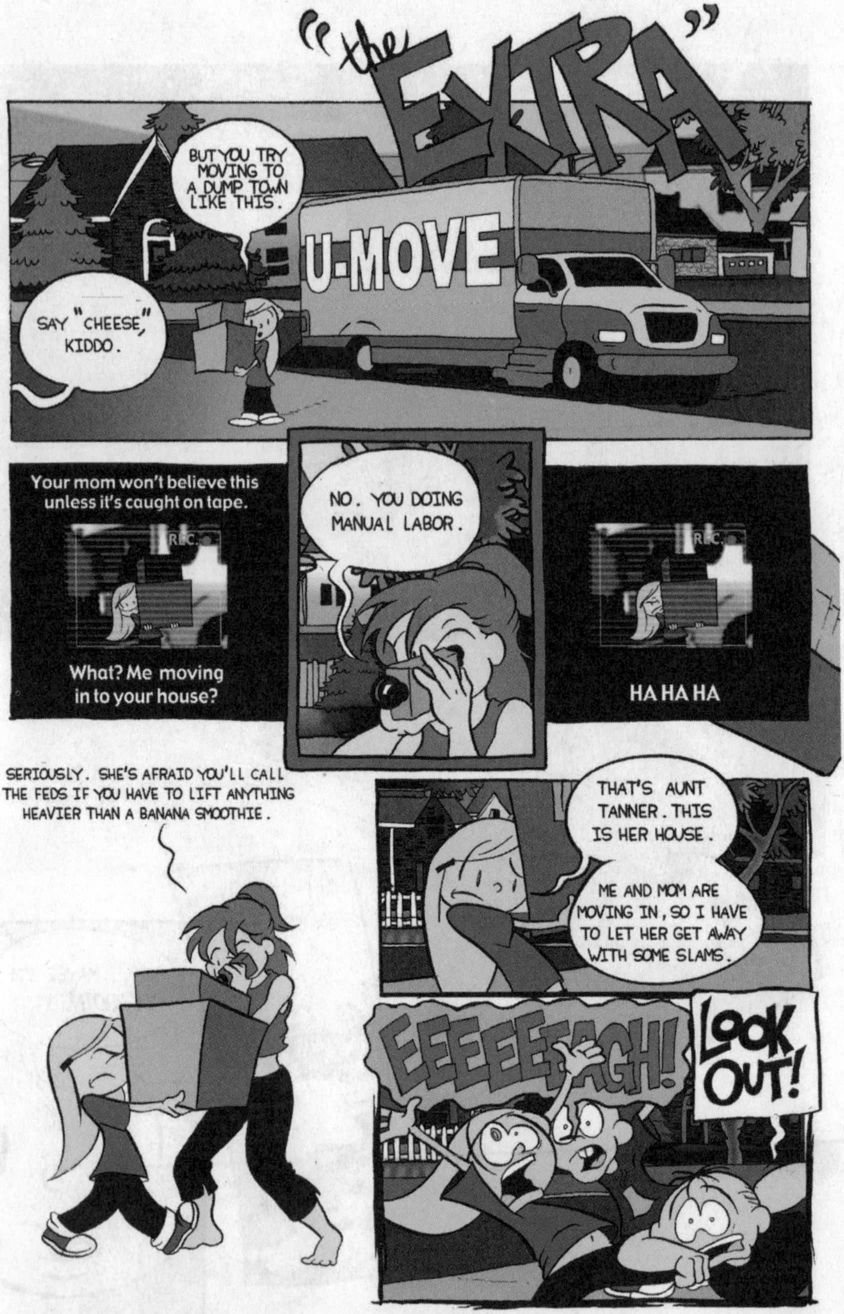
"the EXTRA"
BUT YOU TRY MOVING TO A DUMP TOWN LIKE THIS.
U-MOVE
SAY "CHEESE," KIDDO.
Your mom won't believe this unless it's caught on tape.
REC.
What? Me moving in to your house?
NO. YOU DOING MANUAL LABOR.
REC.
HA HA HA
SERIOUSLY. SHE'S AFRAID YOU'LL CALL THE FEDS IF YOU HAVE TO LIFT ANYTHING HEAVIER THAN A BANANA SMOOTHIE.
THAT'S AUNT TANNER. THIS IS HER HOUSE.
ME AND MOM ARE MOVING IN, SO I HAVE TO LET HER GET AWAY WITH SOME SLAMS.
EEEEEEAGH!
LOOK OUT!

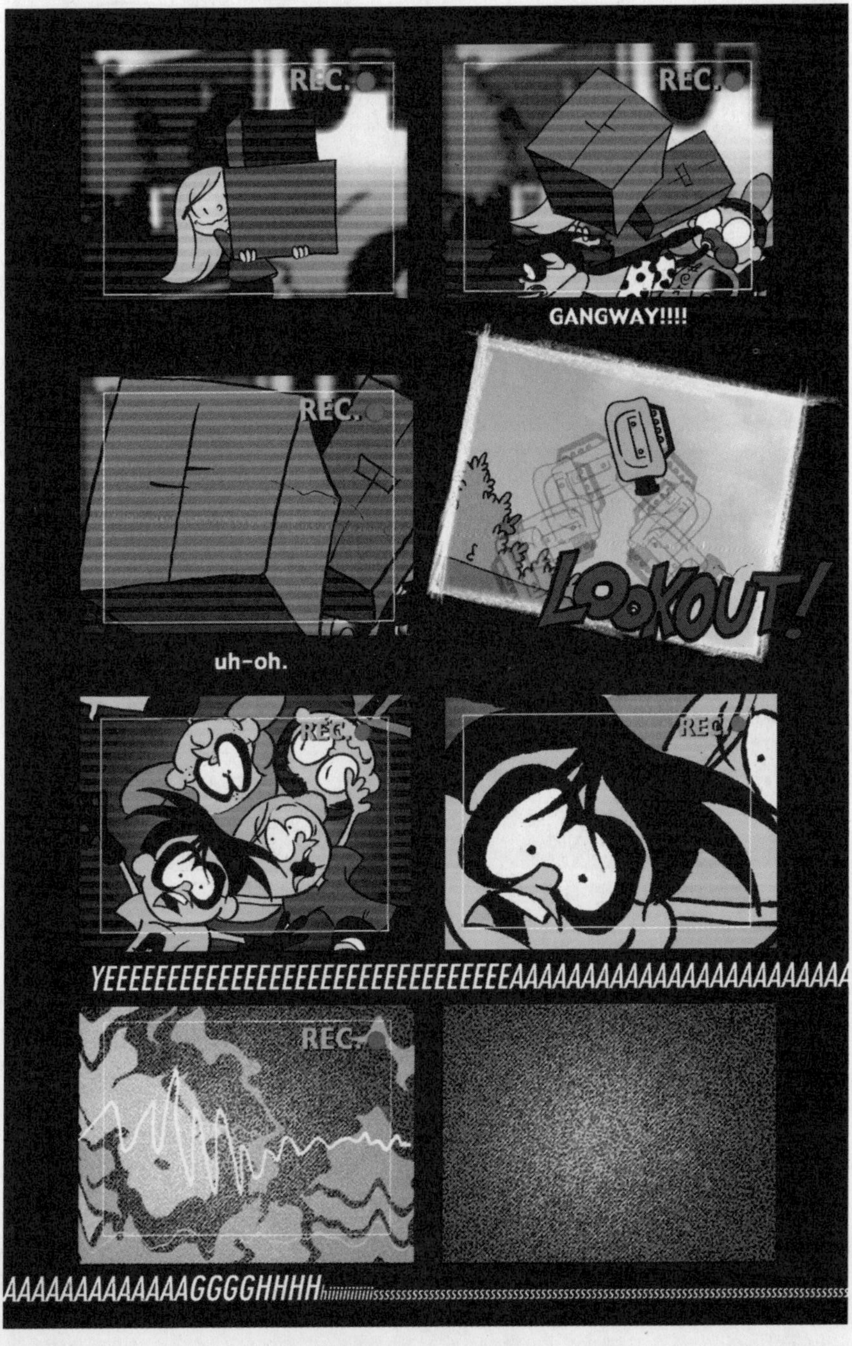

REC.
REC.
GANGWAY!!!!
REC.
LOOKOUT!
uh-oh.
REC.
REC.
YEEEEEEEEEEEEEEEEEEEEEEEEEEEEEEEEAAAAAAAAAAAAAAAAAAAAAAAAA
REC.
AAAAAAAAAAAAAAGGGGHHHHhiiiiiiiiiissssssssssssssssssssssssssssssssssss

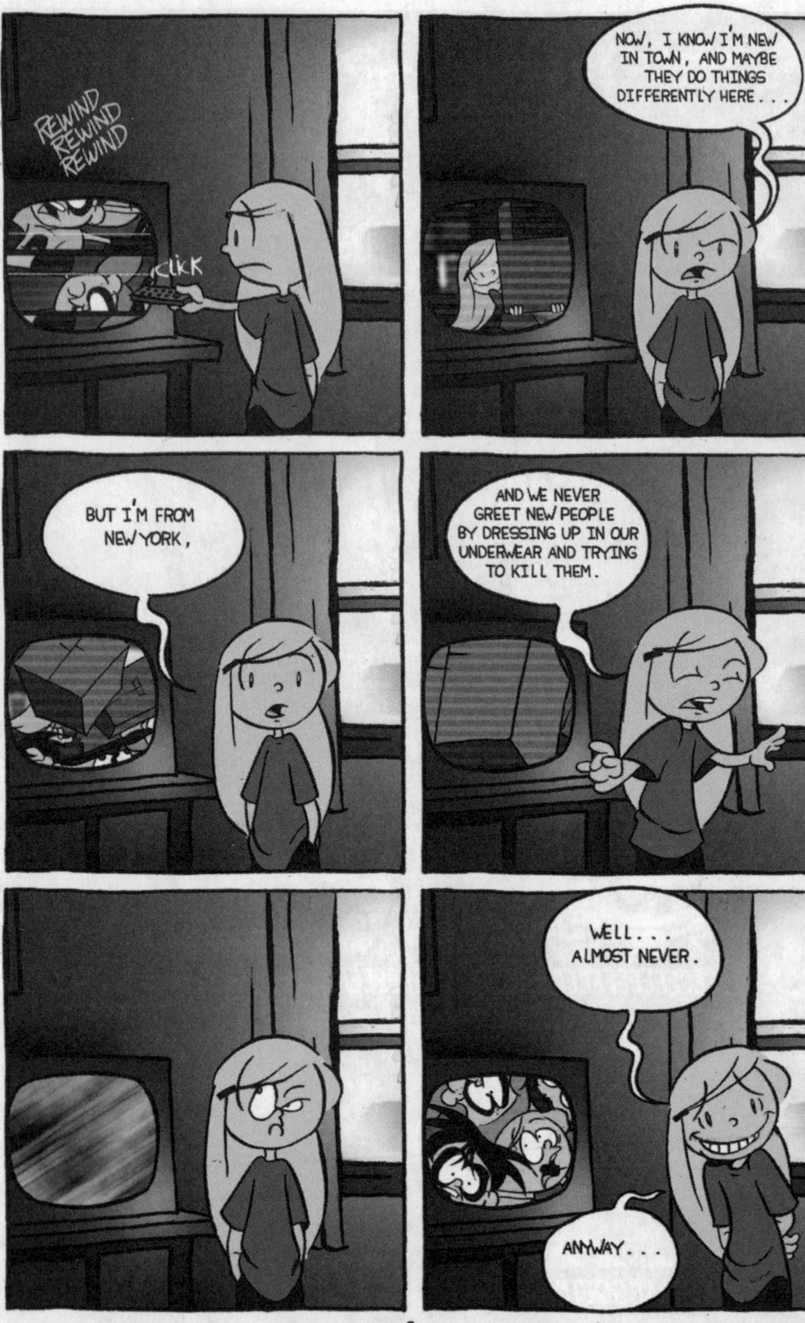
REWIND REWIND REWIND
CLICK
NOW, I KNOW I'M NEW IN TOWN, AND MAYBE THEY DO THINGS DIFFERENTLY HERE...
BUT I'M FROM NEW YORK,
AND WE NEVER GREET NEW PEOPLE BY DRESSING UP IN OUR UNDERWEAR AND TRYING TO KILL THEM.
WELL... ALMOST NEVER.
ANYWAY...

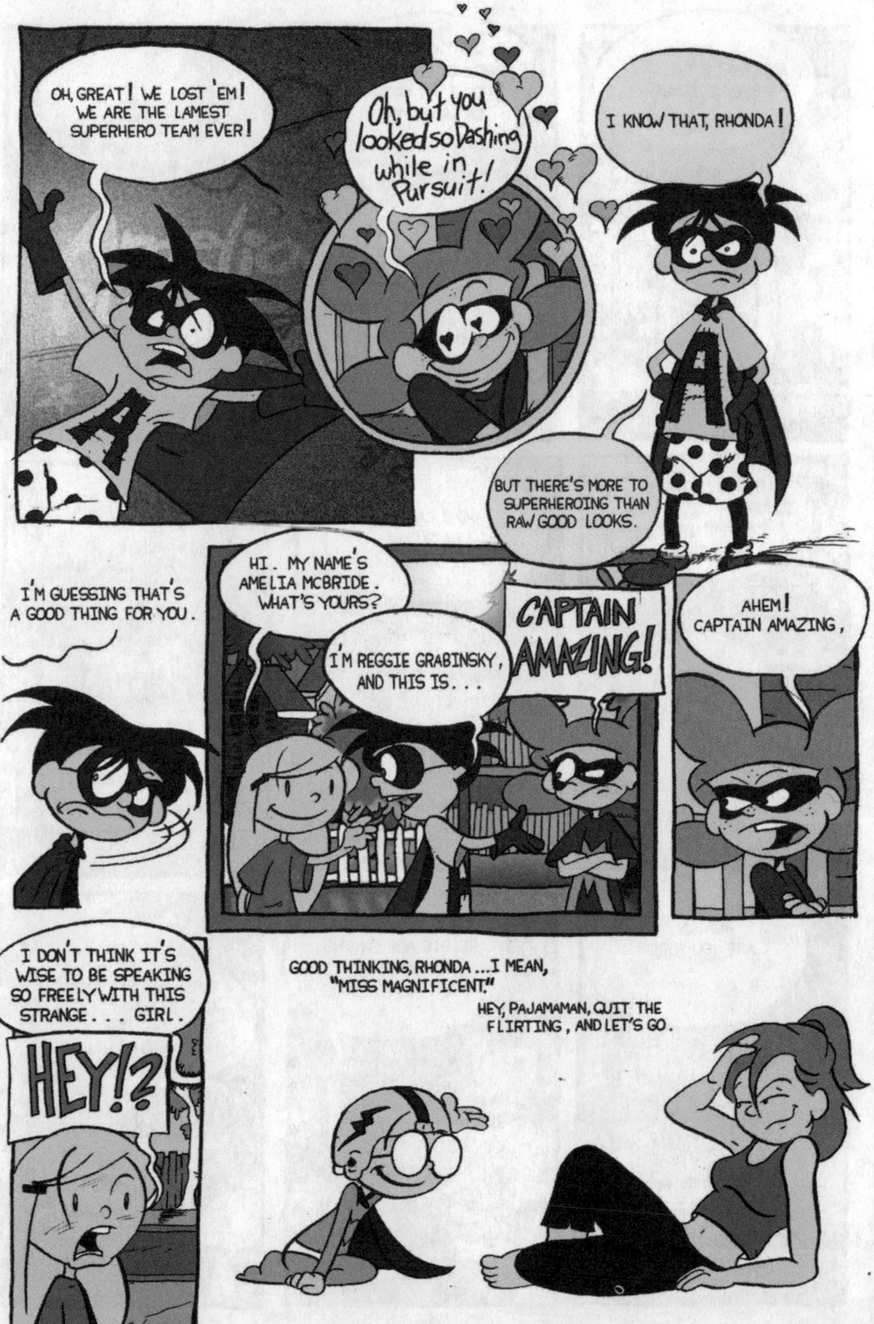
OH, GREAT! WE LOST 'EM! WE ARE THE LAMEST SUPERHERO TEAM EVER!
Oh, but you looked so Dashing while in Pursuit!
I KNOW THAT, RHONDA!
BUT THERE'S MORE TO SUPERHEROING THAN RAW GOOD LOOKS.
I'M GUESSING THAT'S A GOOD THING FOR YOU.
HI. MY NAME'S AMELIA MCBRIDE. WHAT'S YOURS?
I'M REGGIE GRABINSKY, AND THIS IS . . .
CAPTAIN AMAZING!
AHEM! CAPTAIN AMAZING,
I DON'T THINK IT'S WISE TO BE SPEAKING SO FREELY WITH THIS STRANGE . . . GIRL.
HEY!?
GOOD THINKING, RHONDA ...I MEAN, "MISS MAGNIFICENT."
HEY, PAJAMAMAN, QUIT THE FLIRTING, AND LET'S GO.

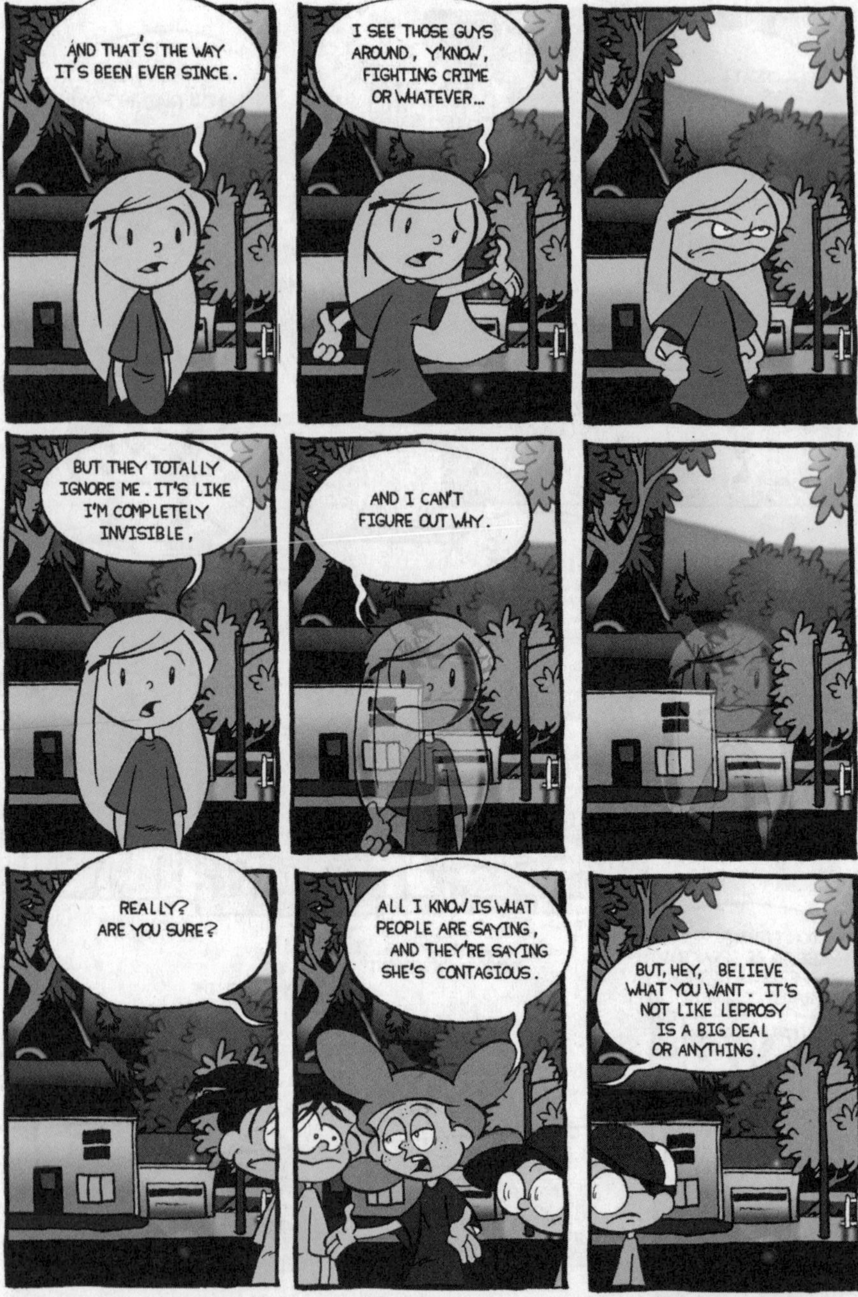
AND THAT'S THE WAY IT'S BEEN EVER SINCE.
I SEE THOSE GUYS AROUND, Y'KNOW, FIGHTING CRIME OR WHATEVER...
BUT THEY TOTALLY IGNORE ME. IT'S LIKE I'M COMPLETELY INVISIBLE,
AND I CAN'T FIGURE OUT WHY.
REALLY? ARE YOU SURE?
ALL I KNOW IS WHAT PEOPLE ARE SAYING, AND THEY'RE SAYING SHE'S CONTAGIOUS.
BUT, HEY, BELIEVE WHAT YOU WANT. IT'S NOT LIKE LEPROSY IS A BIG DEAL OR ANYTHING.

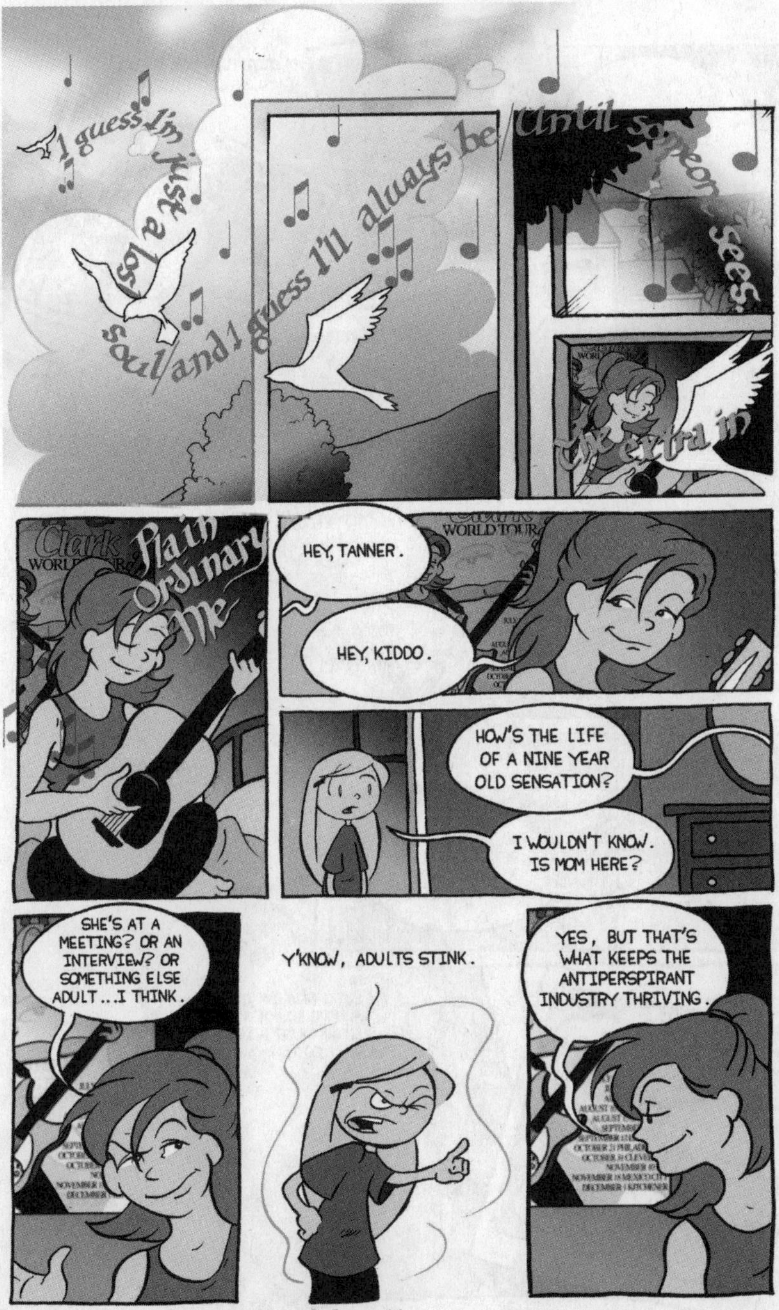
I guess I'm just a lost soul/and I guess I'll always be/Until someone sees
the extra in
Plain Ordinary Me
Clark
WORLD TOUR
HEY, TANNER.
HEY, KIDDO.
HOW'S THE LIFE OF A NINE YEAR OLD SENSATION?
I WOULDN'T KNOW. IS MOM HERE?
SHE'S AT A MEETING? OR AN INTERVIEW? OR SOMETHING ELSE ADULT...I THINK.
Y'KNOW, ADULTS STINK.
YES, BUT THAT'S WHAT KEEPS THE ANTIPERSPIRANT INDUSTRY THRIVING.

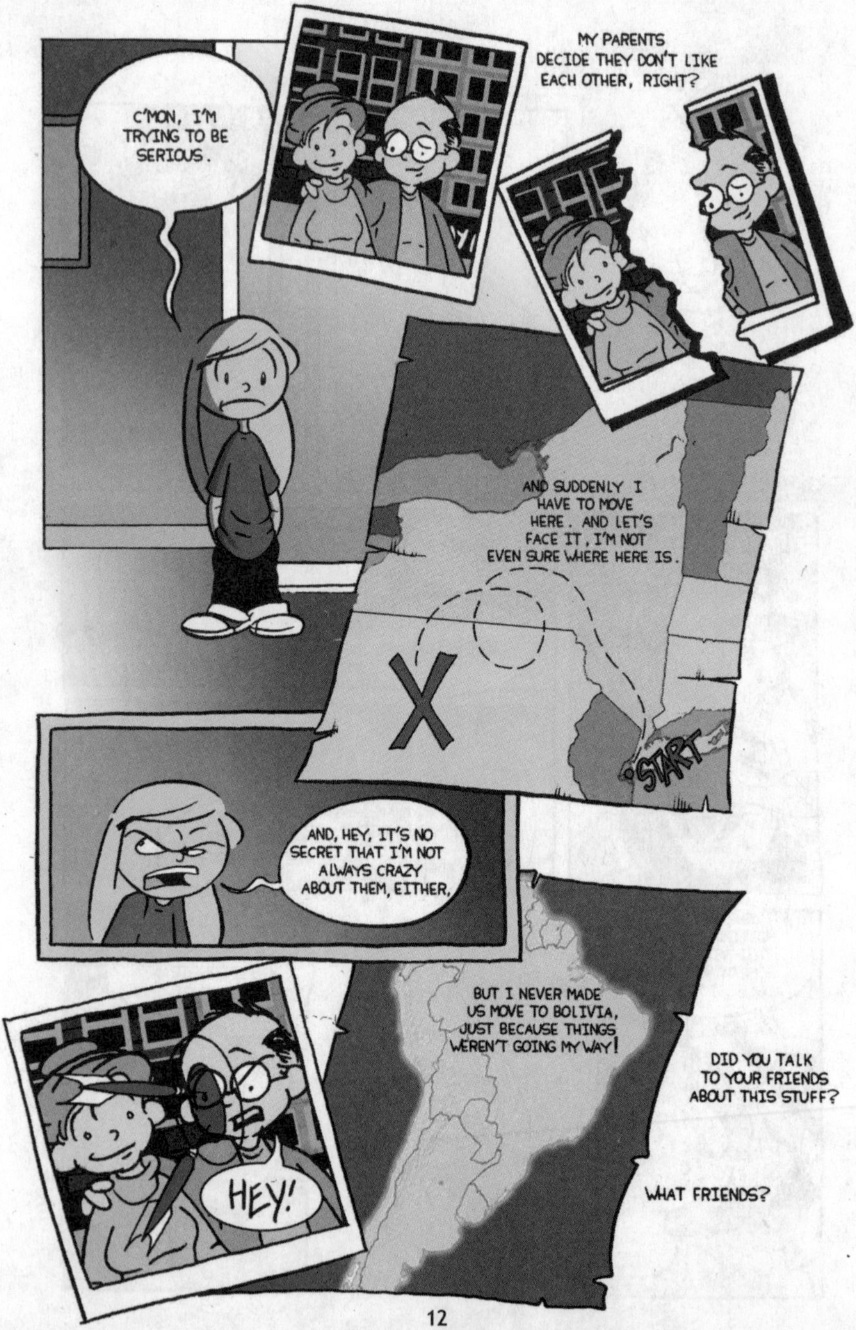
C'MON, I'M TRYING TO BE SERIOUS.
MY PARENTS DECIDE THEY DON'T LIKE EACH OTHER, RIGHT?
AND SUDDENLY I HAVE TO MOVE HERE. AND LET'S FACE IT, I'M NOT EVEN SURE WHERE HERE IS.
X
START
AND, HEY, IT'S NO SECRET THAT I'M NOT ALWAYS CRAZY ABOUT THEM, EITHER,
BUT I NEVER MADE US MOVE TO BOLIVIA, JUST BECAUSE THINGS WEREN'T GOING MY WAY!
HEY!
DID YOU TALK TO YOUR FRIENDS ABOUT THIS STUFF?
WHAT FRIENDS?

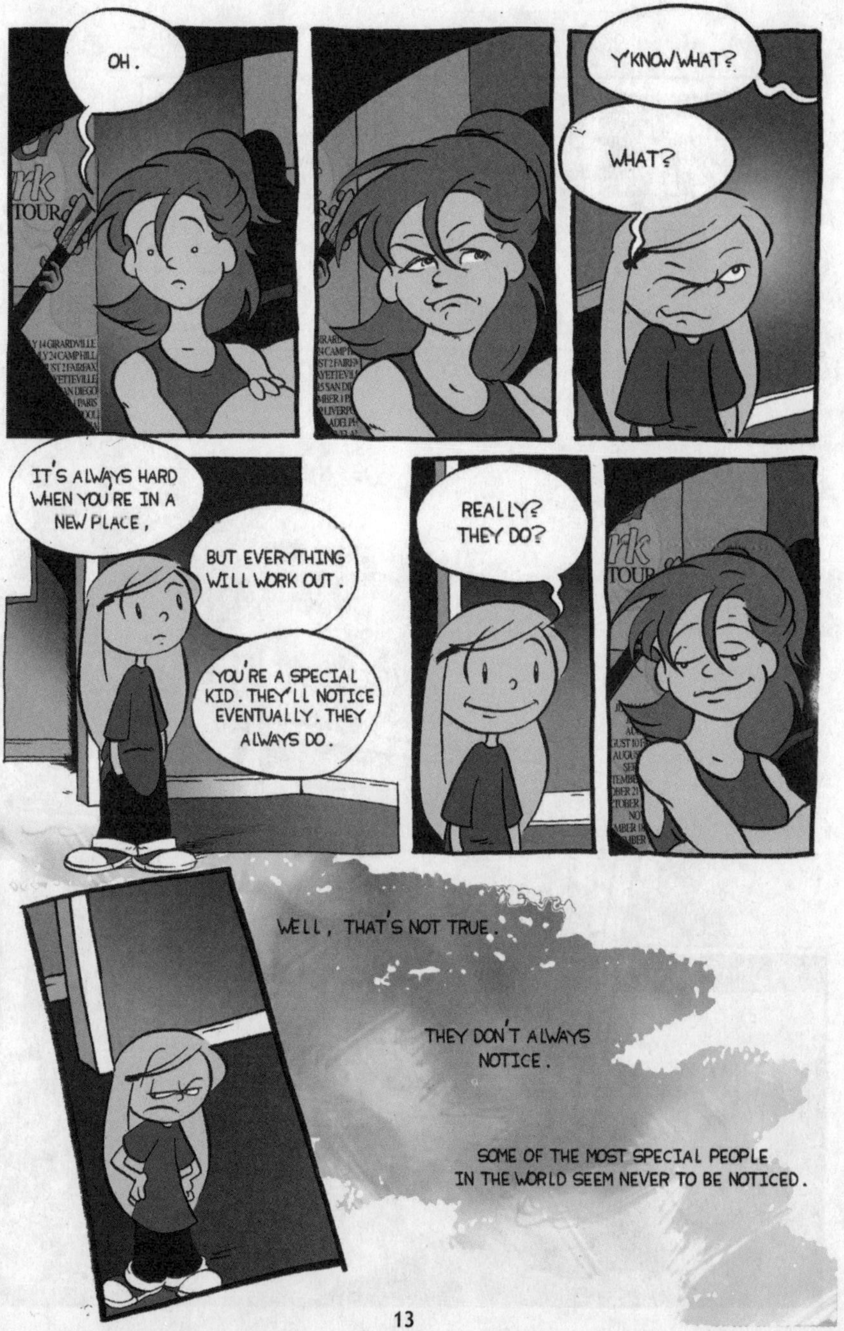
OH.
Y'KNOW WHAT?
WHAT?
IT'S ALWAYS HARD WHEN YOU'RE IN A NEW PLACE,
BUT EVERYTHING WILL WORK OUT.
YOU'RE A SPECIAL KID. THEY'LL NOTICE EVENTUALLY. THEY ALWAYS DO.
REALLY? THEY DO?
WELL, THAT'S NOT TRUE.
THEY DON'T ALWAYS NOTICE.
SOME OF THE MOST SPECIAL PEOPLE IN THE WORLD SEEM NEVER TO BE NOTICED.

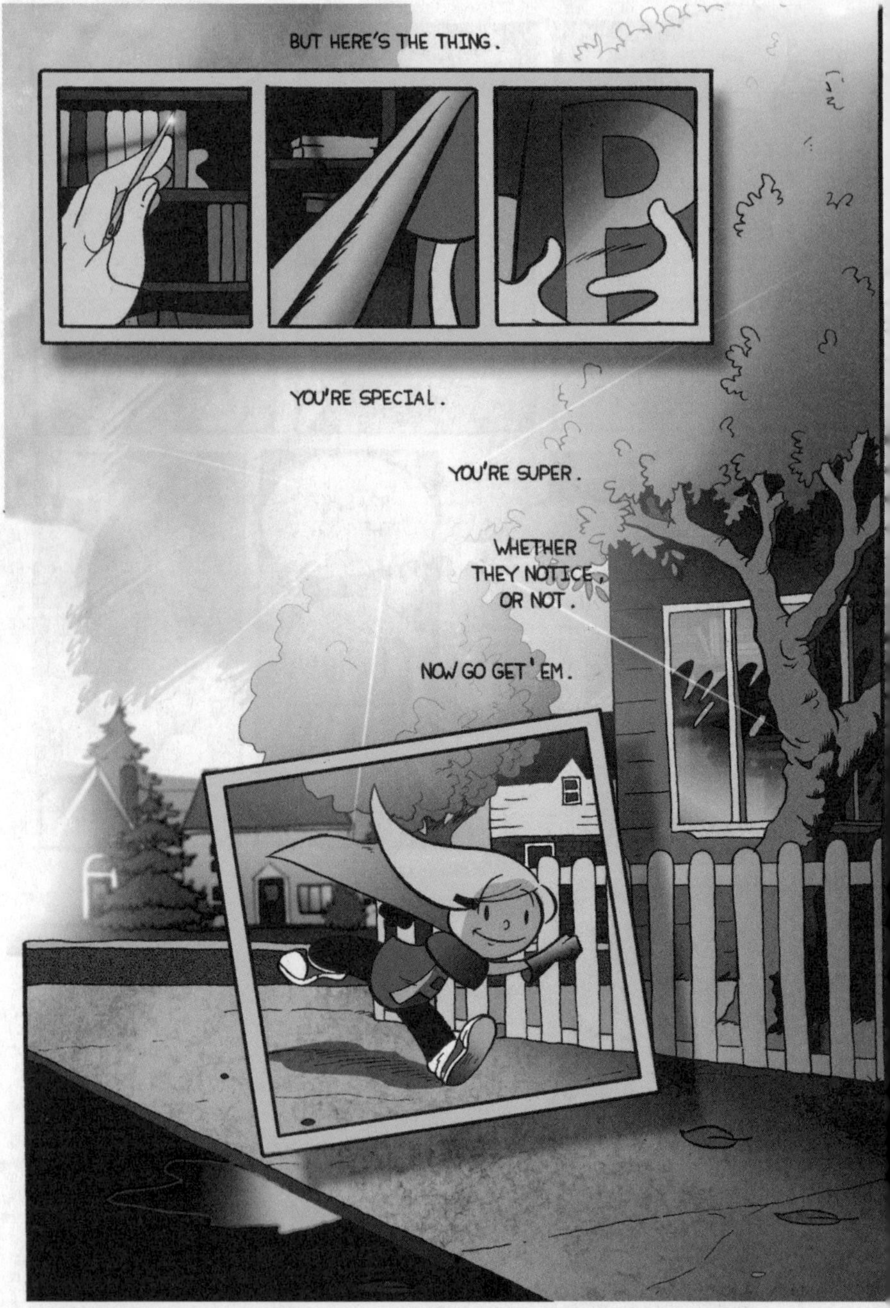
BUT HERE'S THE THING.
YOU'RE SPECIAL.
YOU'RE SUPER.
WHETHER THEY NOTICE, OR NOT.
NOW GO GET 'EM.

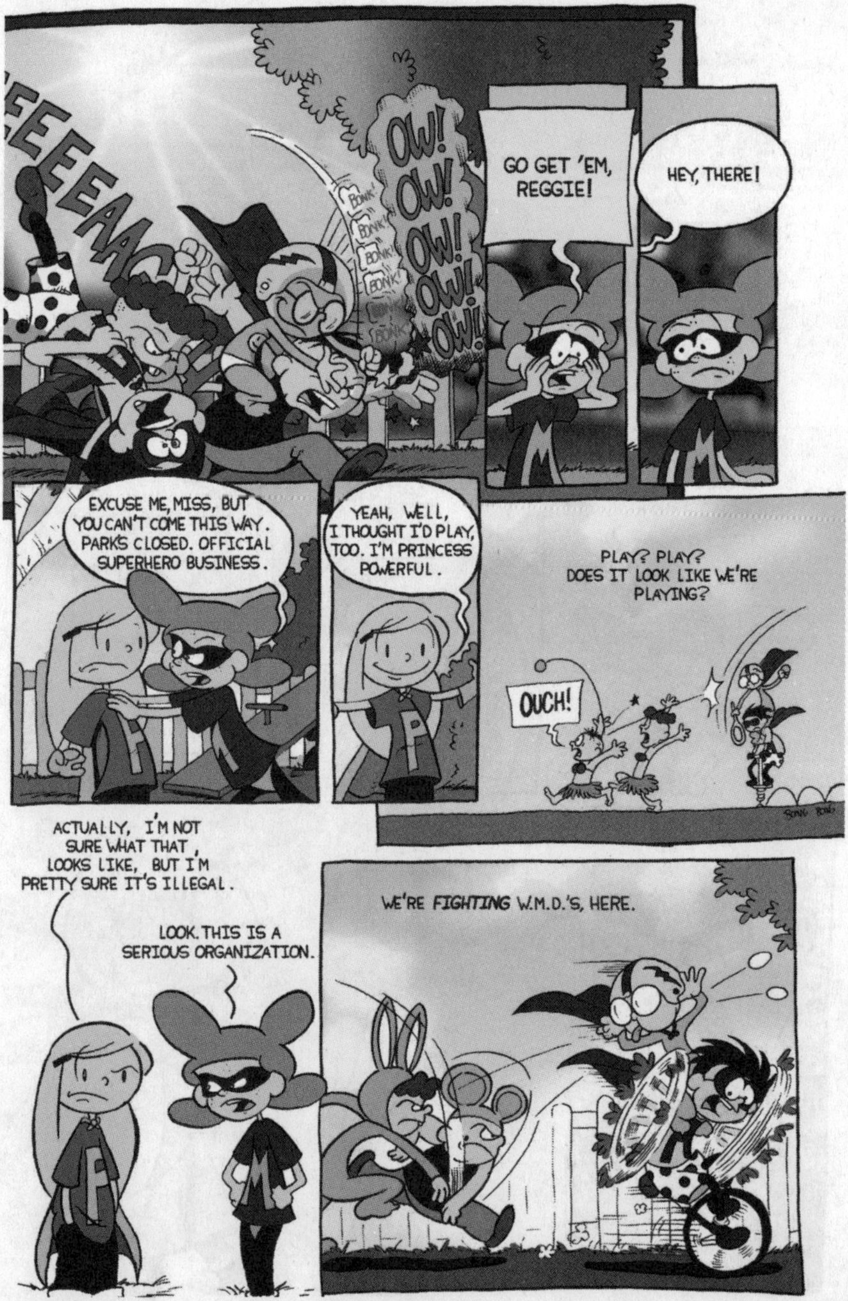

EEEEEAAAG
BONK! BONK! BONK! BONK! BONK! BONK!
OW! OW! OW! OW! OW!
GO GET 'EM, REGGIE!
HEY, THERE!
EXCUSE ME, MISS, BUT YOU CAN'T COME THIS WAY. PARK'S CLOSED. OFFICIAL SUPERHERO BUSINESS.
YEAH, WELL, I THOUGHT I'D PLAY, TOO. I'M PRINCESS POWERFUL.
PLAY? PLAY? DOES IT LOOK LIKE WE'RE PLAYING?
OUCH!
LOOK. THIS IS A SERIOUS ORGANIZATION.
WE'RE *FIGHTING* W.M.D.'S, HERE.
ACTUALLY, I'M NOT SURE WHAT THAT LOOKS LIKE, BUT I'M PRETTY SURE IT'S ILLEGAL.

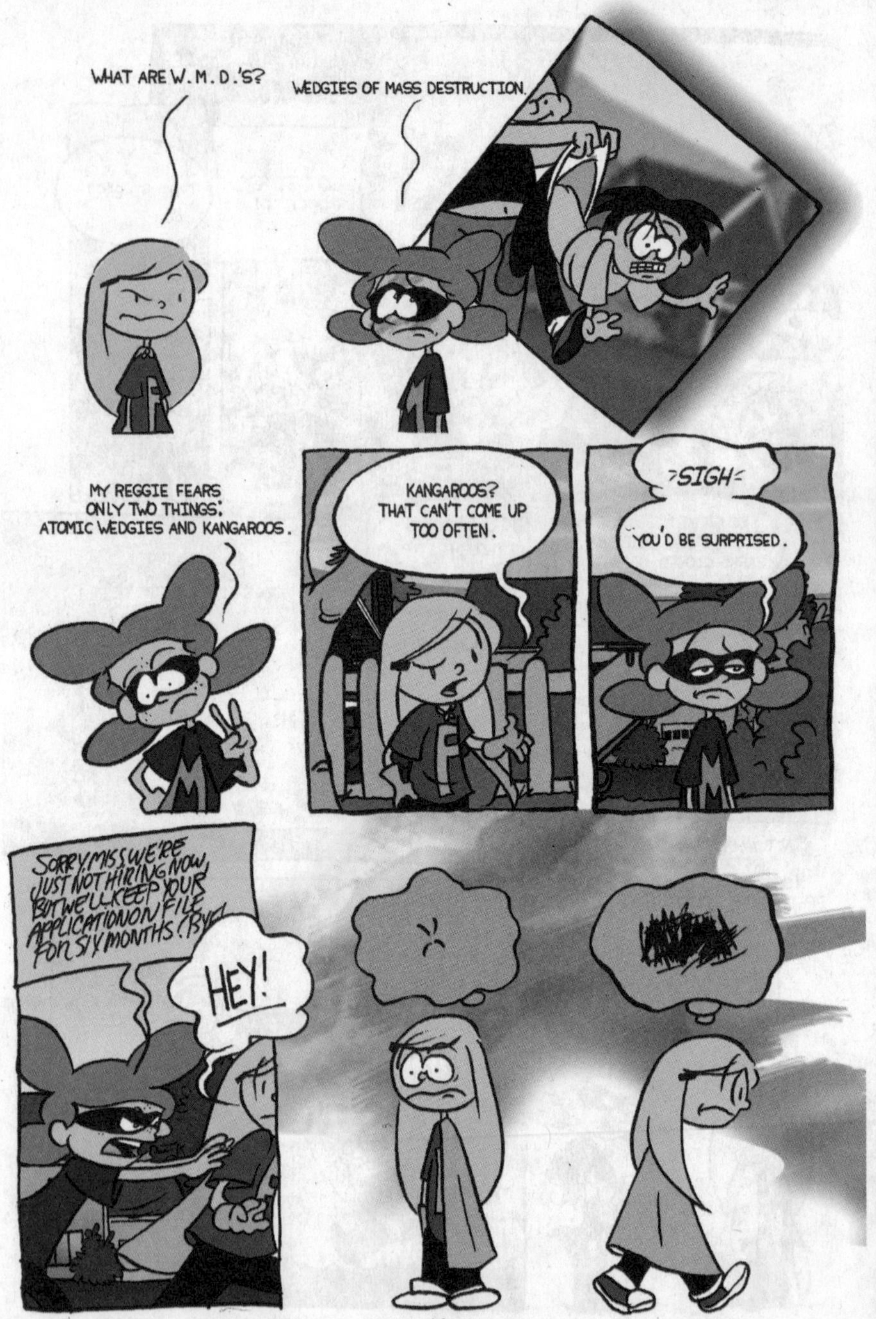
WHAT ARE W. M. D.'S?
WEDGIES OF MASS DESTRUCTION.
MY REGGIE FEARS ONLY TWO THINGS: ATOMIC WEDGIES AND KANGAROOS.
KANGAROOS? THAT CAN'T COME UP TOO OFTEN.
SIGH
YOU'D BE SURPRISED.
SORRY MISS WE'RE JUST NOT HIRING NOW, BUT WE'LL KEEP YOUR APPLICATION ON FILE FOR SIX MONTHS.
HEY!

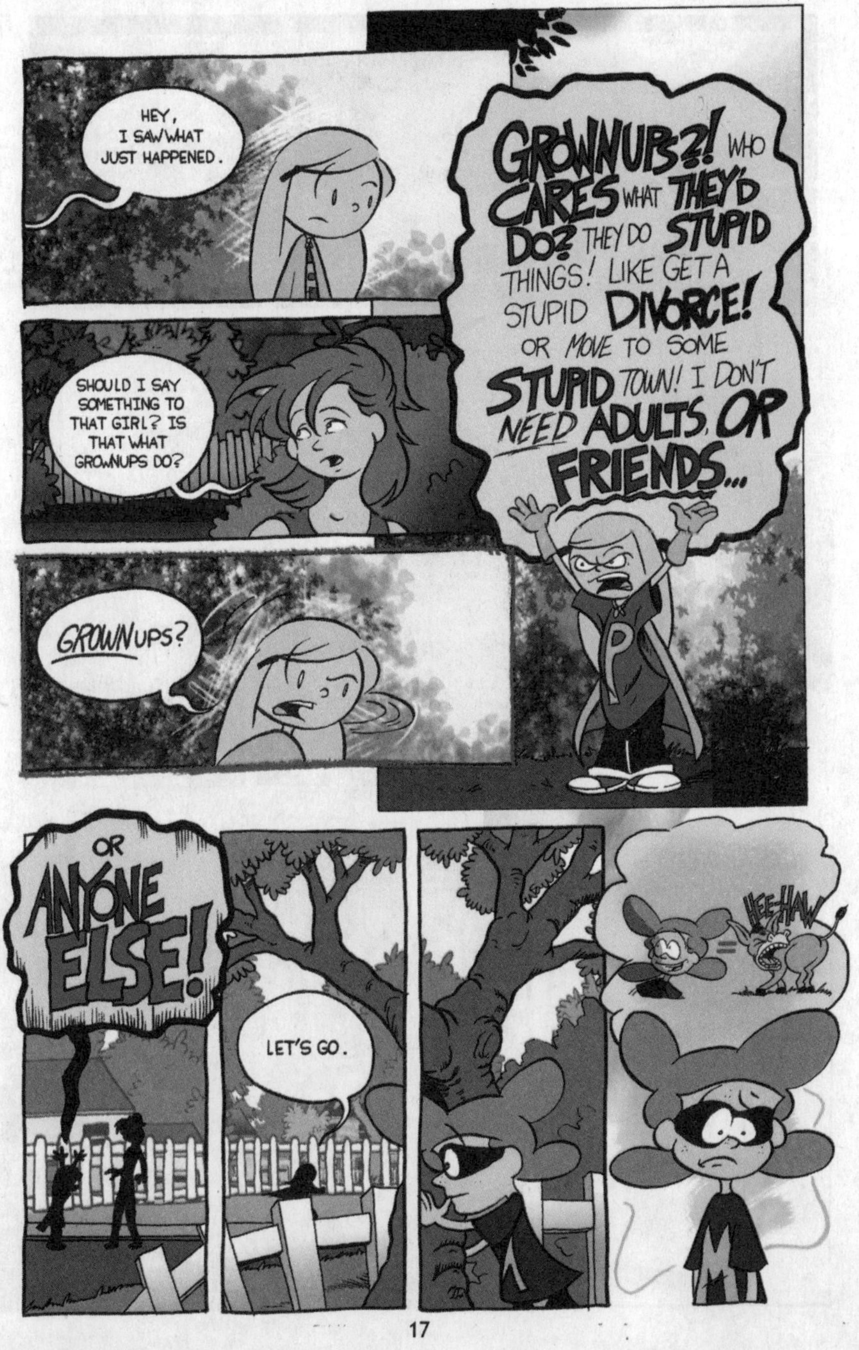
HEY, I SAW WHAT JUST HAPPENED.
SHOULD I SAY SOMETHING TO THAT GIRL? IS THAT WHAT GROWNUPS DO?
GROWNUPS?
GROWNUPS?! WHO CARES WHAT THEY'D DO? THEY DO STUPID THINGS! LIKE GET A STUPID DIVORCE! OR MOVE TO SOME STUPID TOWN! I DON'T NEED ADULTS, OR FRIENDS...
OR ANYONE ELSE!
LET'S GO.
HEE-HAW

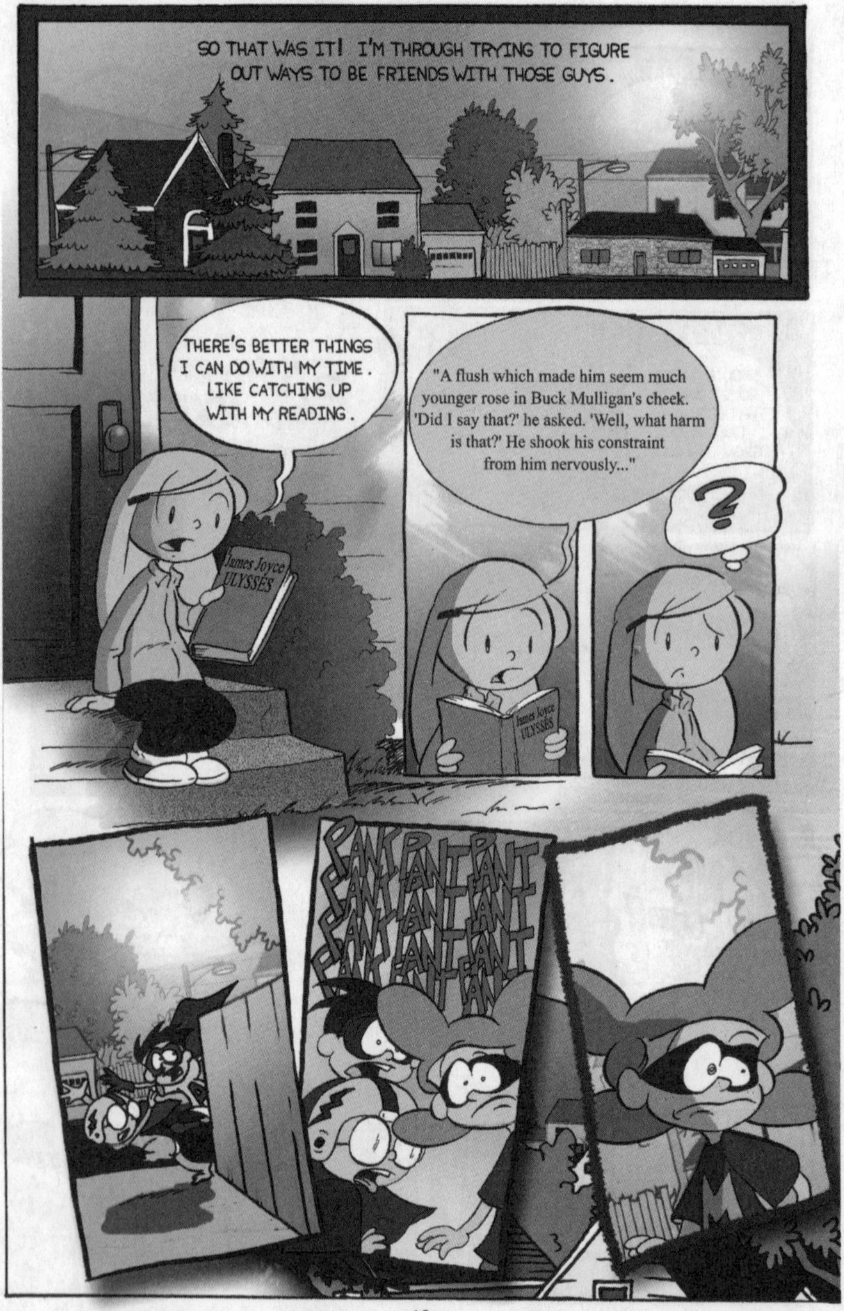
SO THAT WAS IT! I'M THROUGH TRYING TO FIGURE OUT WAYS TO BE FRIENDS WITH THOSE GUYS.
THERE'S BETTER THINGS I CAN DO WITH MY TIME. LIKE CATCHING UP WITH MY READING.
James Joyce ULYSSES
"A flush which made him seem much younger rose in Buck Mulligan's cheek. 'Did I say that?' he asked. 'Well, what harm is that?' He shook his constraint from him nervously..."
James Joyce ULYSSES
?
PANT PANT PANT
PANT PANT PANT
PANT PANT PANT
PANT PANT PANT

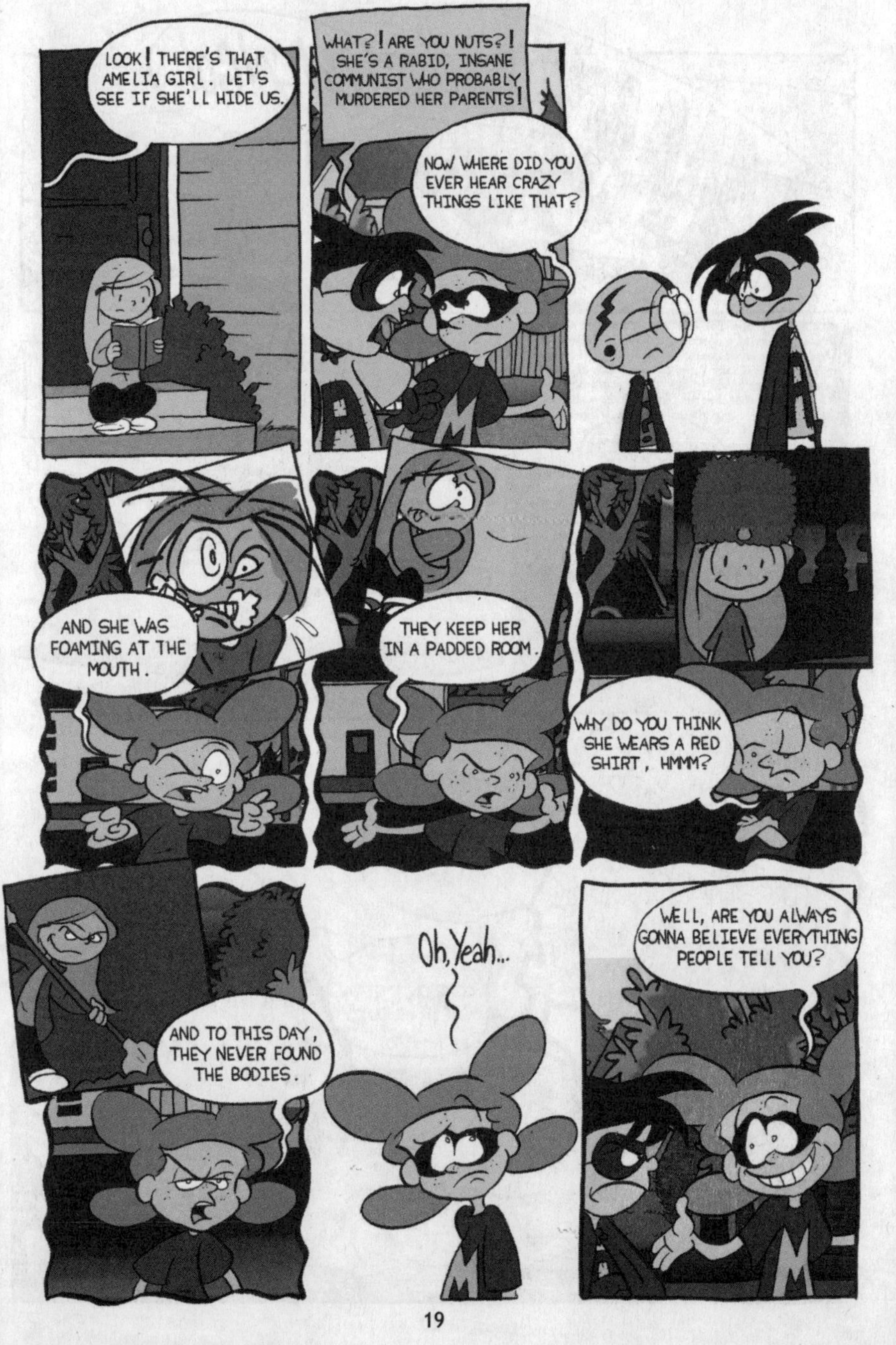
LOOK! THERE'S THAT AMELIA GIRL. LET'S SEE IF SHE'LL HIDE US.
WHAT?! ARE YOU NUTS?! SHE'S A RABID, INSANE COMMUNIST WHO PROBABLY MURDERED HER PARENTS!
NOW WHERE DID YOU EVER HEAR CRAZY THINGS LIKE THAT?
AND SHE WAS FOAMING AT THE MOUTH.
THEY KEEP HER IN A PADDED ROOM.
WHY DO YOU THINK SHE WEARS A RED SHIRT, HMMM?
AND TO THIS DAY, THEY NEVER FOUND THE BODIES.
Oh, Yeah...
WELL, ARE YOU ALWAYS GONNA BELIEVE EVERYTHING PEOPLE TELL YOU?

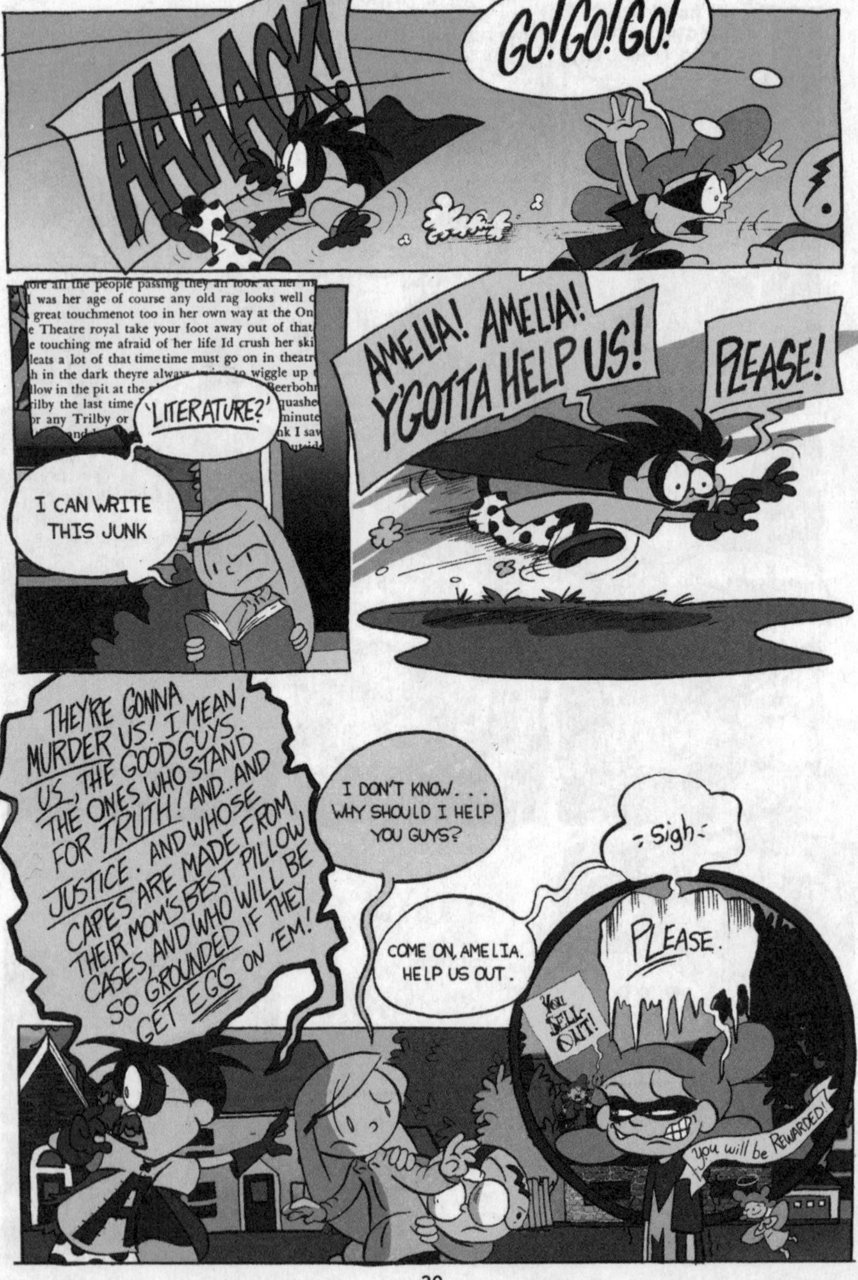

AAAACK!
GO!GO!GO!
fore all the people passing they all look at her m
I was her age of course any old rag looks well c
great touchmenot too in her own way at the On
e Theatre royal take your foot away out of that
e touching me afraid of her life Id crush her ski
leats a lot of that time time must go on in theatr
h in the dark theyre alway trying to wiggle up t
llow in the pit at the Beerbohm
rilby the last time squashed
or any Trilby or minute
'LITERATURE?'
I CAN WRITE THIS JUNK
AMELIA! AMELIA! Y'GOTTA HELP US!
PLEASE!
THEY'RE GONNA MURDER US! I MEAN, US, THE GOOD GUYS. THE ONES WHO STAND FOR TRUTH! AND... AND JUSTICE. AND WHOSE CAPES ARE MADE FROM THEIR MOM'S BEST PILLOW CASES AND WHO WILL BE SO GROUNDED IF THEY GET EGG ON 'EM!
I DON'T KNOW... WHY SHOULD I HELP YOU GUYS?
COME ON, AMELIA. HELP US OUT.
Sigh
PLEASE.
YOU SELL-OUT!
you will be REWARDED!

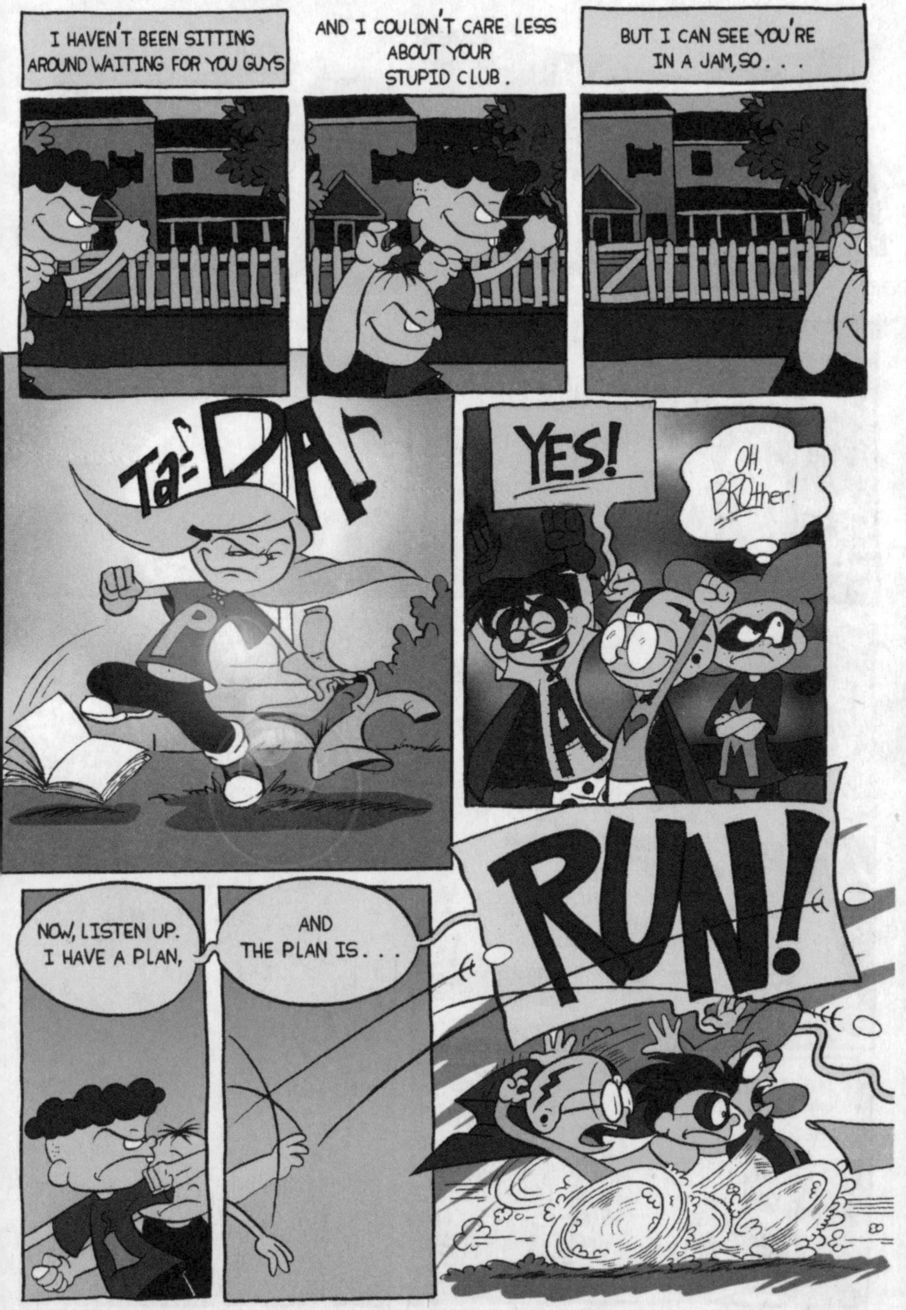
I HAVEN'T BEEN SITTING AROUND WAITING FOR YOU GUYS
AND I COULDN'T CARE LESS ABOUT YOUR STUPID CLUB.
BUT I CAN SEE YOU'RE IN A JAM, SO . . .
TA-DA!
YES!
OH, BROther!
NOW, LISTEN UP. I HAVE A PLAN,
AND THE PLAN IS . . .
RUN!

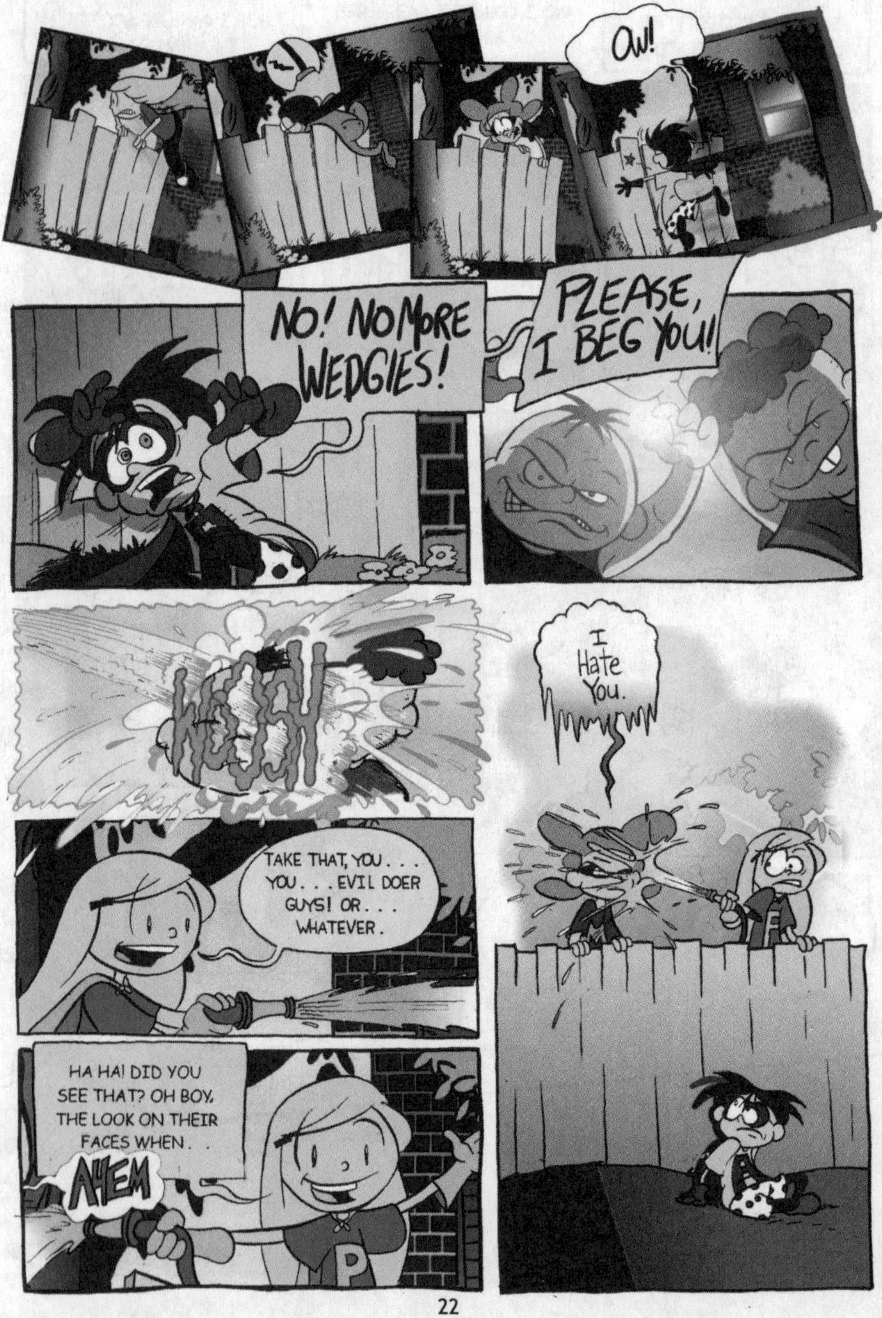
OW!
NO! NO MORE WEDGIES!
PLEASE, I BEG YOU!!
WOOSH
TAKE THAT, YOU . . . YOU . . . EVIL DOER GUYS! OR . . . WHATEVER.
I Hate You.
HA HA! DID YOU SEE THAT? OH BOY, THE LOOK ON THEIR FACES WHEN . .
AHEM

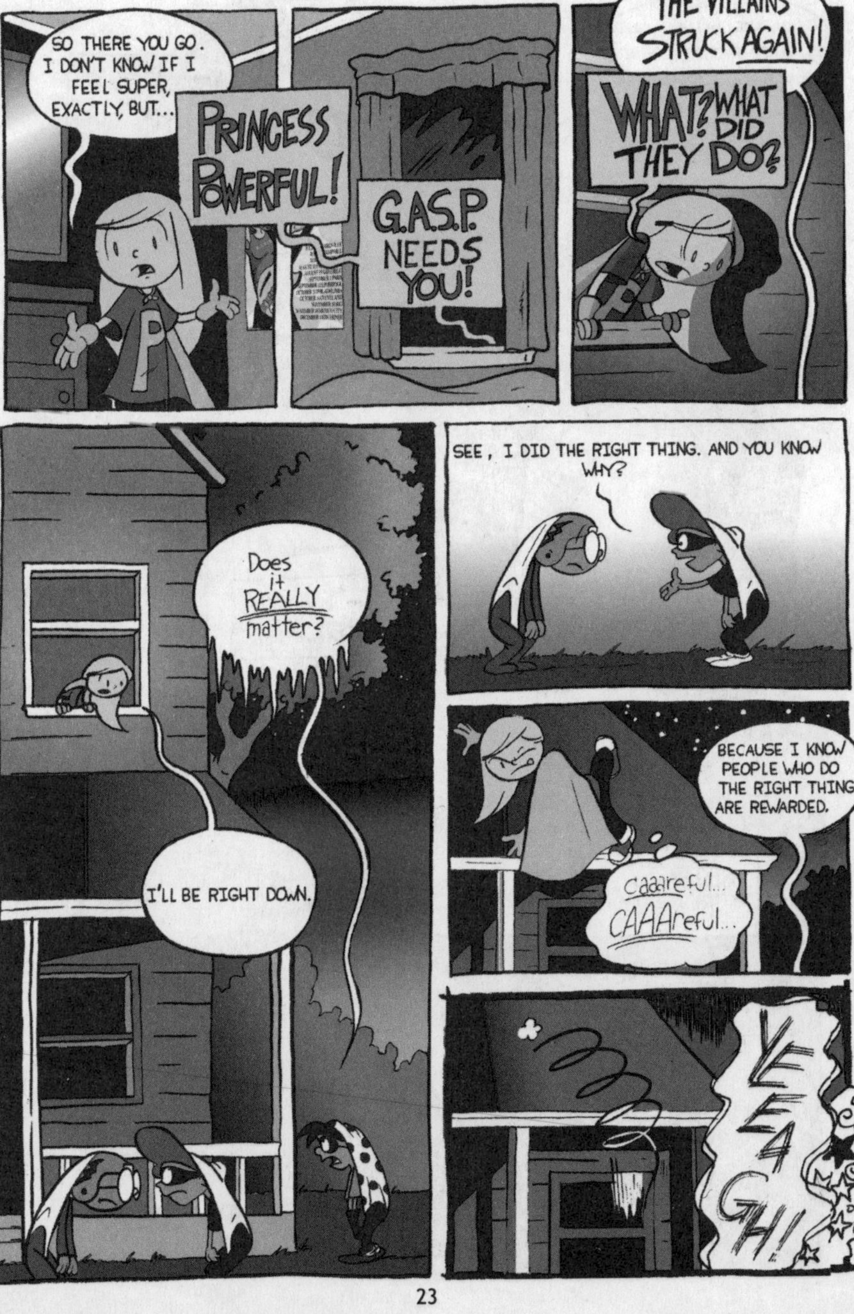

SO THERE YOU GO. I DON'T KNOW IF I FEEL SUPER, EXACTLY, BUT...
PRINCESS POWERFUL!
G.A.S.P. NEEDS YOU!
THE VILLAINS STRUCK AGAIN!
WHAT? WHAT DID THEY DO?
Does it REALLY matter?
I'LL BE RIGHT DOWN.
SEE, I DID THE RIGHT THING. AND YOU KNOW WHY?
BECAUSE I KNOW PEOPLE WHO DO THE RIGHT THING ARE REWARDED.
caaareful... CAAAreful...
YEEAGH!

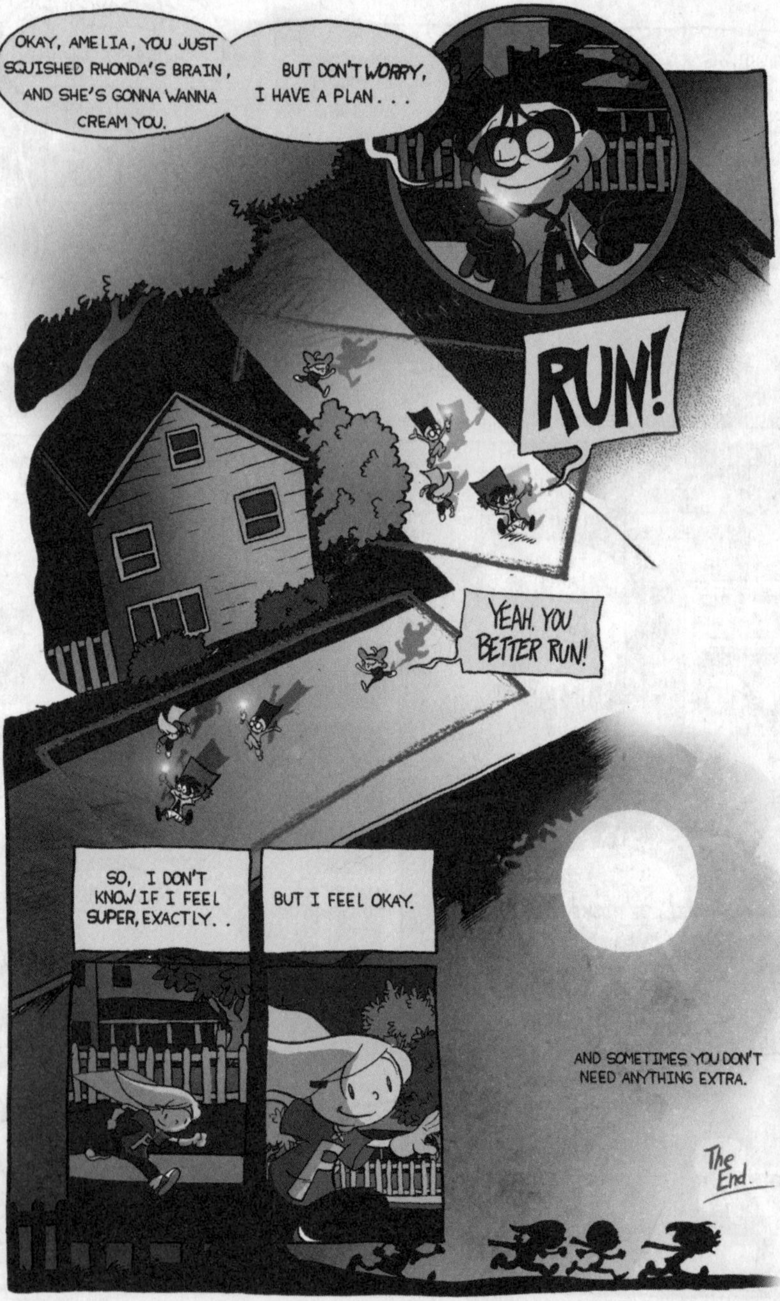
OKAY, AMELIA, YOU JUST SQUISHED RHONDA'S BRAIN, AND SHE'S GONNA WANNA CREAM YOU.
BUT DON'T WORRY, I HAVE A PLAN . . .
RUN!
YEAH. YOU BETTER RUN!
SO, I DON'T KNOW IF I FEEL SUPER, EXACTLY. .
BUT I FEEL OKAY.
AND SOMETIMES YOU DON'T NEED ANYTHING EXTRA.
The End.

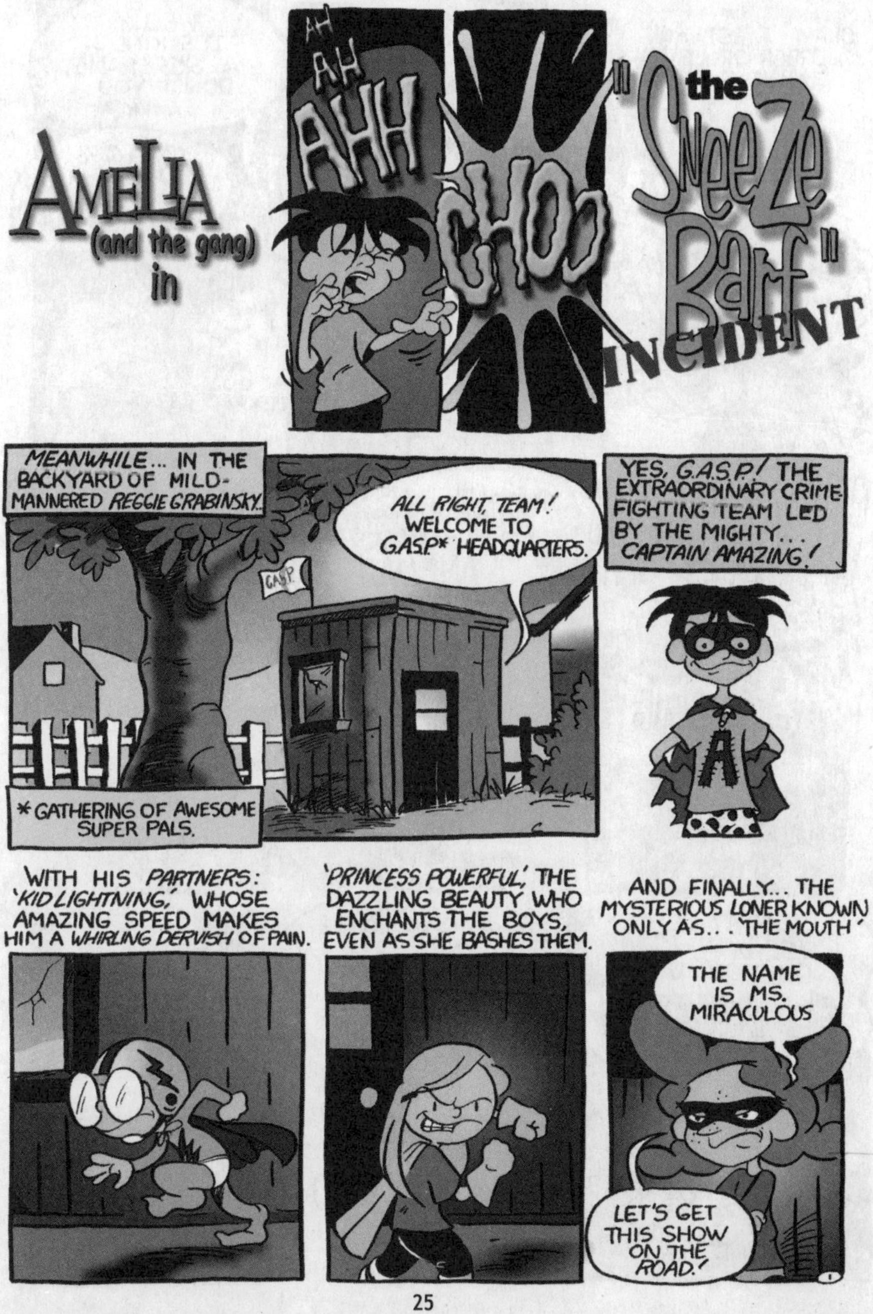
AMELIA
(and the gang)
in
AH
AH
AHH
CHOO
"the SneeZe Barf"
INCIDENT
MEANWHILE... IN THE BACKYARD OF MILD-MANNERED REGGIE GRABINSKY...
ALL RIGHT, TEAM! WELCOME TO G.A.S.P.* HEADQUARTERS.
G.A.S.P.
*GATHERING OF AWESOME SUPER PALS.
YES, G.A.S.P.! THE EXTRAORDINARY CRIME-FIGHTING TEAM LED BY THE MIGHTY... CAPTAIN AMAZING!
WITH HIS PARTNERS: 'KID LIGHTNING,' WHOSE AMAZING SPEED MAKES HIM A WHIRLING DERVISH OF PAIN.
'PRINCESS POWERFUL,' THE DAZZLING BEAUTY WHO ENCHANTS THE BOYS, EVEN AS SHE BASHES THEM.
AND FINALLY... THE MYSTERIOUS LONER KNOWN ONLY AS... 'THE MOUTH'
THE NAME IS MS. MIRACULOUS
LET'S GET THIS SHOW ON THE ROAD!

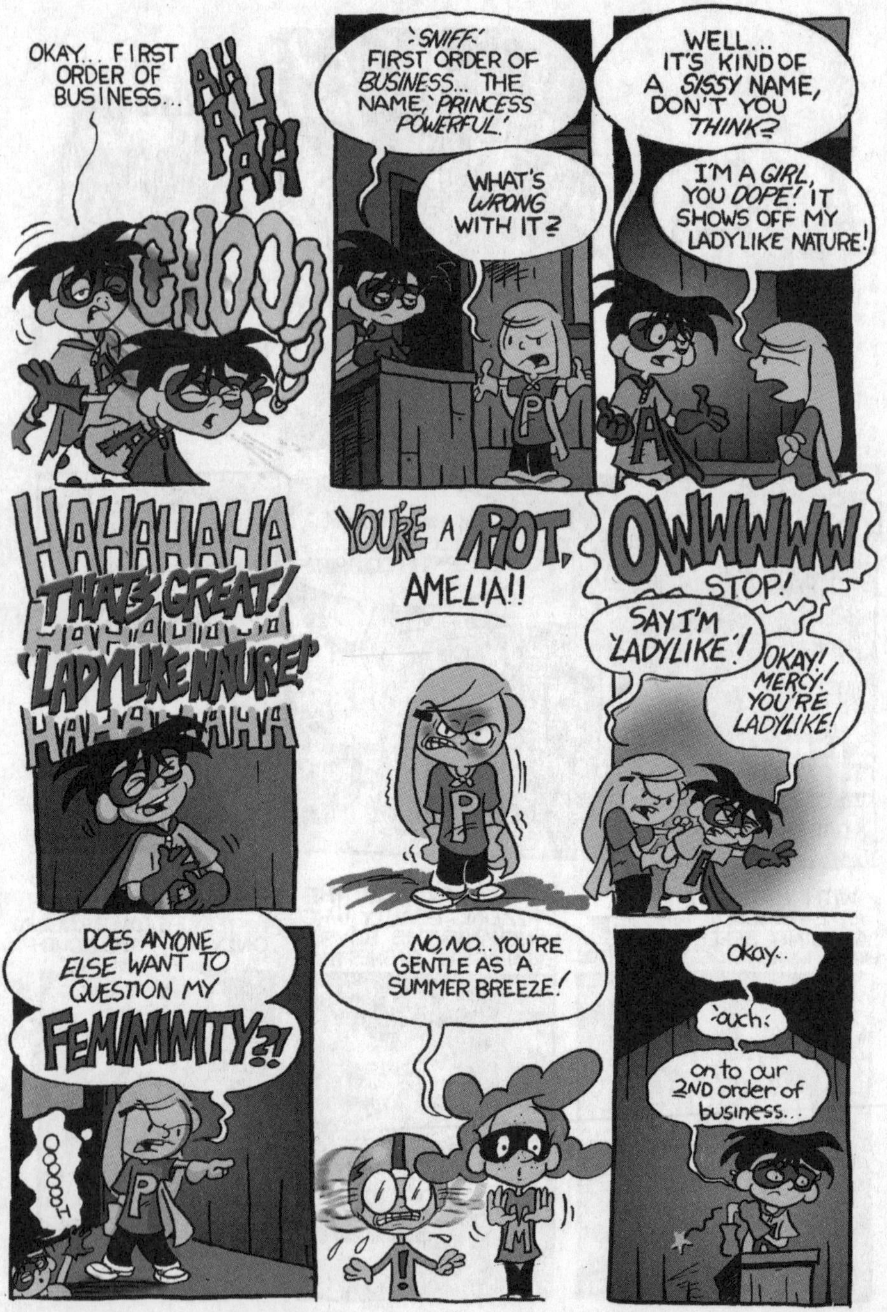
OKAY... FIRST ORDER OF BUSINESS...
AH AH AH
CHOO
:SNIFF: FIRST ORDER OF BUSINESS... THE NAME, 'PRINCESS POWERFUL.'
WHAT'S WRONG WITH IT?
WELL... IT'S KIND OF A SISSY NAME, DON'T YOU THINK?
I'M A GIRL, YOU DOPE! IT SHOWS OFF MY LADYLIKE NATURE!
HAHAHAHA
THAT'S GREAT!
'LADYLIKE NATURE!'
YOU'RE A RIOT, AMELIA!!
OWWWWW
STOP!
SAY I'M 'LADYLIKE'!
OKAY! MERCY! YOU'RE LADYLIKE!
DOES ANYONE ELSE WANT TO QUESTION MY FEMININITY?!
OOOOOH
NO, NO.. YOU'RE GENTLE AS A SUMMER BREEZE!
okay..
:ouch:
on to our 2ND order of business...

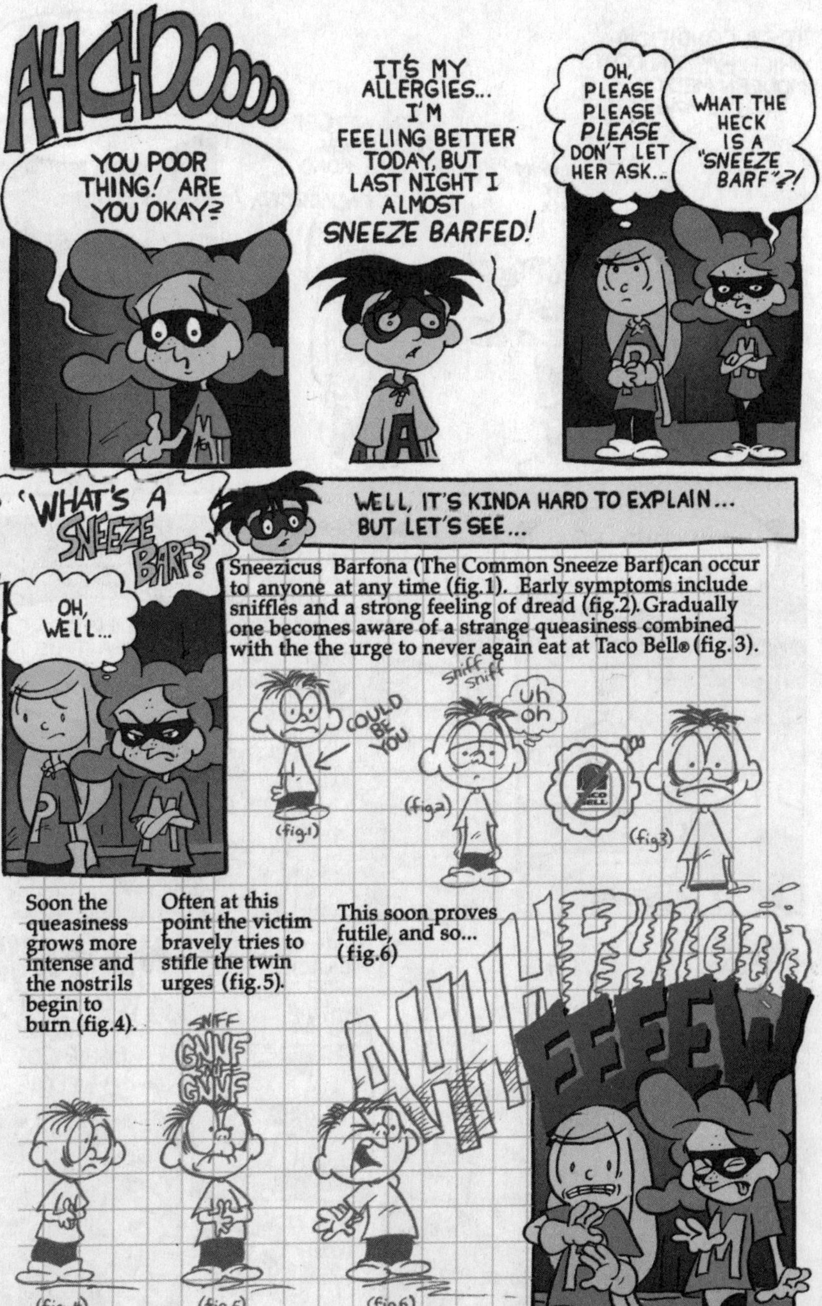

AHCHOOOOO
YOU POOR THING! ARE YOU OKAY?
IT'S MY ALLERGIES... I'M FEELING BETTER TODAY, BUT LAST NIGHT I ALMOST SNEEZE BARFED!
OH, PLEASE PLEASE PLEASE DON'T LET HER ASK...
WHAT THE HECK IS A "SNEEZE BARF"?!
"WHAT'S A SNEEZE BARF?"
OH, WELL...
WELL, IT'S KINDA HARD TO EXPLAIN... BUT LET'S SEE...
Sneezicus Barfona (The Common Sneeze Barf)can occur to anyone at any time (fig.1). Early symptoms include sniffles and a strong feeling of dread (fig.2). Gradually one becomes aware of a strange queasiness combined with the the urge to never again eat at Taco Bell® (fig. 3).
COULD BE YOU
(fig.1)
sniff sniff
uh oh
(fig.2)
TACO BELL
(fig.3)
Soon the queasiness grows more intense and the nostrils begin to burn (fig.4).
Often at this point the victim bravely tries to stifle the twin urges (fig.5).
This soon proves futile, and so... (fig.6)
SNIFF
GNNF
GNNF
AHHHPHOOO
EEEEW
(fig.4)
(fig.5)
(fig.6)

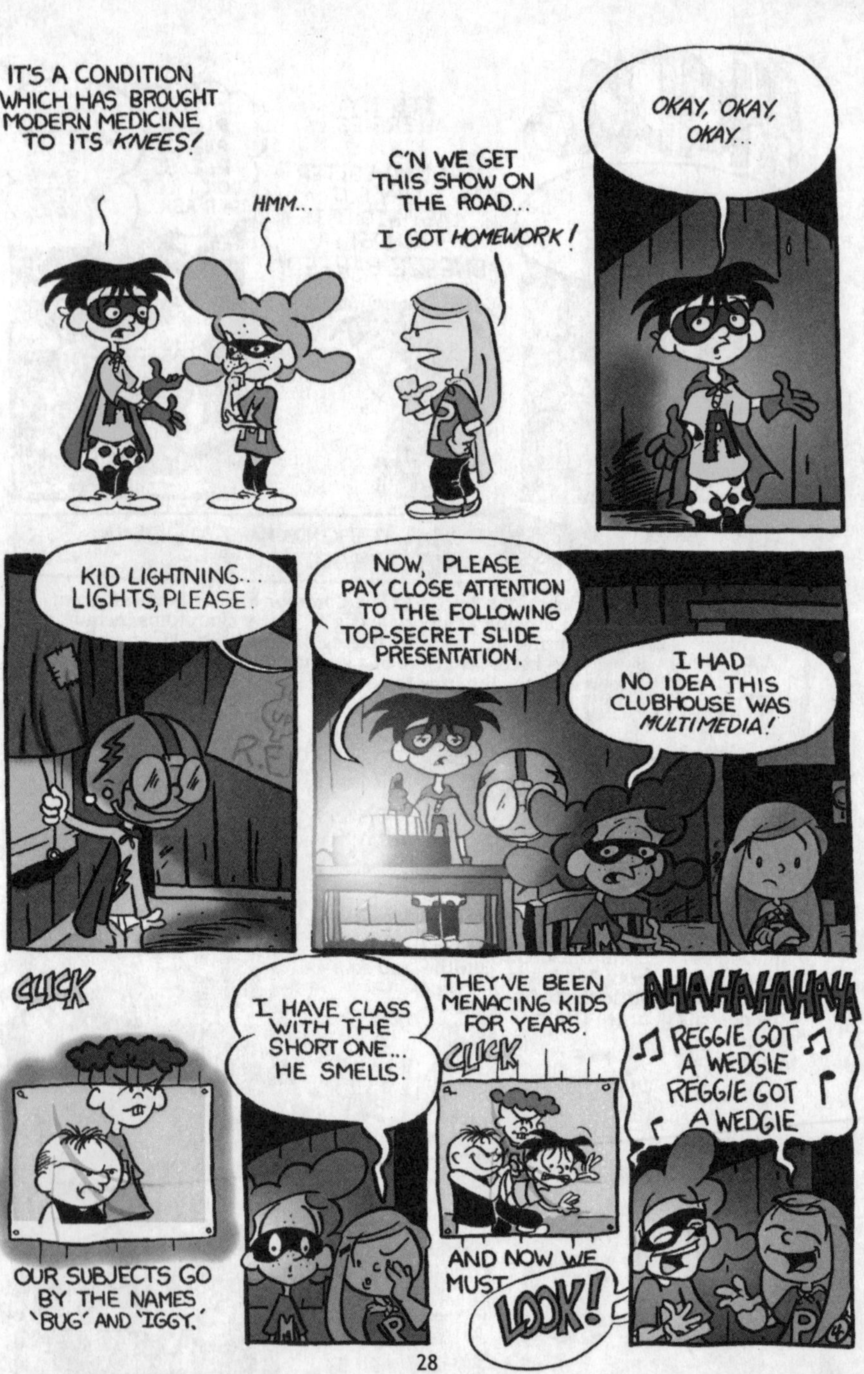
IT'S A CONDITION WHICH HAS BROUGHT MODERN MEDICINE TO ITS KNEES!
HMM...
C'N WE GET THIS SHOW ON THE ROAD...
I GOT HOMEWORK!
OKAY, OKAY, OKAY...
KID LIGHTNING... LIGHTS, PLEASE.
NOW, PLEASE PAY CLOSE ATTENTION TO THE FOLLOWING TOP-SECRET SLIDE PRESENTATION.
I HAD NO IDEA THIS CLUBHOUSE WAS MULTIMEDIA!
CLICK
OUR SUBJECTS GO BY THE NAMES 'BUG' AND 'IGGY.'
I HAVE CLASS WITH THE SHORT ONE... HE SMELLS.
THEY'VE BEEN MENACING KIDS FOR YEARS.
CLICK
AND NOW WE MUST
LOOK!
AHAHAHAHAHA
REGGIE GOT A WEDGIE REGGIE GOT A WEDGIE

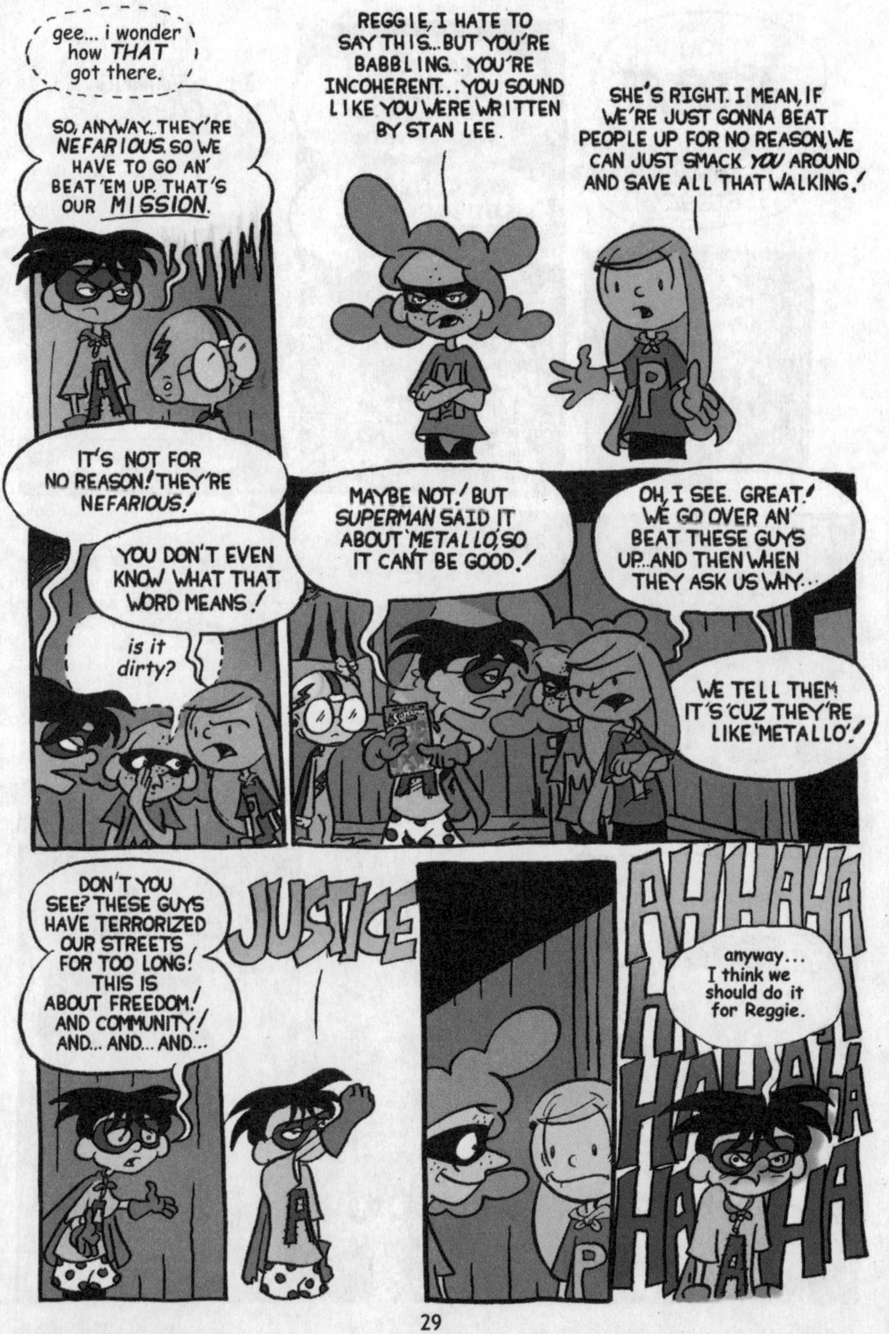
gee... i wonder how THAT got there.
SO, ANYWAY...THEY'RE NEFARIOUS. SO WE HAVE TO GO AN' BEAT 'EM UP. THAT'S OUR MISSION.
REGGIE, I HATE TO SAY THIS...BUT YOU'RE BABBLING...YOU'RE INCOHERENT...YOU SOUND LIKE YOU WERE WRITTEN BY STAN LEE.
SHE'S RIGHT. I MEAN, IF WE'RE JUST GONNA BEAT PEOPLE UP FOR NO REASON, WE CAN JUST SMACK YOU AROUND AND SAVE ALL THAT WALKING!
IT'S NOT FOR NO REASON! THEY'RE NEFARIOUS!
YOU DON'T EVEN KNOW WHAT THAT WORD MEANS!
is it dirty?
MAYBE NOT! BUT SUPERMAN SAID IT ABOUT 'METALLO', SO IT CAN'T BE GOOD!
OH, I SEE. GREAT! WE GO OVER AN' BEAT THESE GUYS UP...AND THEN WHEN THEY ASK US WHY...
WE TELL THEM: IT'S 'CUZ THEY'RE LIKE 'METALLO'!
DON'T YOU SEE? THESE GUYS HAVE TERRORIZED OUR STREETS FOR TOO LONG! THIS IS ABOUT FREEDOM! AND COMMUNITY! AND... AND... AND...
JUSTICE
AHHAHA HAHAHA HAHAHA
anyway... I think we should do it for Reggie.

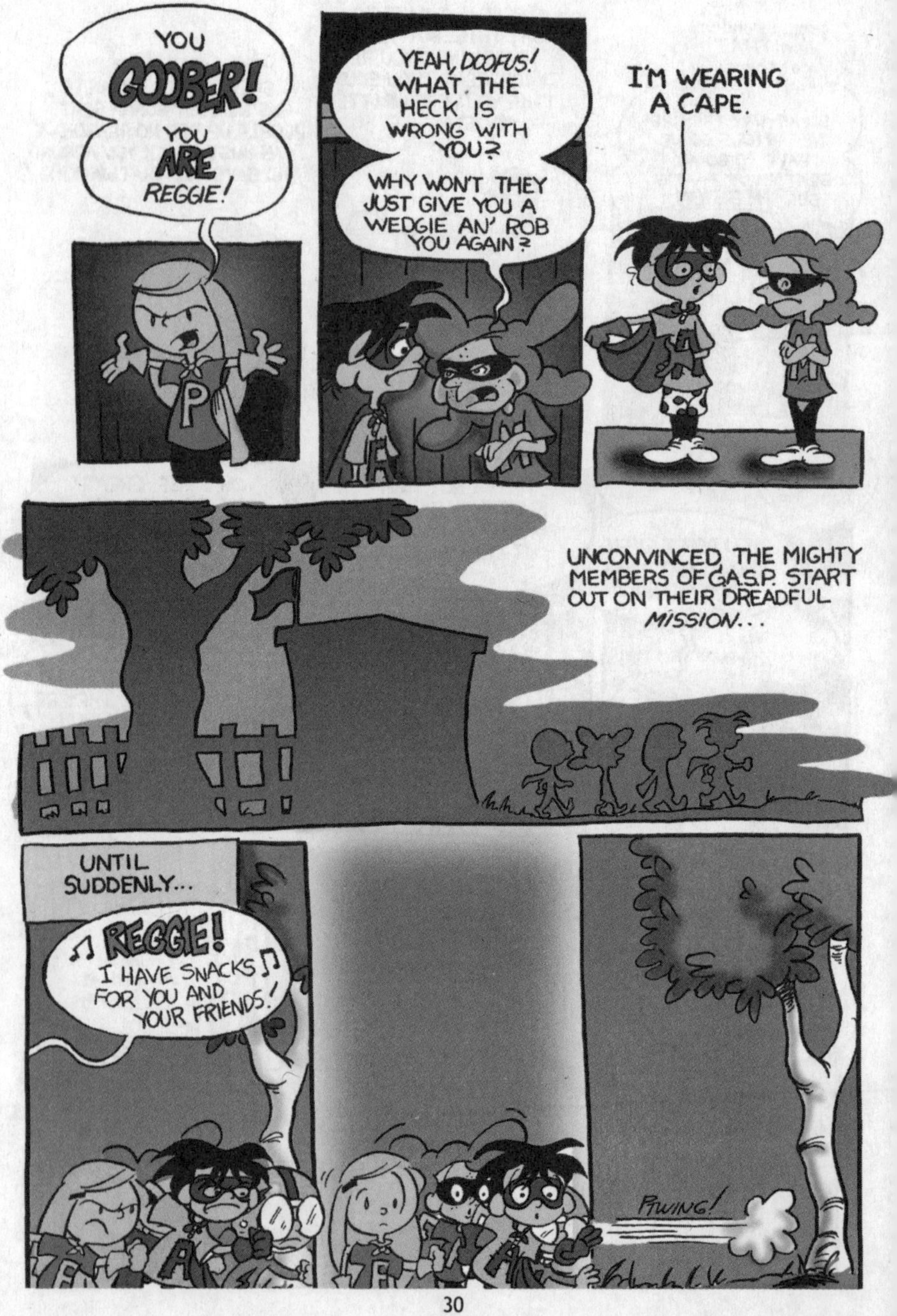
YOU GOOBER! YOU ARE REGGIE!
YEAH, DOOFUS! WHAT. THE HECK IS WRONG WITH YOU?
WHY WON'T THEY JUST GIVE YOU A WEDGIE AN' ROB YOU AGAIN?
I'M WEARING A CAPE.
UNCONVINCED, THE MIGHTY MEMBERS OF G.A.S.P. START OUT ON THEIR DREADFUL MISSION...
UNTIL SUDDENLY...
REGGIE! I HAVE SNACKS FOR YOU AND YOUR FRIENDS!
PTWING!

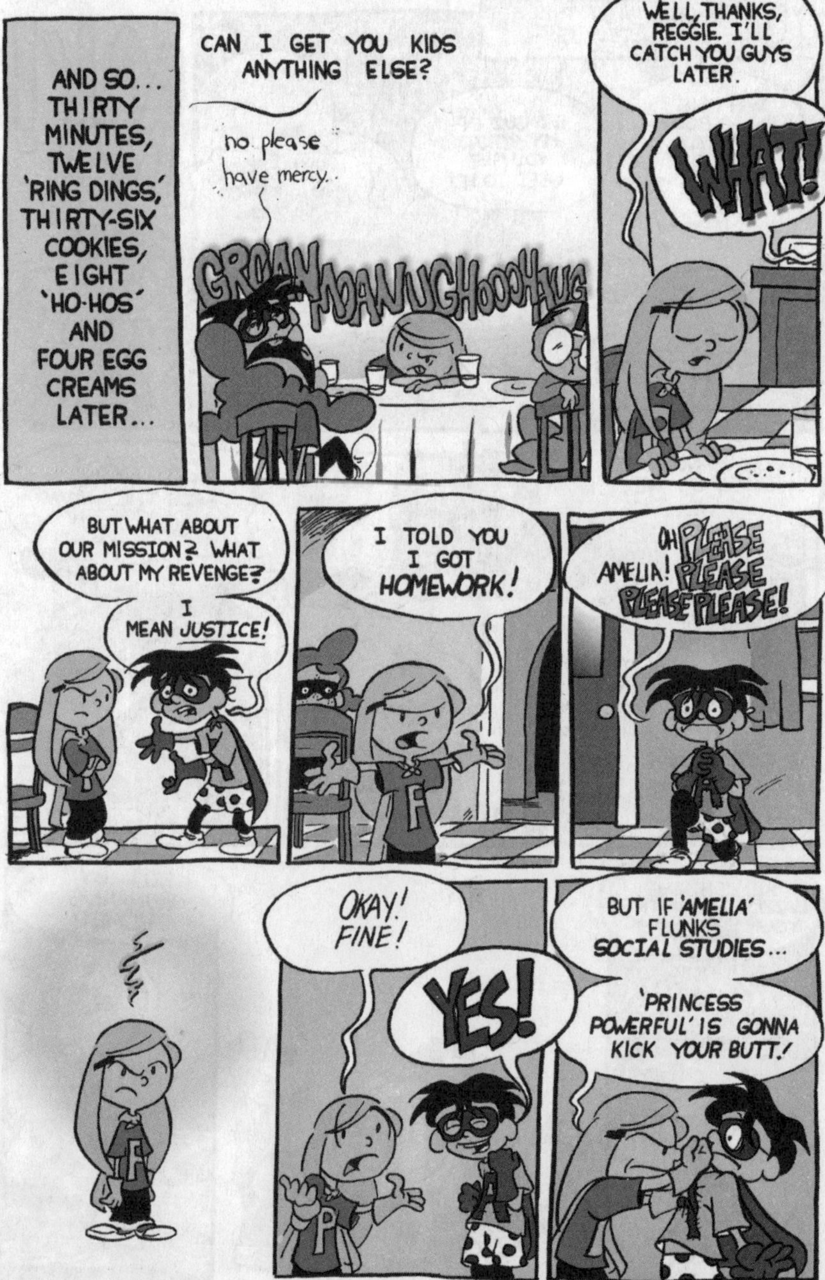
AND SO... THIRTY MINUTES, TWELVE 'RING DINGS,' THIRTY-SIX COOKIES, EIGHT 'HO-HOS' AND FOUR EGG CREAMS LATER...
CAN I GET YOU KIDS ANYTHING ELSE?
no please have mercy..
GROANMOANUGHOOOHAUG
WELL, THANKS, REGGIE. I'LL CATCH YOU GUYS LATER.
WHAT!
BUT WHAT ABOUT OUR MISSION? WHAT ABOUT MY REVENGE?
I MEAN JUSTICE!
I TOLD YOU I GOT HOMEWORK!
OH PLEASE AMELIA! PLEASE PLEASE PLEASE PLEASE!
OKAY! FINE!
YES!
BUT IF 'AMELIA' FLUNKS SOCIAL STUDIES...
'PRINCESS POWERFUL' IS GONNA KICK YOUR BUTT!

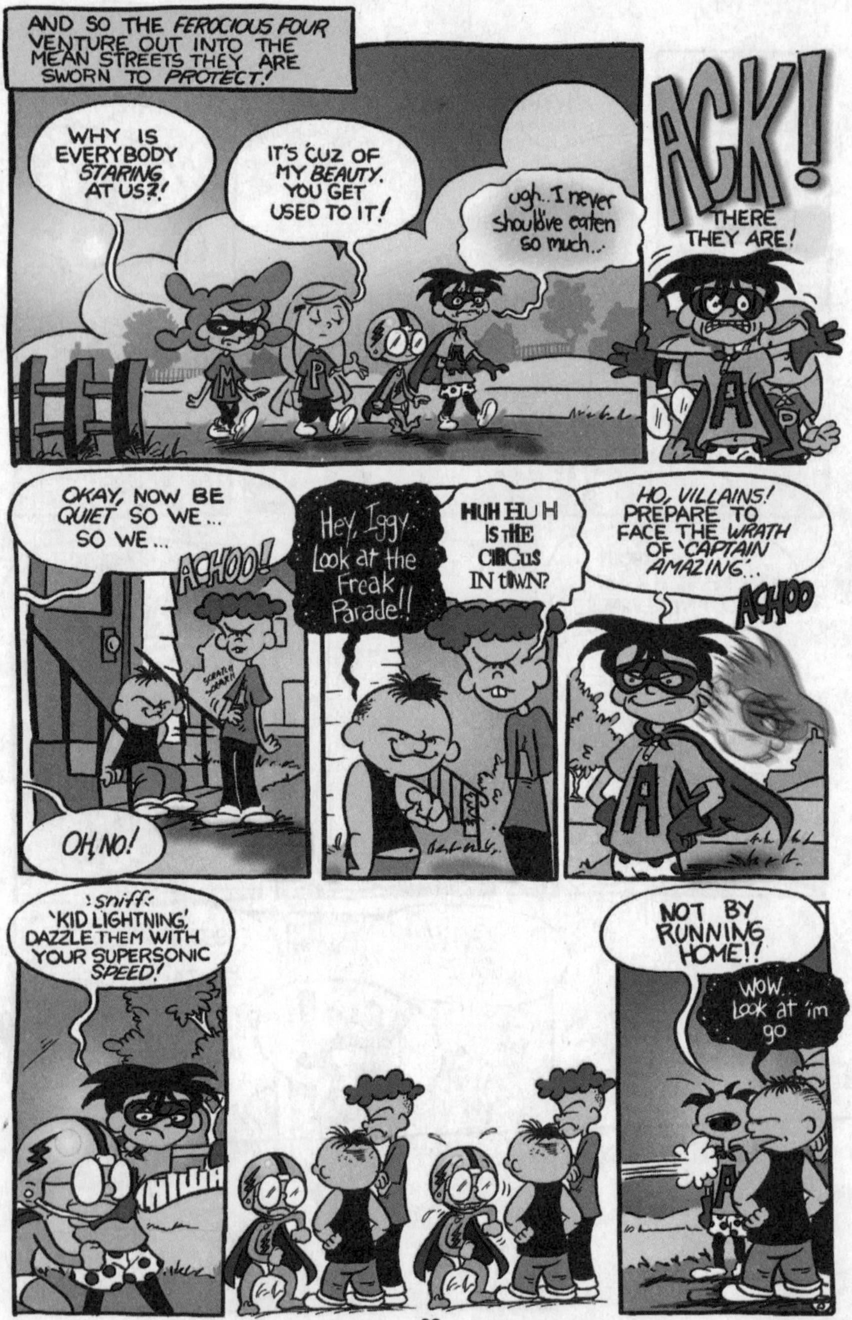
AND SO THE FEROCIOUS FOUR VENTURE OUT INTO THE MEAN STREETS THEY ARE SWORN TO PROTECT!
WHY IS EVERYBODY STARING AT US?!
IT'S 'CUZ OF MY BEAUTY. YOU GET USED TO IT!
ugh.. I never should've eaten so much...
ACK!
THERE THEY ARE!
OKAY, NOW BE QUIET SO WE... SO WE...
ACHOO!
SCRATCH SCRATCH
OH, NO!
Hey, Iggy. Look at the Freak Parade!!
HUH HUH IS THE CIRCUS IN TOWN?
HO, VILLAINS! PREPARE TO FACE THE WRATH OF 'CAPTAIN AMAZING'...
ACHOO
:sniff:
'KID LIGHTNING,' DAZZLE THEM WITH YOUR SUPERSONIC SPEED!
NOT BY RUNNING HOME!!
WOW.. Look at 'im go

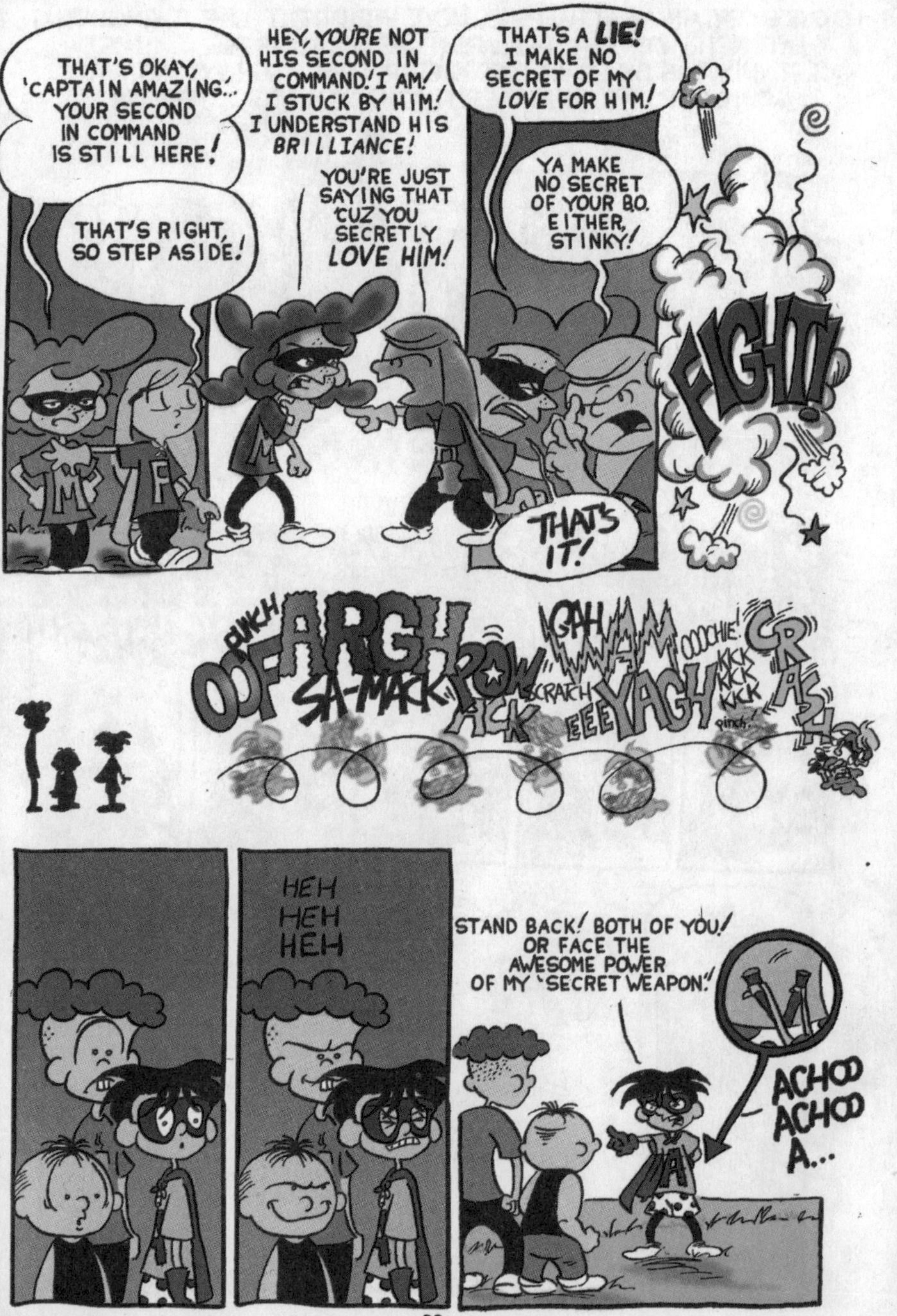
THAT'S OKAY, 'CAPTAIN AMAZING'... YOUR SECOND IN COMMAND IS STILL HERE!
THAT'S RIGHT, SO STEP ASIDE!
HEY, YOU'RE NOT HIS SECOND IN COMMAND! I AM! I STUCK BY HIM! I UNDERSTAND HIS BRILLIANCE!
YOU'RE JUST SAYING THAT 'CUZ YOU SECRETLY LOVE HIM!
THAT'S A LIE! I MAKE NO SECRET OF MY LOVE FOR HIM!
YA MAKE NO SECRET OF YOUR B.O. EITHER, STINKY!
THAT'S IT!
FIGHT!
PUNCH
OOF
ARGH
SA-MACK
POW
ACK
SCRATCH
GAH
WAM
OOOCHIE!
EEE
YAGH
KICK KICK KICK
pinch!
CRASH
HEH HEH HEH
STAND BACK! BOTH OF YOU! OR FACE THE AWESOME POWER OF MY 'SECRET WEAPON'!
ACHOO ACHOO A...

NO ONE'S CERTAIN WHAT HAPPENED NEXT. PERHAPS IT WAS THE GLARING LATE AFTERNOON SUN. PERHAPS IT WAS THE ALLERGIES. IT ALMOST CERTAINLY WAS THE SNACK FOOD... REGARDLESS... THE NEXT INSTANT WOULD BE BURNED INTO THESE FIVE YOUNG MINDS ... FOREVER.

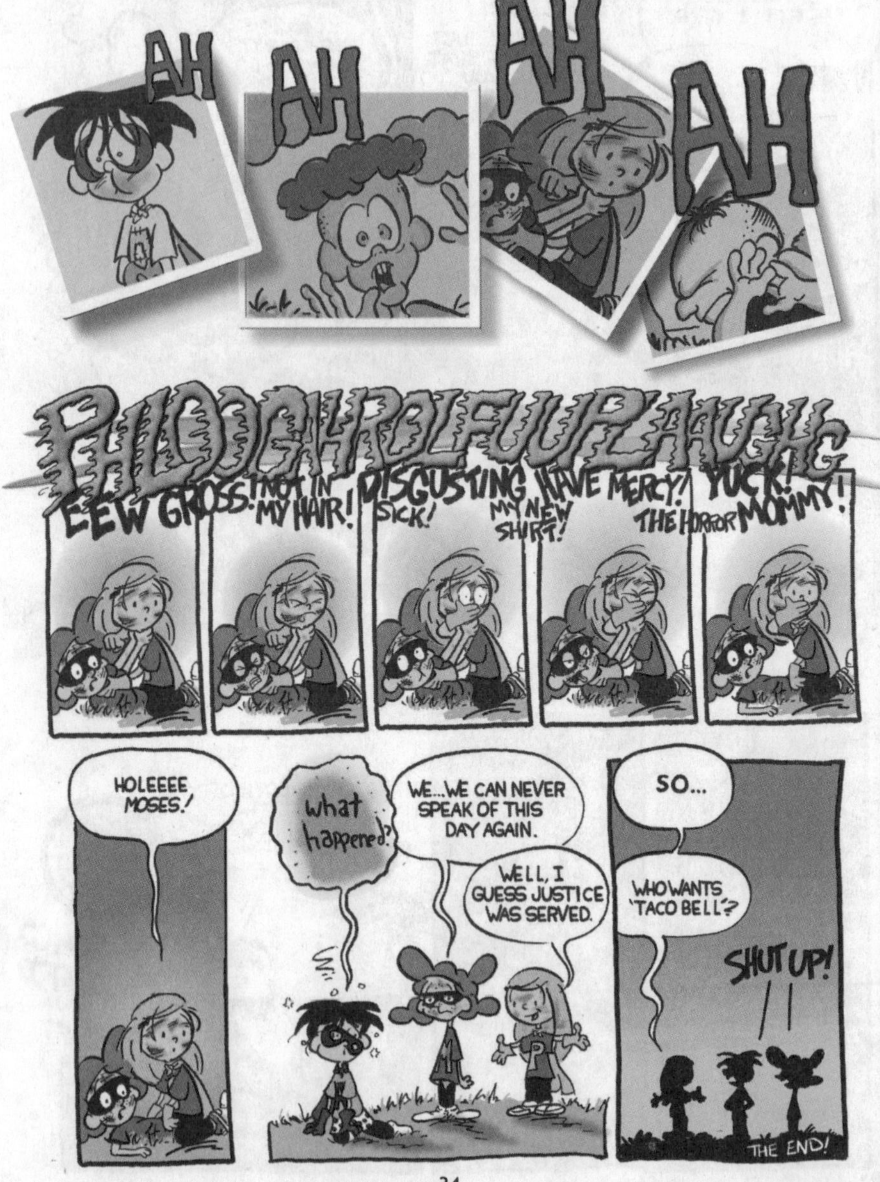
AH
AH
AH
AH
PHLOOGHROLFUUPLAUGHG
EEW GROSS!
NOT IN MY HAIR!
DISGUSTING
SICK!
HAVE MERCY!
MY NEW SHIRT!
YUCK!
THE HORROR
MOMMY!
HOLEEEE MOSES!
what happened?
WE...WE CAN NEVER SPEAK OF THIS DAY AGAIN.
WELL, I GUESS JUSTICE WAS SERVED.
SO...
WHO WANTS 'TACO BELL'?
SHUT UP!
THE END!

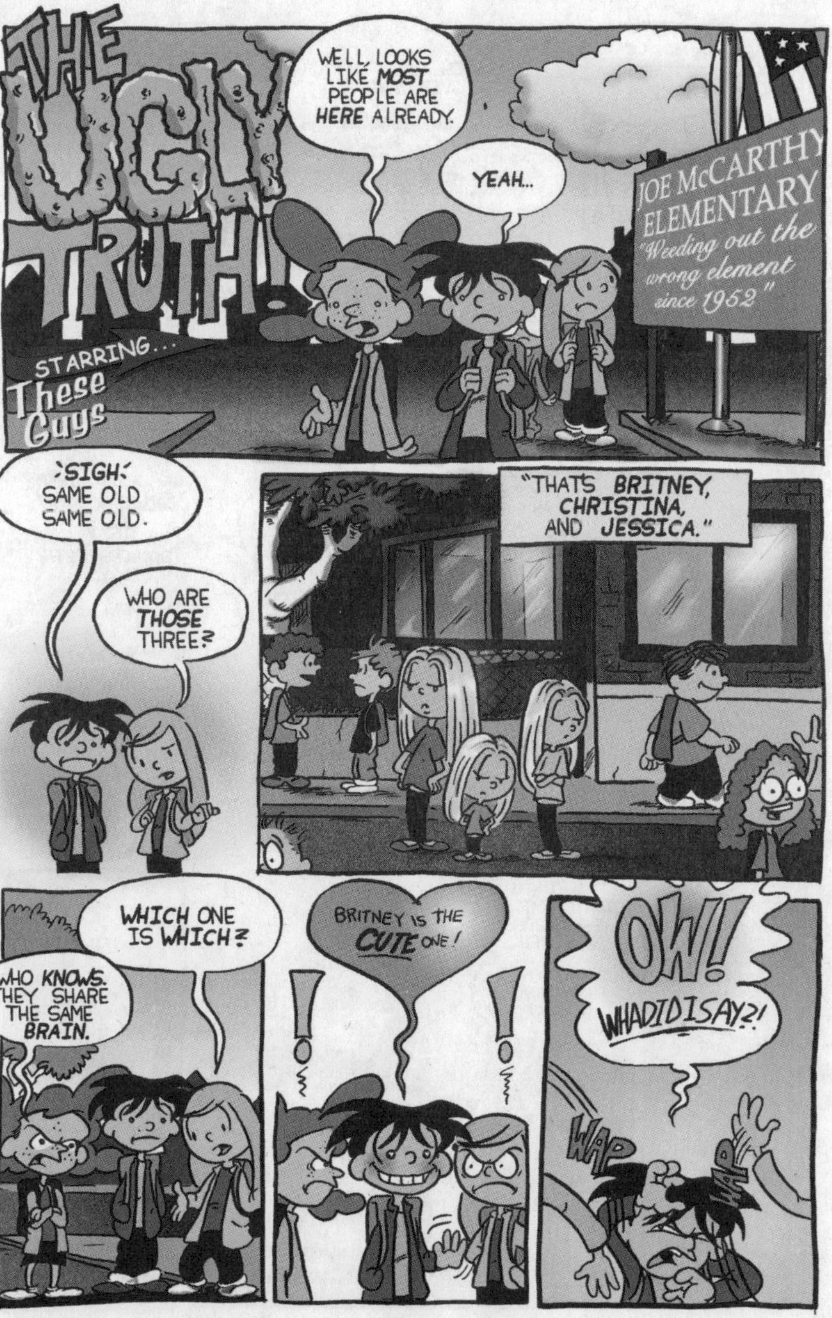
THE UGLY TRUTH!
STARRING...
These Guys
WELL, LOOKS LIKE MOST PEOPLE ARE HERE ALREADY.
YEAH...
JOE McCARTHY ELEMENTARY "Weeding out the wrong element since 1952"
SIGH SAME OLD SAME OLD.
WHO ARE THOSE THREE?
"THAT'S BRITNEY, CHRISTINA, AND JESSICA."
WHICH ONE IS WHICH?
WHO KNOWS. THEY SHARE THE SAME BRAIN.
BRITNEY IS THE CUTE ONE!
!
!
OW!
WHADIDISAY?!
WAP
WAP

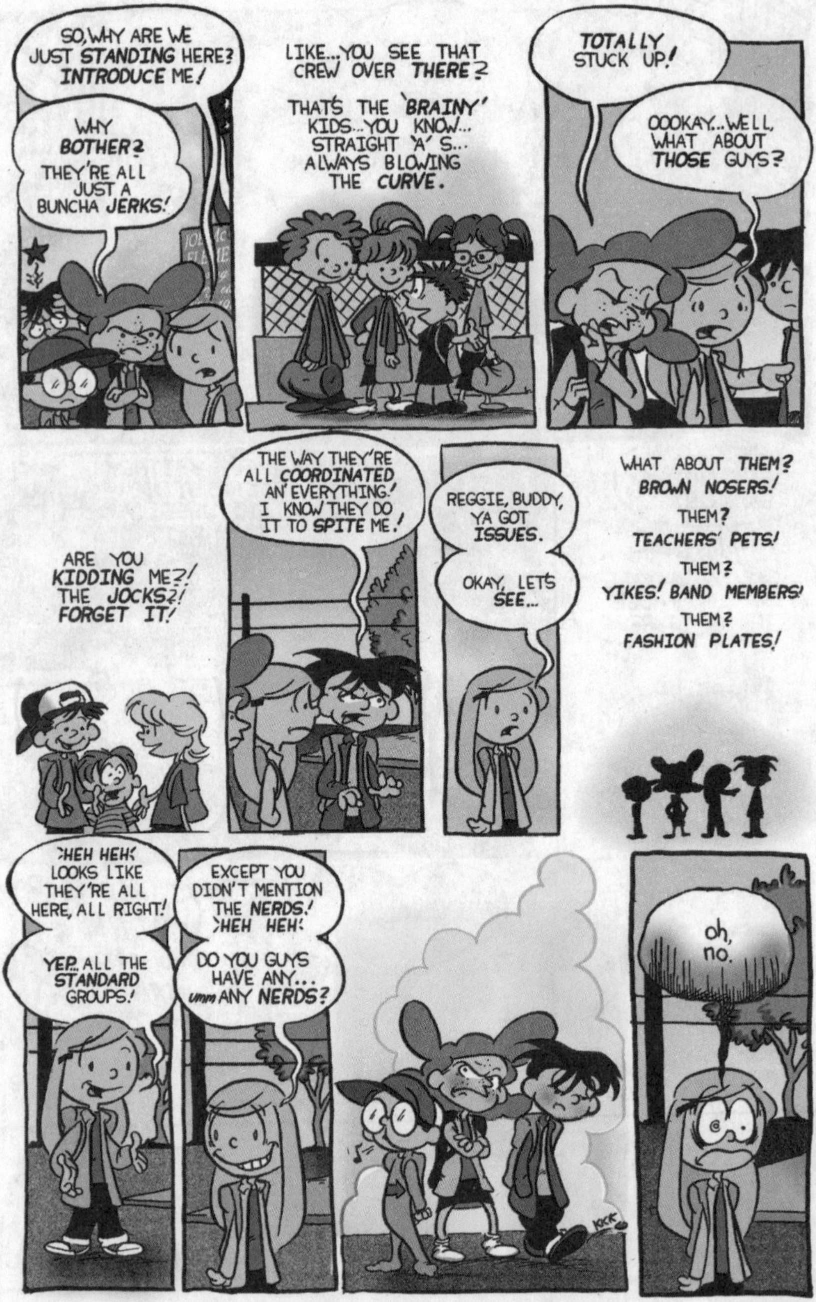

SO, WHY ARE WE JUST STANDING HERE? INTRODUCE ME!
WHY BOTHER? THEY'RE ALL JUST A BUNCHA JERKS!
LIKE... YOU SEE THAT CREW OVER THERE?
THAT'S THE 'BRAINY' KIDS... YOU KNOW... STRAIGHT 'A' S... ALWAYS BLOWING THE CURVE.
TOTALLY STUCK UP!
OOOKAY... WELL, WHAT ABOUT THOSE GUYS?
ARE YOU KIDDING ME?! THE JOCKS?! FORGET IT!
THE WAY THEY'RE ALL COORDINATED AN' EVERYTHING! I KNOW THEY DO IT TO SPITE ME!
REGGIE, BUDDY, YA GOT ISSUES.
OKAY, LET'S SEE...
WHAT ABOUT THEM? BROWN NOSERS!
THEM? TEACHERS' PETS!
THEM? YIKES! BAND MEMBERS!
THEM? FASHION PLATES!
HEH HEH LOOKS LIKE THEY'RE ALL HERE, ALL RIGHT!
YEP... ALL THE STANDARD GROUPS!
EXCEPT YOU DIDN'T MENTION THE NERDS! HEH HEH
DO YOU GUYS HAVE ANY... umm ANY NERDS?
KICK
oh, no.

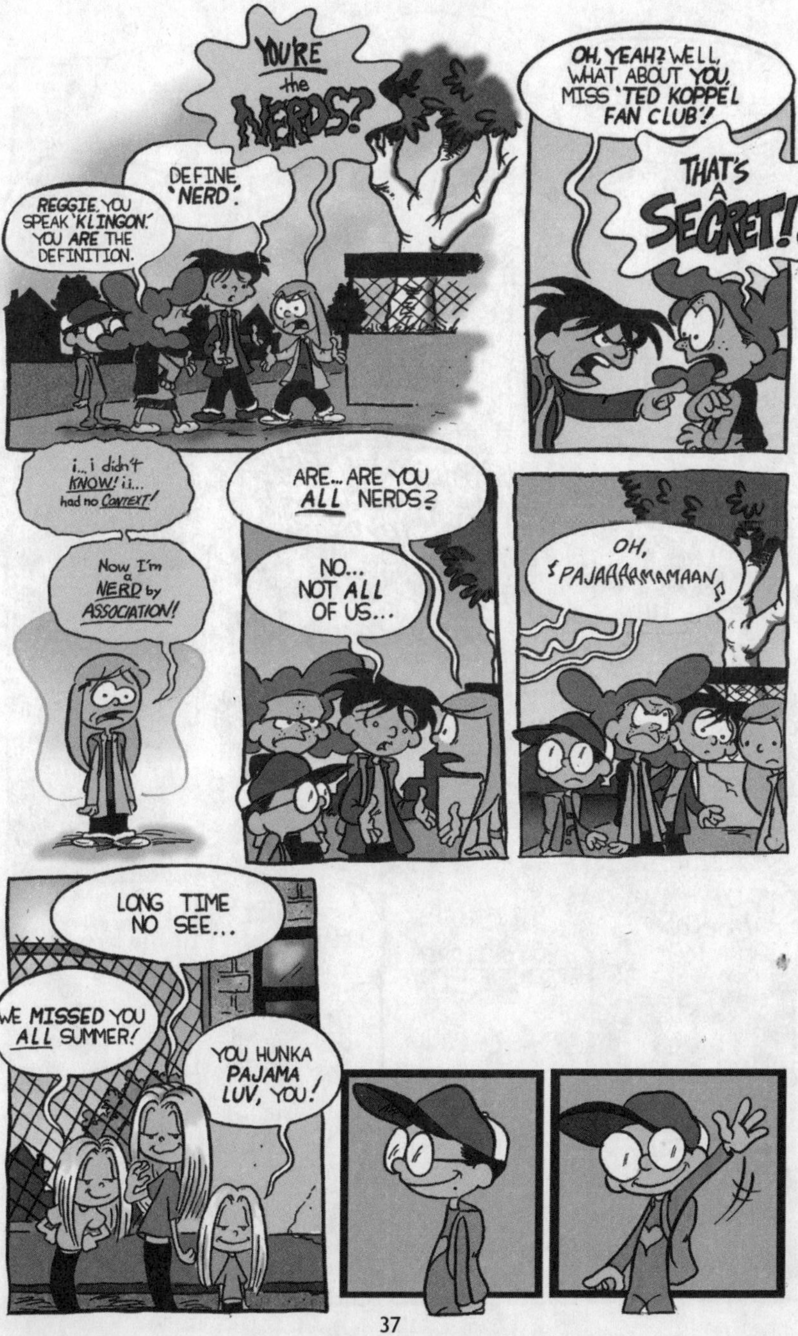
REGGIE, YOU SPEAK 'KLINGON.' YOU ARE THE DEFINITION.
DEFINE 'NERD.'
YOU'RE the NERDS?
OH, YEAH? WELL, WHAT ABOUT YOU, MISS 'TED KOPPEL FAN CLUB'!
THAT'S A SECRET!
i.. i didn't KNOW! i.i... had no CONTEXT!
Now I'm a NERD by ASSOCIATION!
ARE... ARE YOU ALL NERDS?
NO... NOT ALL OF US...
OH, PAJAAAAMAMAAN
LONG TIME NO SEE...
WE MISSED YOU ALL SUMMER!
YOU HUNKA PAJAMA LUV, YOU!

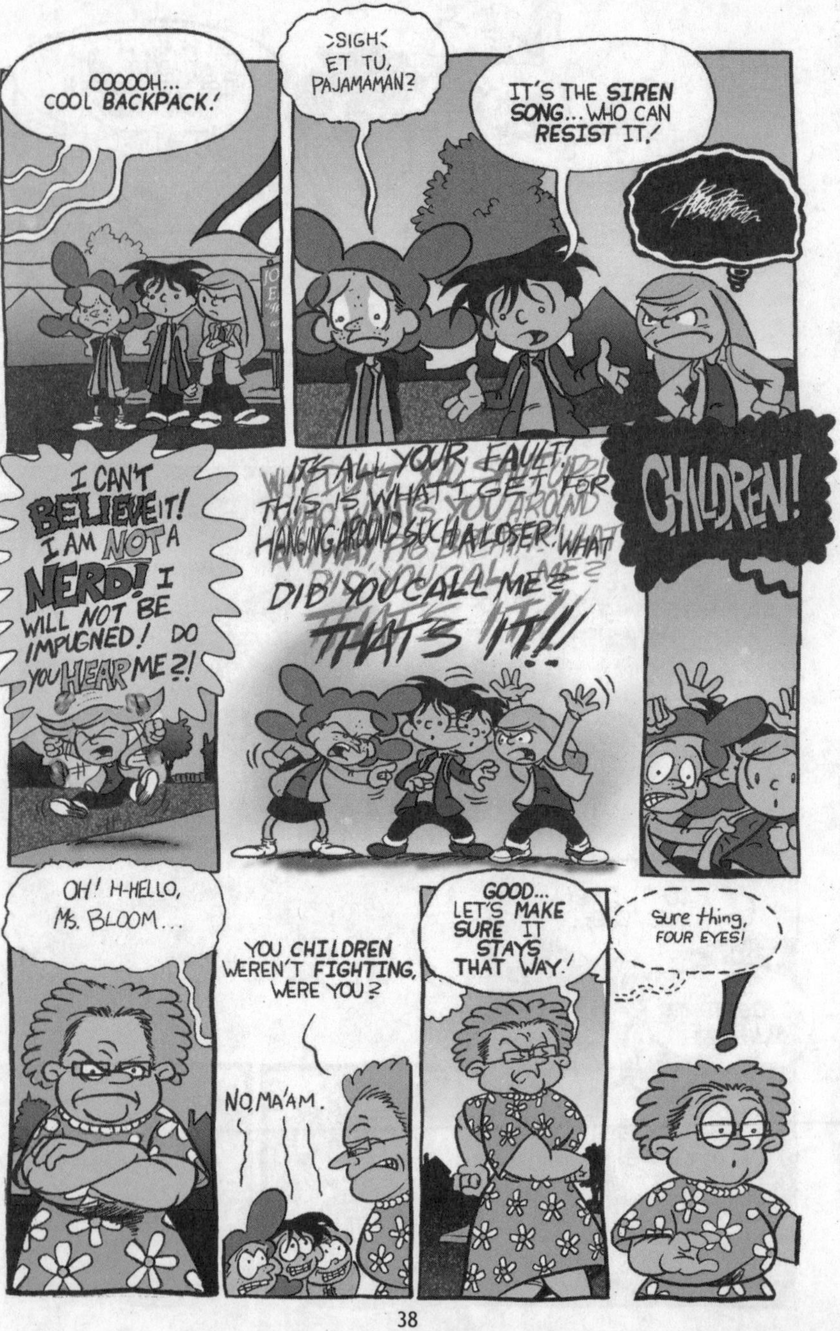
OOOOOH... COOL BACKPACK!
SIGH ET TU, PAJAMAMAN?
IT'S THE SIREN SONG... WHO CAN RESIST IT!
I CAN'T BELIEVE IT! I AM NOT A NERD! I WILL NOT BE IMPUGNED! DO YOU HEAR ME?!
IT'S ALL YOUR FAULT!
THIS IS WHAT I GET FOR HANGING AROUND SUCH A LOSER!
WHAT DID YOU CALL ME?
THAT'S IT!!
CHILDREN!
OH! H-HELLO, MS. BLOOM...
YOU CHILDREN WEREN'T FIGHTING, WERE YOU?
NO, MA'AM.
GOOD... LET'S MAKE SURE IT STAYS THAT WAY!
Sure thing, FOUR EYES!
!

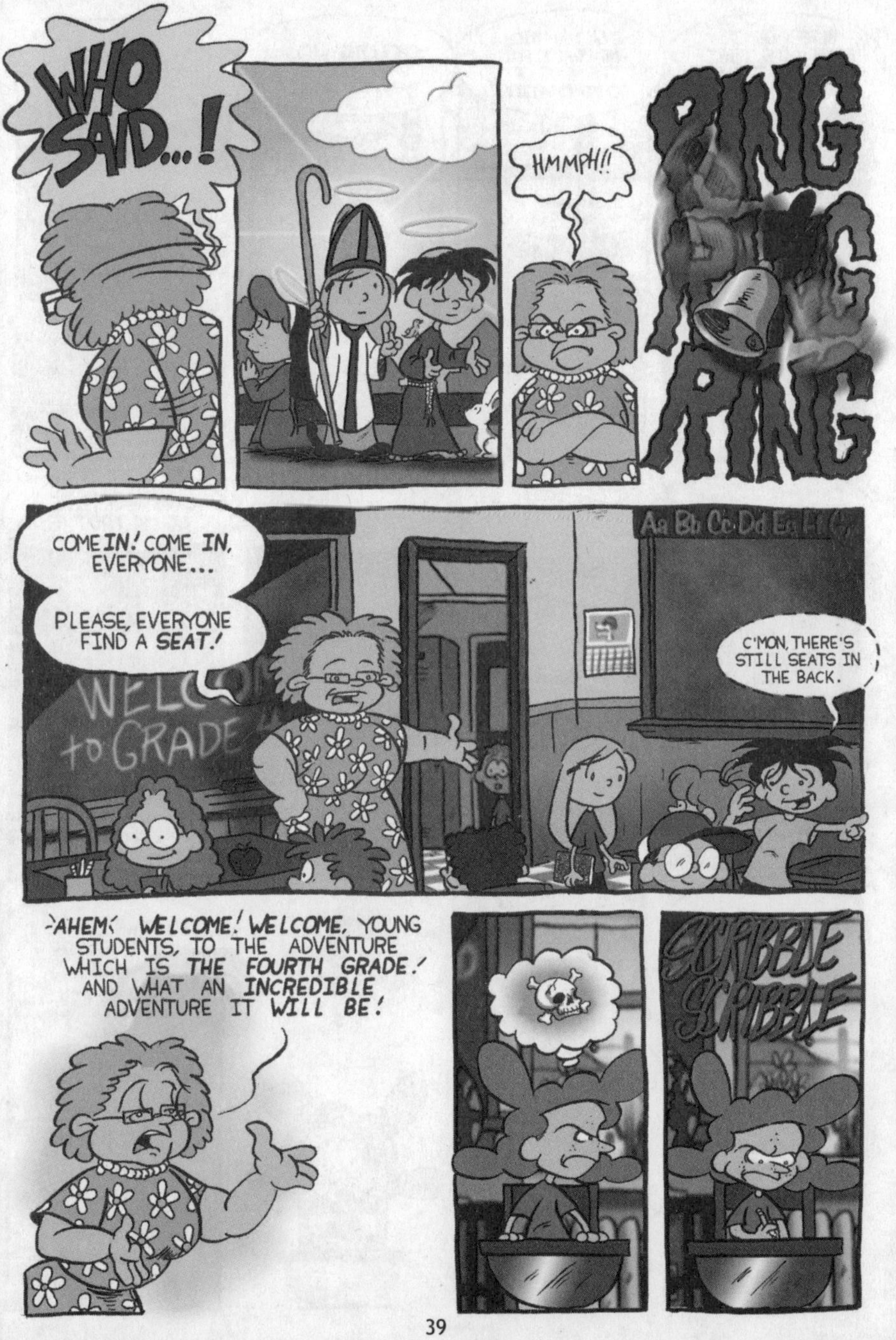
WHO SAID...!
HMMPH!!
RING RING RING
COME IN! COME IN, EVERYONE...
PLEASE, EVERYONE FIND A SEAT!
WELCOME to GRADE
C'MON, THERE'S STILL SEATS IN THE BACK.
Aa Bb Cc Dd Ee
-AHEM- WELCOME! WELCOME, YOUNG STUDENTS, TO THE ADVENTURE WHICH IS THE FOURTH GRADE! AND WHAT AN INCREDIBLE ADVENTURE IT WILL BE!
SCRIBBLE SCRIBBLE

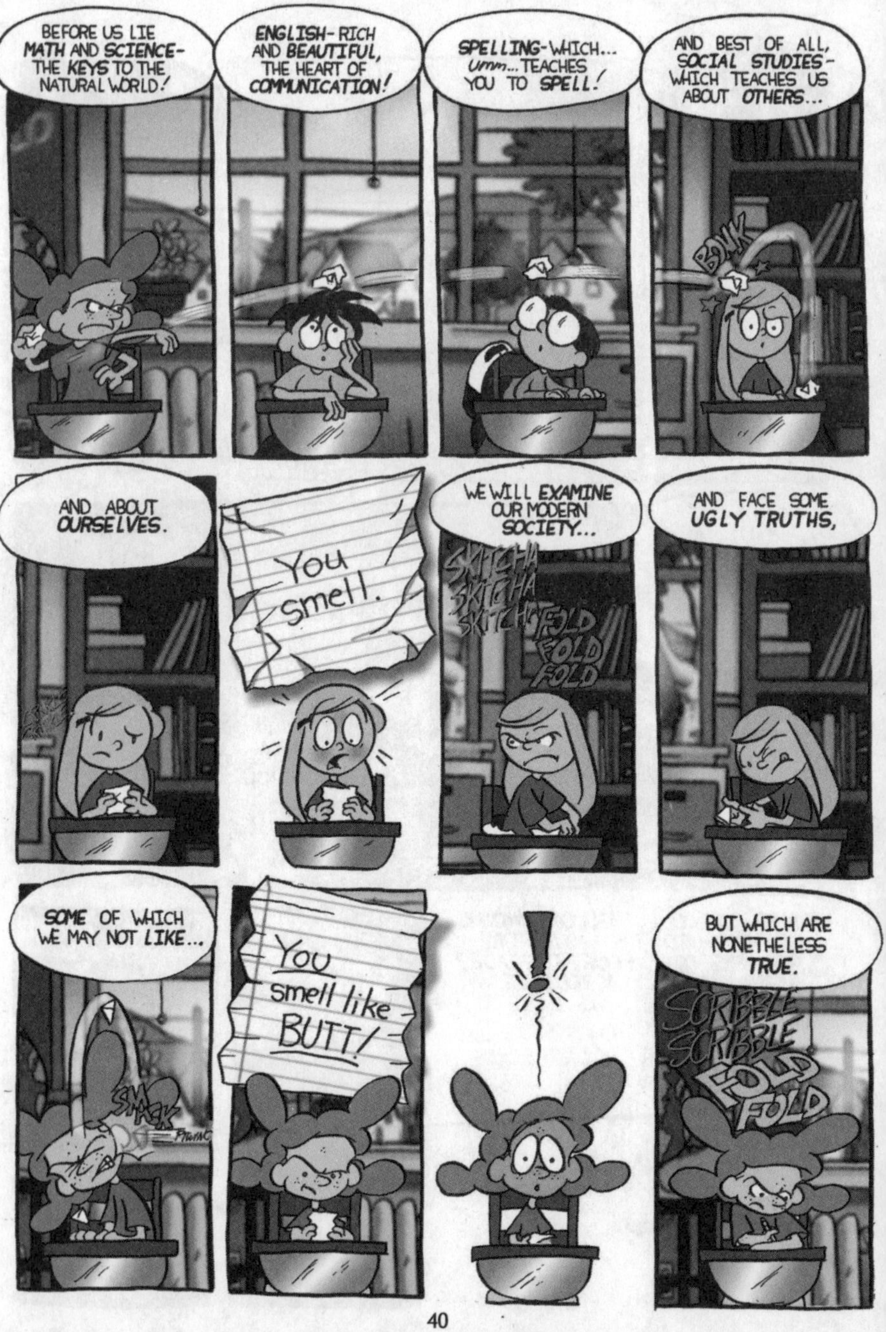
BEFORE US LIE MATH AND SCIENCE- THE KEYS TO THE NATURAL WORLD!
ENGLISH- RICH AND BEAUTIFUL, THE HEART OF COMMUNICATION!
SPELLING- WHICH... Umm... TEACHES YOU TO SPELL!
AND BEST OF ALL, SOCIAL STUDIES- WHICH TEACHES US ABOUT OTHERS...
BONK
AND ABOUT OURSELVES.
You smell.
WE WILL EXAMINE OUR MODERN SOCIETY...
SKITCHA SKITCHA SKITCHA
FOLD FOLD FOLD
AND FACE SOME UGLY TRUTHS,
SOME OF WHICH WE MAY NOT LIKE...
SMACK
You smell like BUTT!
!
BUT WHICH ARE NONETHELESS TRUE.
SCRIBBLE SCRIBBLE
FOLD FOLD

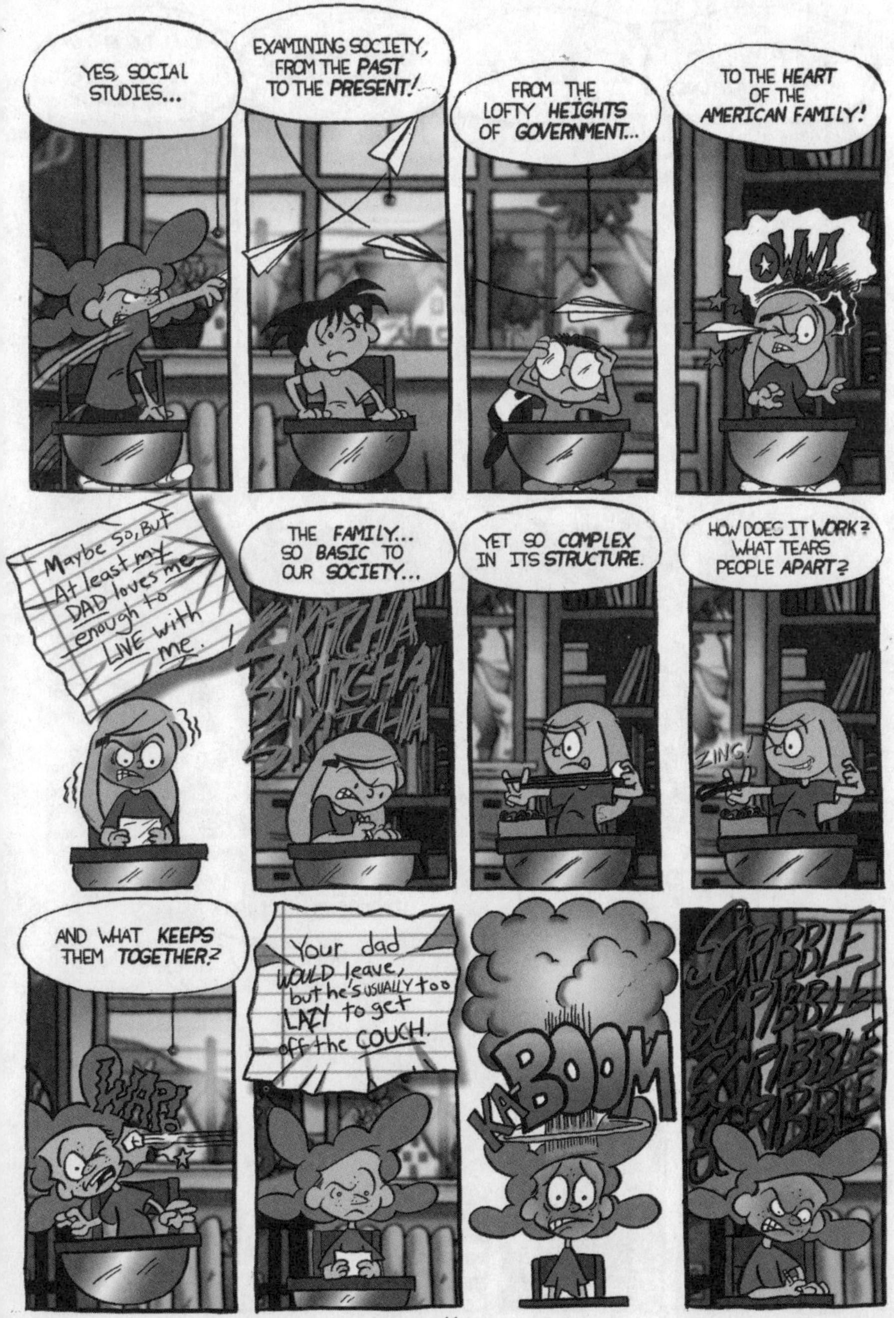
YES, SOCIAL STUDIES...
EXAMINING SOCIETY, FROM THE PAST TO THE PRESENT!
FROM THE LOFTY HEIGHTS OF GOVERNMENT...
TO THE HEART OF THE AMERICAN FAMILY!
OWW!
Maybe so, But At least my DAD loves me enough to LIVE with me.
THE FAMILY... SO BASIC TO OUR SOCIETY...
SKITCHA SKITCHA SKITCHA
YET SO COMPLEX IN ITS STRUCTURE.
HOW DOES IT WORK? WHAT TEARS PEOPLE APART?
ZING!
AND WHAT KEEPS THEM TOGETHER?
WAP!
Your dad WOULD leave, but he's USUALLY too LAZY to get off the COUCH.
KA-BOOM
SCRIBBLE SCRIBBLE SCRIBBLE SCRIBBLE

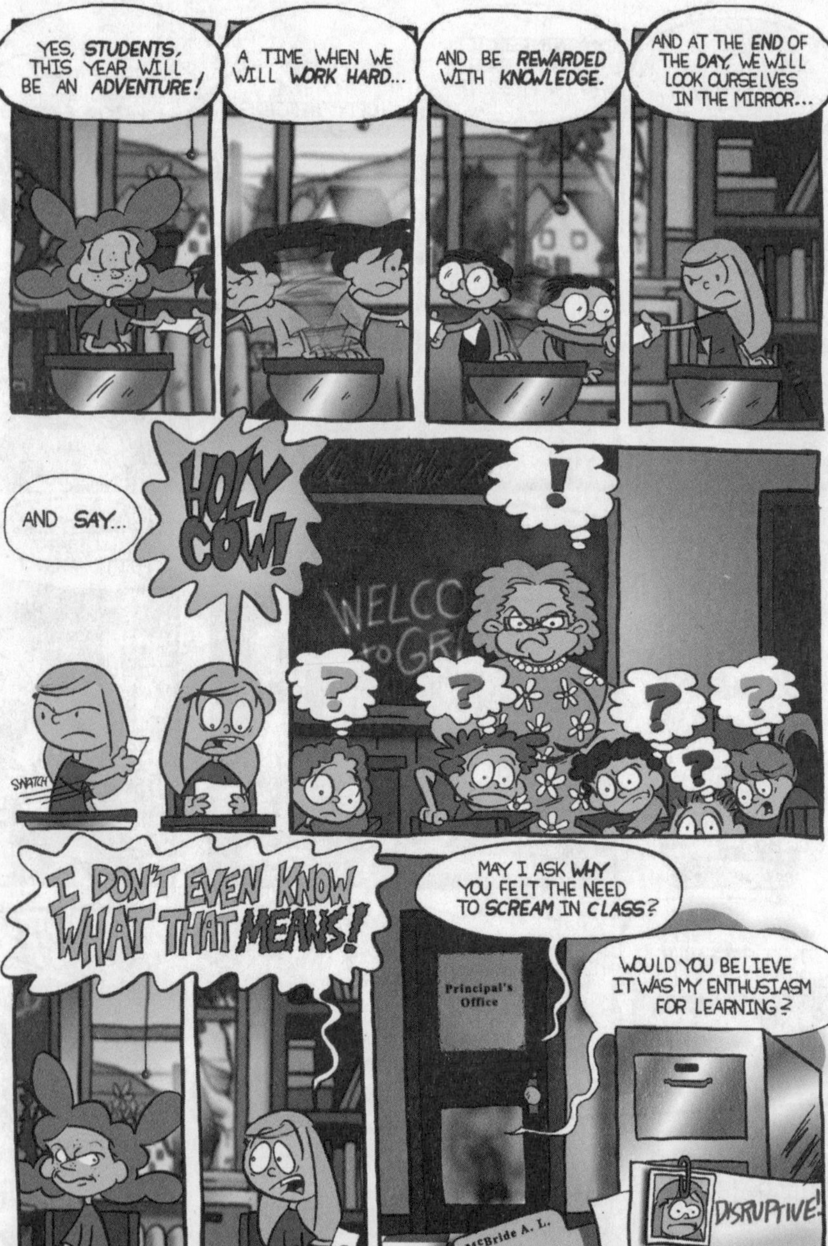
YES, STUDENTS, THIS YEAR WILL BE AN ADVENTURE!
A TIME WHEN WE WILL WORK HARD...
AND BE REWARDED WITH KNOWLEDGE.
AND AT THE END OF THE DAY, WE WILL LOOK OURSELVES IN THE MIRROR...
AND SAY...
HOLY COW!
!
WELCO to GR
?
?
?
?
?
SWATCH
I DON'T EVEN KNOW WHAT THAT MEANS!
MAY I ASK WHY YOU FELT THE NEED TO SCREAM IN CLASS?
Principal's Office
WOULD YOU BELIEVE IT WAS MY ENTHUSIASM FOR LEARNING?
DISRUPTIVE!
McBride A. L.
PERMANENT RECORD

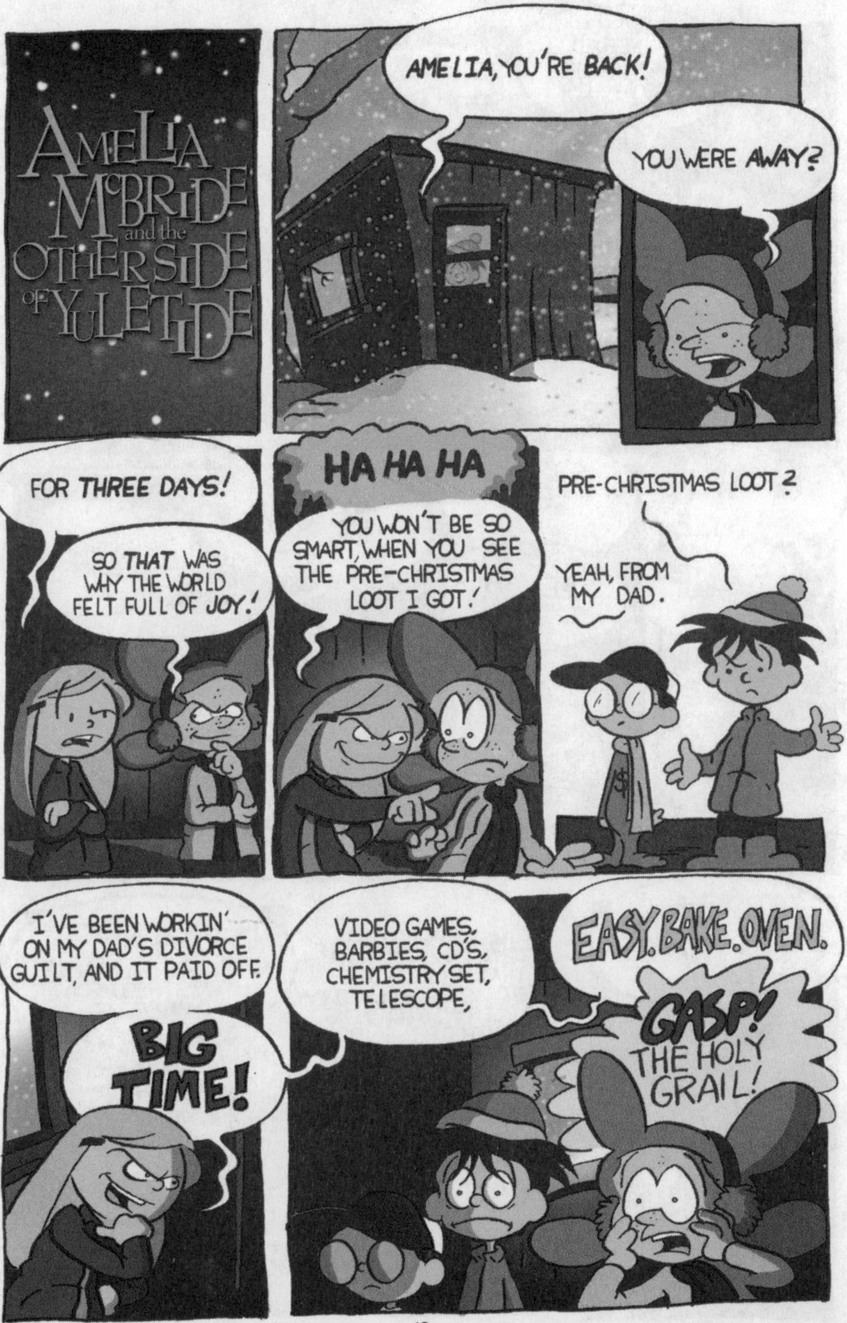
AMELIA McBRIDE and the OTHER SIDE of YULETIDE
AMELIA, YOU'RE BACK!
YOU WERE AWAY?
FOR THREE DAYS!
SO THAT WAS WHY THE WORLD FELT FULL OF JOY!
HA HA HA
YOU WON'T BE SO SMART, WHEN YOU SEE THE PRE-CHRISTMAS LOOT I GOT!
PRE-CHRISTMAS LOOT?
YEAH, FROM MY DAD.
I'VE BEEN WORKIN' ON MY DAD'S DIVORCE GUILT, AND IT PAID OFF.
BIG TIME!
VIDEO GAMES, BARBIES, CD'S, CHEMISTRY SET, TELESCOPE,
EASY. BAKE. OVEN.
GASP! THE HOLY GRAIL!

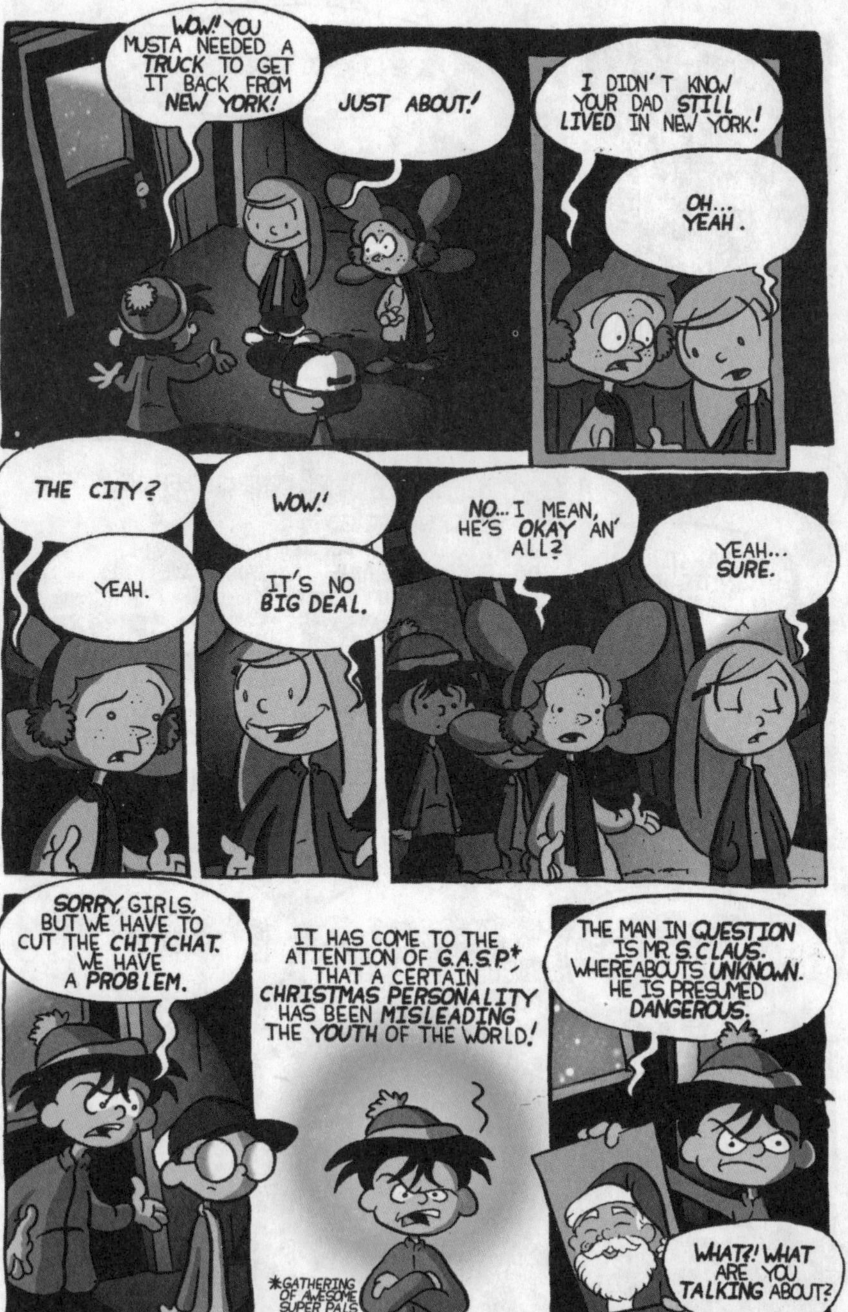
WOW! YOU MUSTA NEEDED A TRUCK TO GET IT BACK FROM NEW YORK!
JUST ABOUT!
I DIDN'T KNOW YOUR DAD STILL LIVED IN NEW YORK!
OH... YEAH.
THE CITY?
YEAH.
WOW!
IT'S NO BIG DEAL.
NO... I MEAN, HE'S OKAY AN' ALL?
YEAH... SURE.
SORRY, GIRLS, BUT WE HAVE TO CUT THE CHITCHAT. WE HAVE A PROBLEM.
IT HAS COME TO THE ATTENTION OF G.A.S.P.* THAT A CERTAIN CHRISTMAS PERSONALITY HAS BEEN MISLEADING THE YOUTH OF THE WORLD!
*GATHERING OF AWESOME SUPER PALS
THE MAN IN QUESTION IS MR. S. CLAUS. WHEREABOUTS UNKNOWN. HE IS PRESUMED DANGEROUS.
WHAT?! WHAT ARE YOU TALKING ABOUT?

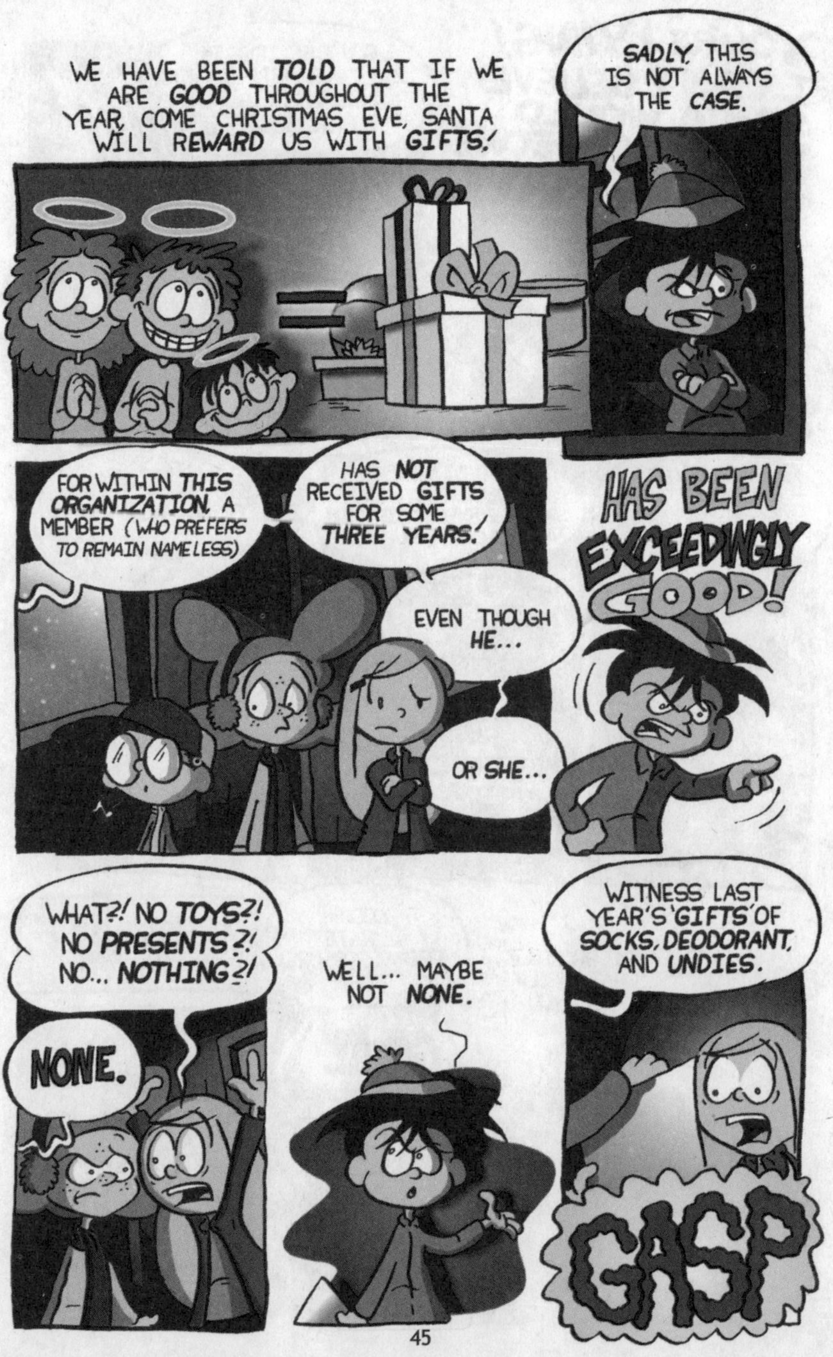
WE HAVE BEEN TOLD THAT IF WE ARE GOOD THROUGHOUT THE YEAR, COME CHRISTMAS EVE, SANTA WILL REWARD US WITH GIFTS!
SADLY, THIS IS NOT ALWAYS THE CASE.
FOR WITHIN THIS ORGANIZATION, A MEMBER (WHO PREFERS TO REMAIN NAMELESS)
HAS NOT RECEIVED GIFTS FOR SOME THREE YEARS!
EVEN THOUGH HE...
OR SHE...
HAS BEEN EXCEEDINGLY GOOD!
WHAT?! NO TOYS?! NO PRESENTS?! NO... NOTHING?!
NONE.
WELL... MAYBE NOT NONE.
WITNESS LAST YEAR'S 'GIFTS' OF SOCKS, DEODORANT, AND UNDIES.
GASP

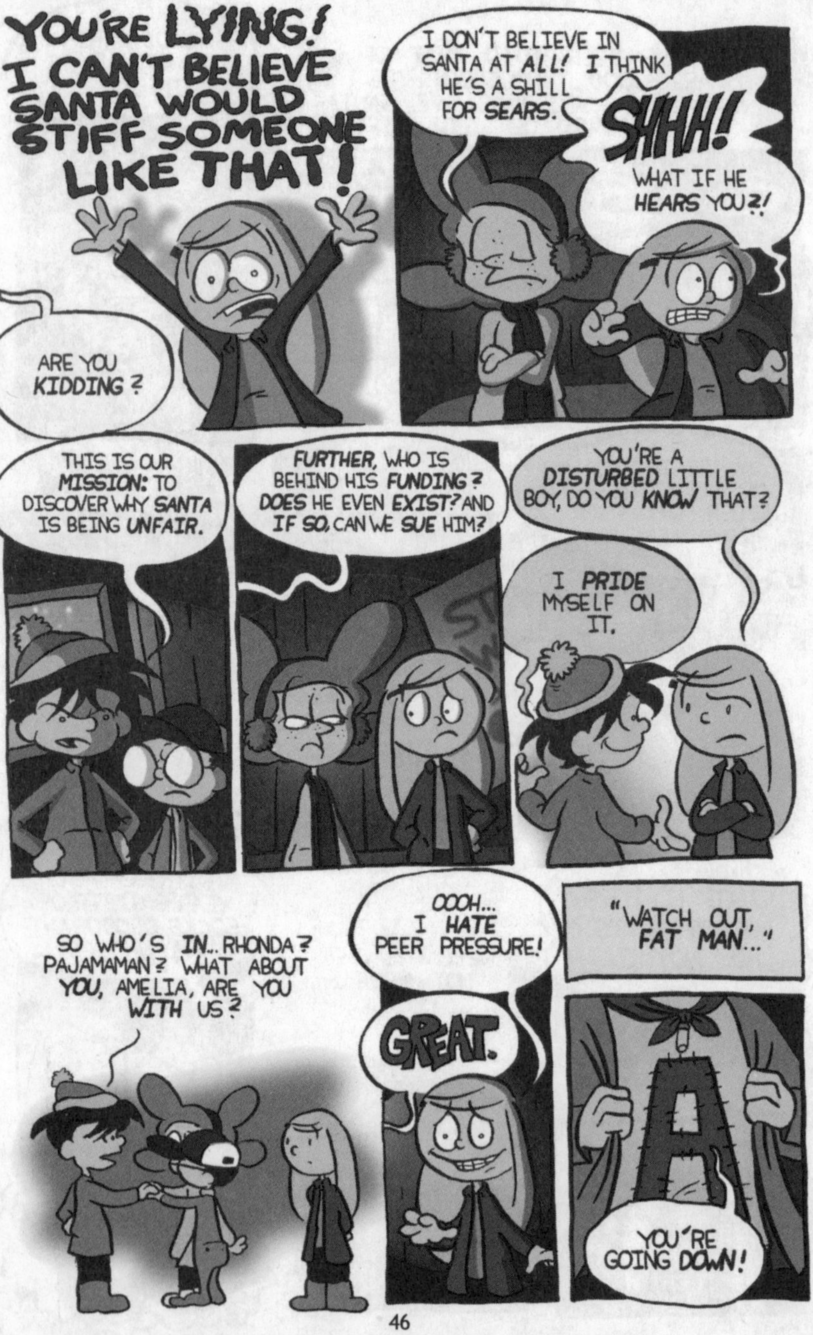
YOU'RE LYING! I CAN'T BELIEVE SANTA WOULD STIFF SOMEONE LIKE THAT!
ARE YOU KIDDING?
I DON'T BELIEVE IN SANTA AT ALL! I THINK HE'S A SHILL FOR SEARS.
SHHH!
WHAT IF HE HEARS YOU?!
THIS IS OUR MISSION: TO DISCOVER WHY SANTA IS BEING UNFAIR.
FURTHER, WHO IS BEHIND HIS FUNDING? DOES HE EVEN EXIST? AND IF SO, CAN WE SUE HIM?
YOU'RE A DISTURBED LITTLE BOY, DO YOU KNOW THAT?
I PRIDE MYSELF ON IT.
SO WHO'S IN... RHONDA? PAJAMAMAN? WHAT ABOUT YOU, AMELIA, ARE YOU WITH US?
OOOH... I HATE PEER PRESSURE!
GREAT.
"WATCH OUT, FAT MAN..."
YOU'RE GOING DOWN!

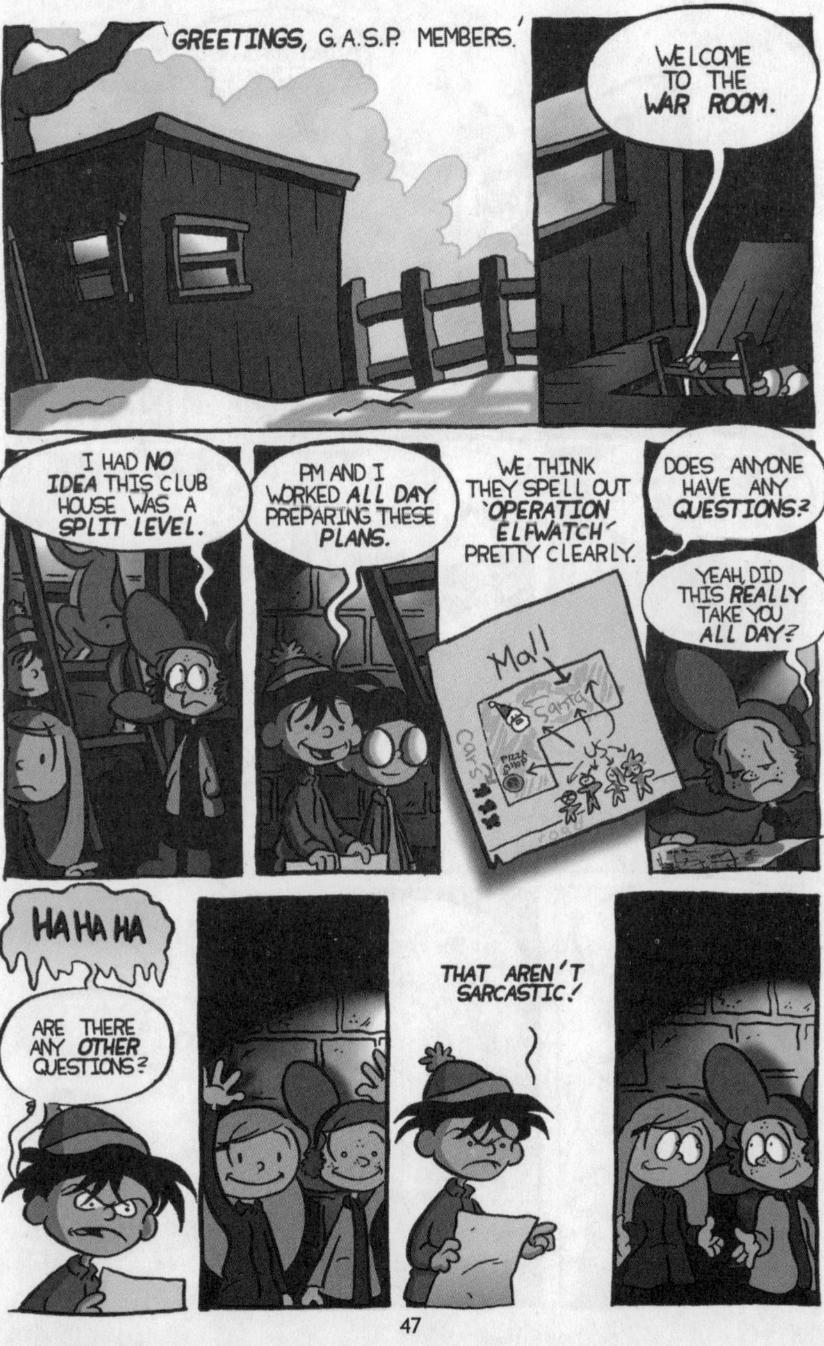
'GREETINGS, G.A.S.P. MEMBERS.'
WELCOME TO THE WAR ROOM.
I HAD NO IDEA THIS CLUB HOUSE WAS A SPLIT LEVEL.
PM AND I WORKED ALL DAY PREPARING THESE PLANS.
WE THINK THEY SPELL OUT 'OPERATION ELFWATCH' PRETTY CLEARLY.
Mall
Santa
Cars
PIZZA SHOP
US
DOES ANYONE HAVE ANY QUESTIONS?
YEAH, DID THIS REALLY TAKE YOU ALL DAY?
HA HA HA
ARE THERE ANY OTHER QUESTIONS?
THAT AREN'T SARCASTIC!

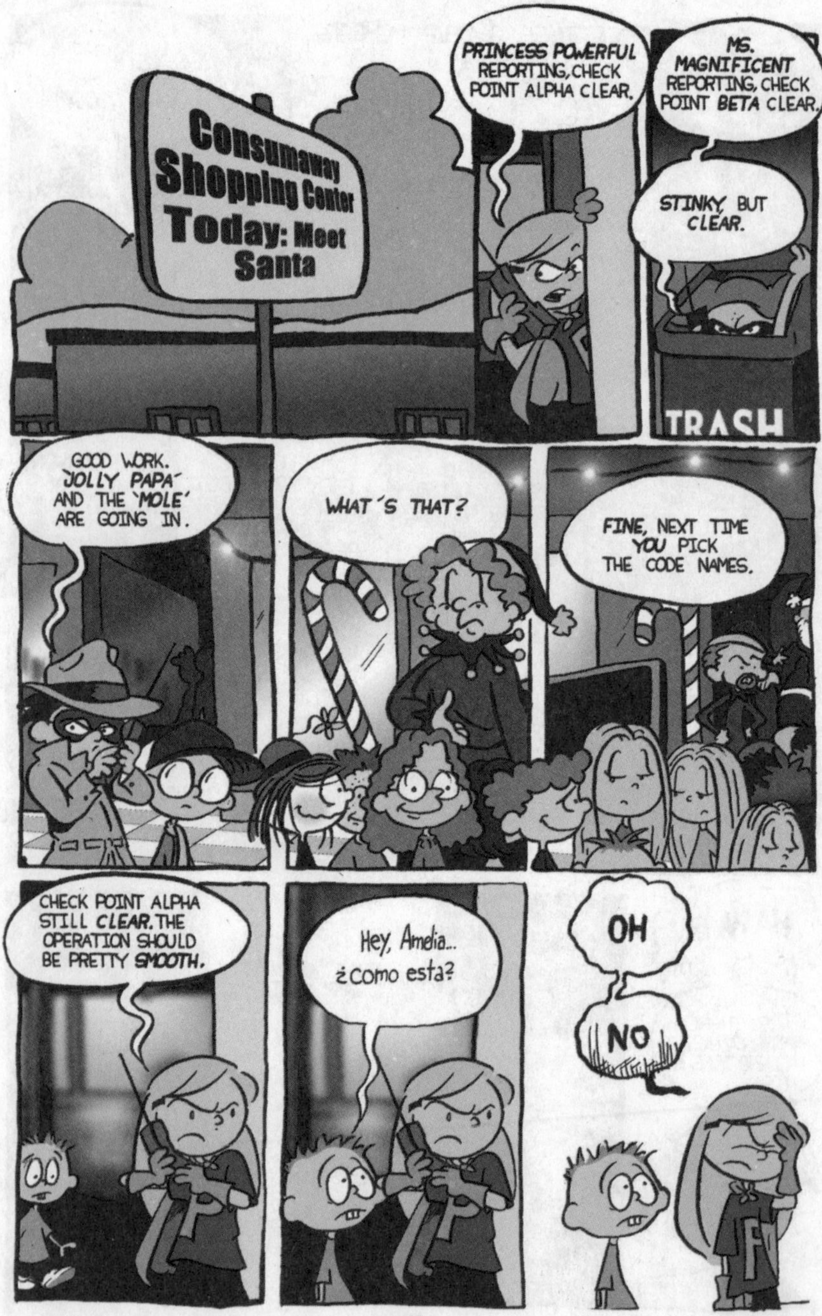
Consumaway Shopping Center Today: Meet Santa
PRINCESS POWERFUL REPORTING, CHECK POINT ALPHA CLEAR.
MS. MAGNIFICENT REPORTING, CHECK POINT BETA CLEAR.
STINKY, BUT CLEAR.
TRASH
GOOD WORK. 'JOLLY PAPA' AND THE 'MOLE' ARE GOING IN.
WHAT'S THAT?
FINE, NEXT TIME YOU PICK THE CODE NAMES.
CHECK POINT ALPHA STILL CLEAR. THE OPERATION SHOULD BE PRETTY SMOOTH.
Hey, Amelia... ¿como esta?
OH
NO

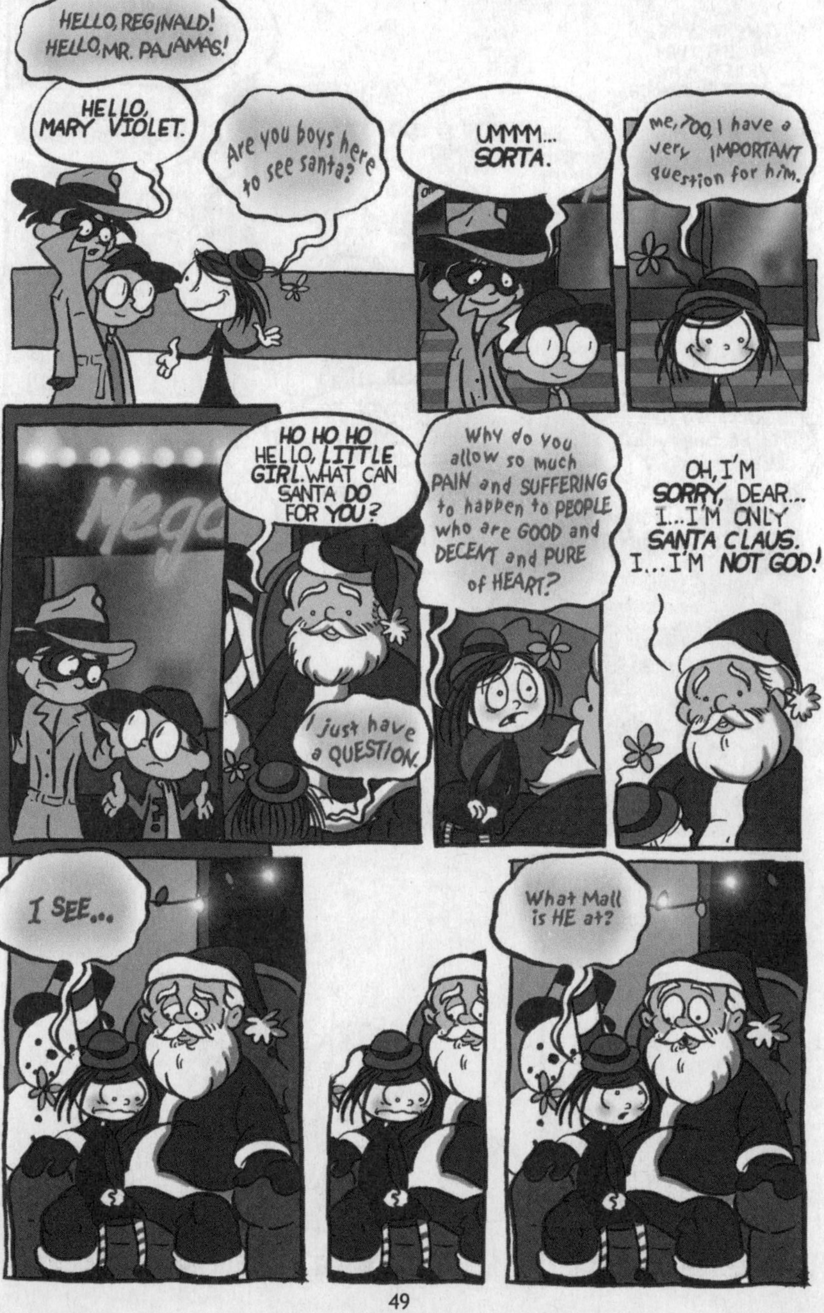

HELLO, REGINALD! HELLO, MR. PAJAMAS!
HELLO, MARY VIOLET.
Are you boys here to see santa?
UMMMM... SORTA.
me, TOO, I have a very IMPORTANT question for him.
HO HO HO HELLO, LITTLE GIRL. WHAT CAN SANTA DO FOR YOU?
I just have a QUESTION.
Why do you allow so much PAIN and SUFFERING to happen to PEOPLE who are GOOD and DECENT and PURE of HEART?
OH, I'M SORRY, DEAR... I... I'M ONLY SANTA CLAUS. I... I'M NOT GOD!
I SEE...
What Mall is HE at?

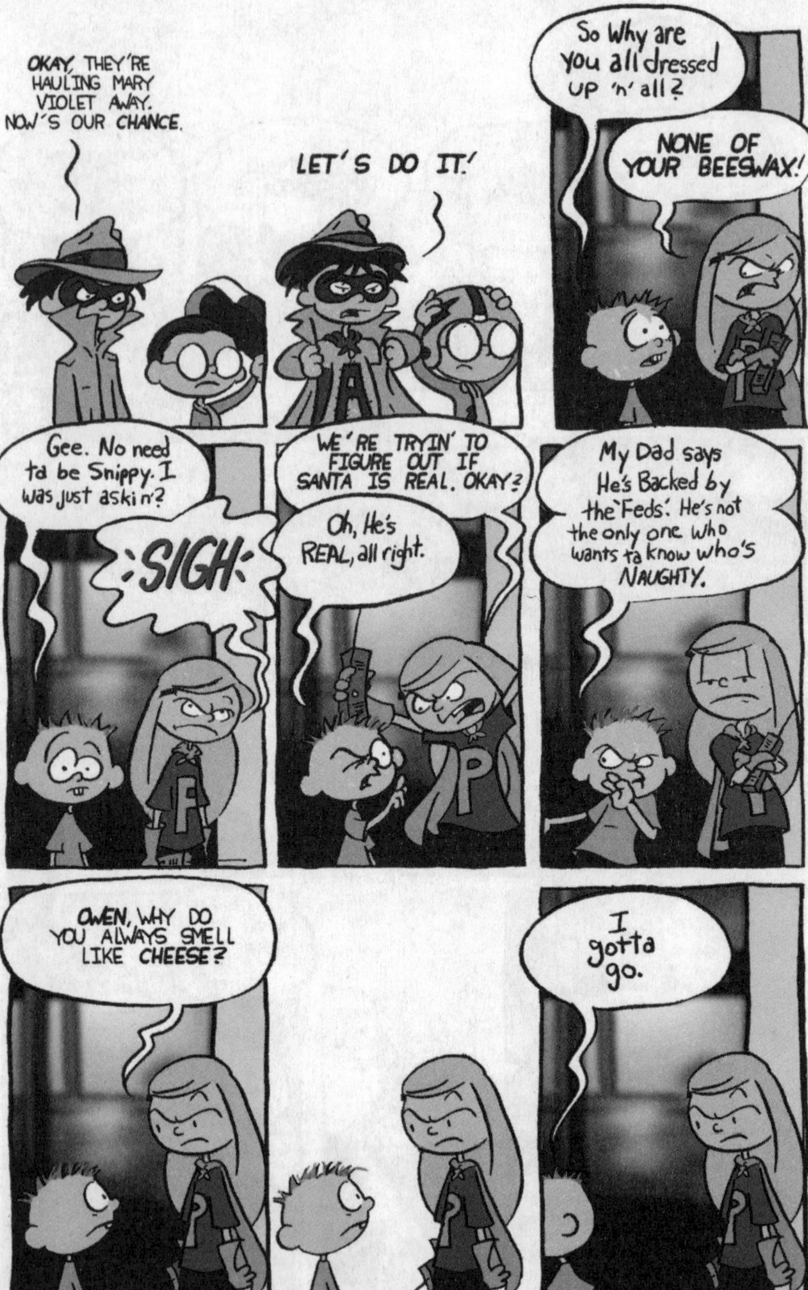
OKAY, THEY'RE HAULING MARY VIOLET AWAY. NOW'S OUR CHANCE.
LET'S DO IT!
So Why are you all dressed up 'n' all?
NONE OF YOUR BEESWAX!
Gee. No need ta be Snippy. I was just askin'?
SIGH
WE'RE TRYIN' TO FIGURE OUT IF SANTA IS REAL. OKAY?
Oh, He's REAL, all right.
My Dad says He's Backed by the 'Feds'. He's not the only one who wants ta know who's NAUGHTY.
OWEN, WHY DO YOU ALWAYS SMELL LIKE CHEESE?
I gotta go.

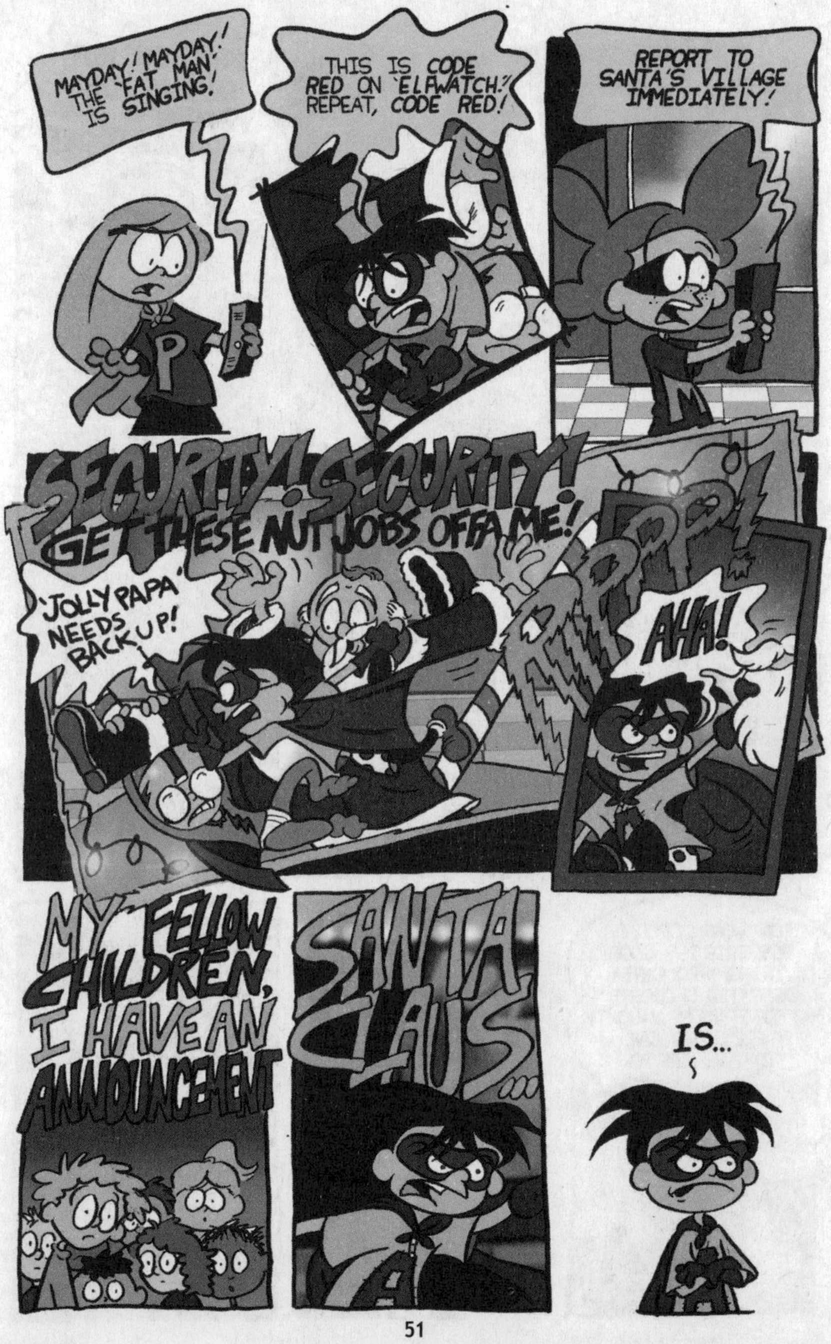
MAYDAY! MAYDAY! THE 'FAT MAN' IS SINGING!
THIS IS CODE RED ON 'ELFWATCH!' REPEAT, CODE RED!
REPORT TO SANTA'S VILLAGE IMMEDIATELY!
SECURITY! SECURITY! GET THESE NUT JOBS OFFA ME!
'JOLLY PAPA' NEEDS BACK UP!
AHA!
MY FELLOW CHILDREN, I HAVE AN ANNOUNCEMENT
SANTA CLAUS...
IS...

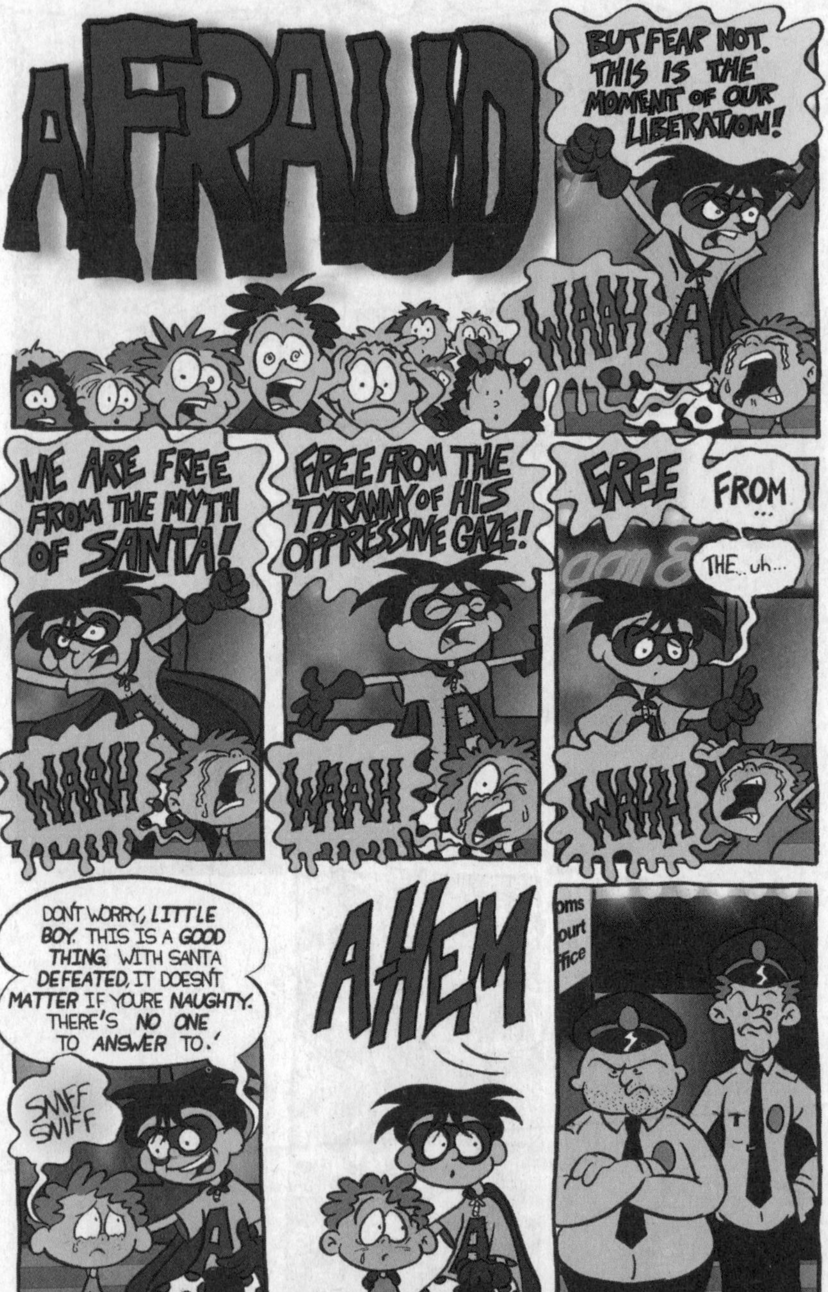
A FRAUD
BUT FEAR NOT. THIS IS THE MOMENT OF OUR LIBERATION!
WAAH
WE ARE FREE FROM THE MYTH OF SANTA!
WAAH
FREE FROM THE TYRANNY OF HIS OPPRESSIVE GAZE!
WAAH
FREE
FROM ...
THE... uh...
WAHH
DON'T WORRY, LITTLE BOY. THIS IS A GOOD THING. WITH SANTA DEFEATED, IT DOESN'T MATTER IF YOU'RE NAUGHTY. THERE'S NO ONE TO ANSWER TO.
SNIFF SNIFF
A-HEM

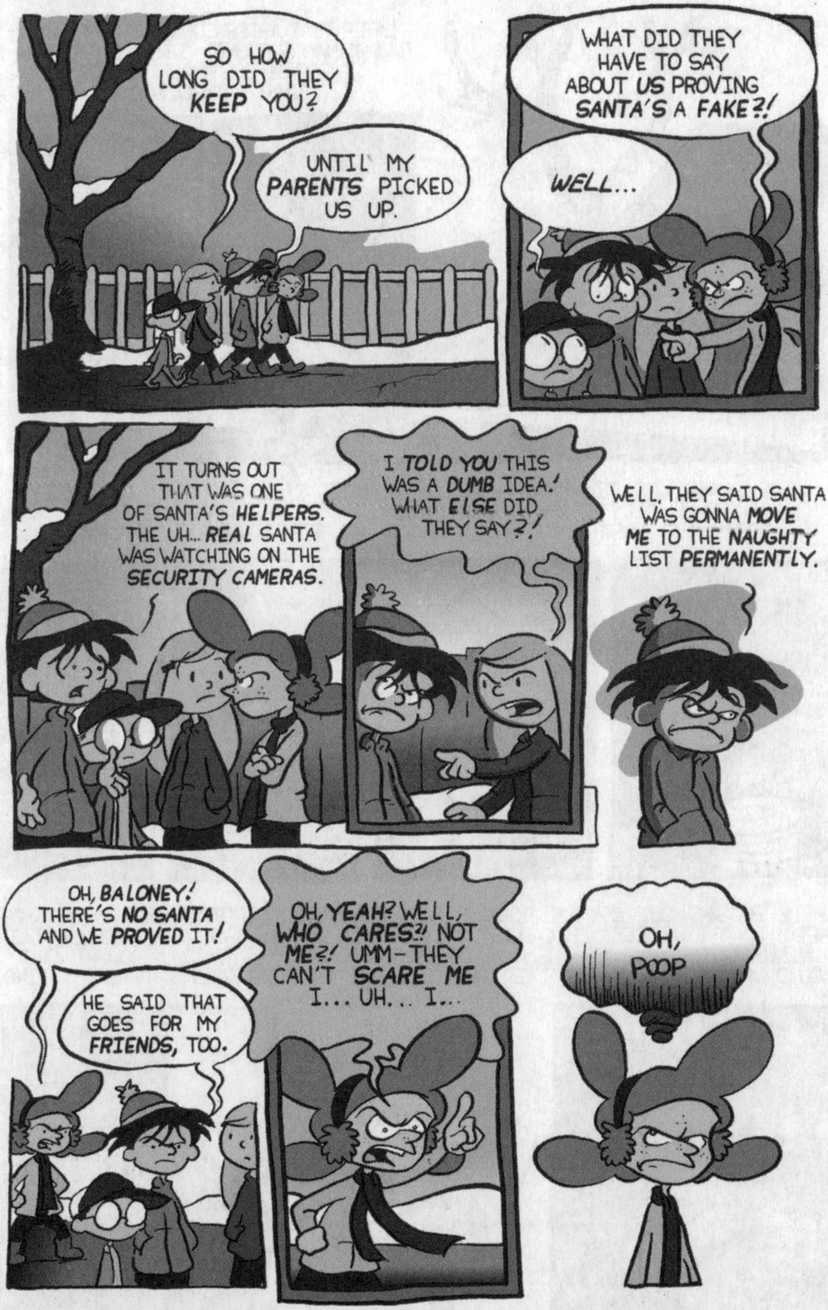
SO HOW LONG DID THEY KEEP YOU?
UNTIL MY PARENTS PICKED US UP.
WHAT DID THEY HAVE TO SAY ABOUT US PROVING SANTA'S A FAKE?!
WELL...
IT TURNS OUT THAT WAS ONE OF SANTA'S HELPERS. THE UH... REAL SANTA WAS WATCHING ON THE SECURITY CAMERAS.
I TOLD YOU THIS WAS A DUMB IDEA! WHAT ELSE DID THEY SAY?!
WELL, THEY SAID SANTA WAS GONNA MOVE ME TO THE NAUGHTY LIST PERMANENTLY.
OH, BALONEY! THERE'S NO SANTA AND WE PROVED IT!
HE SAID THAT GOES FOR MY FRIENDS, TOO.
OH, YEAH? WELL, WHO CARES?! NOT ME?! UMM-THEY CAN'T SCARE ME I... UH... I...
OH, POOP

LATER THAT AFTERNOON WE STOPPED BY ***PAJAMAMAN'S HOUSE.*** I HAD NEVER BEEN THERE BEFORE, AND IT WASN'T WHAT I ***EXPECTED.***

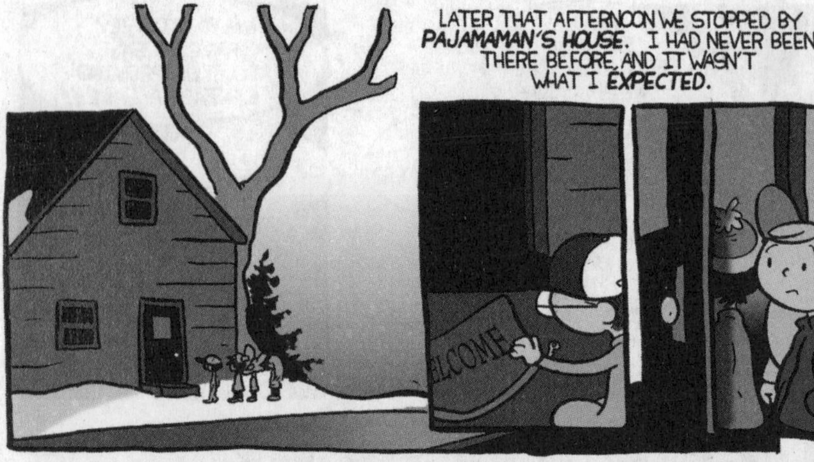
ELCOME

THE PLACE WAS ***TINY*** AND KIND OF A ***MESS.*** IT WAS PRETTY ***OBVIOUS*** HIS FOLKS DIDN'T HAVE MUCH ***MONEY.*** I HAD BEEN FEELING SORTA SORRY FOR MYSELF, BUT SUDDENLY I WAS FEELING PRETTY ***LUCKY.***

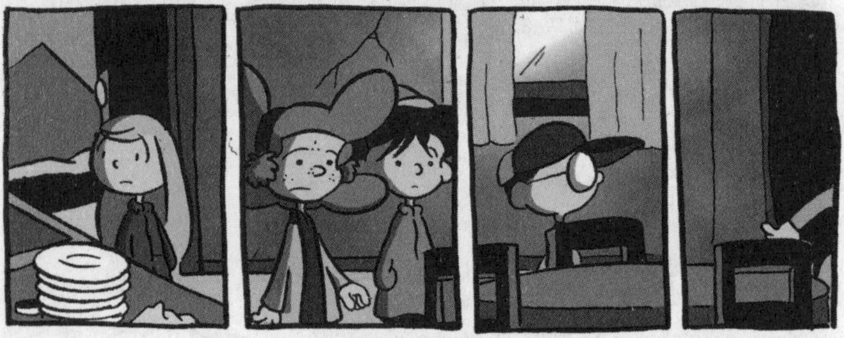

WHILE PM WAS OUT OF THE ROOM, I NOTICED THIS ***CLIPPING*** FROM A CATALOG TAPED TO THE FRIDGE. IT CAUGHT MY EYE 'CUZ IT WAS FOR THE ***'RED CAPTAIN NINJA'*** WHICH WAS AT THE TOP OF ***MY*** 'WANT LIST.' I REALLY THOUGHT DAD WOULD ***COME THROUGH*** WITH IT, BUT I GUESS THEY'RE PRETTY HARD TO FIND.

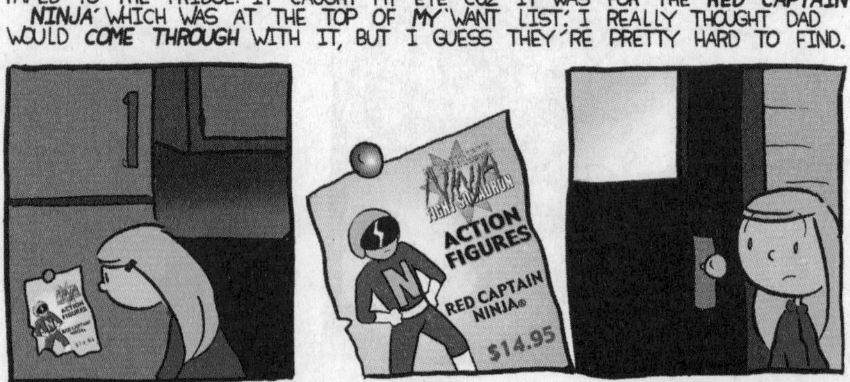
NINJA
FIGHT SQUADRON
ACTION FIGURES
RED CAPTAIN NINJA®
$14.95

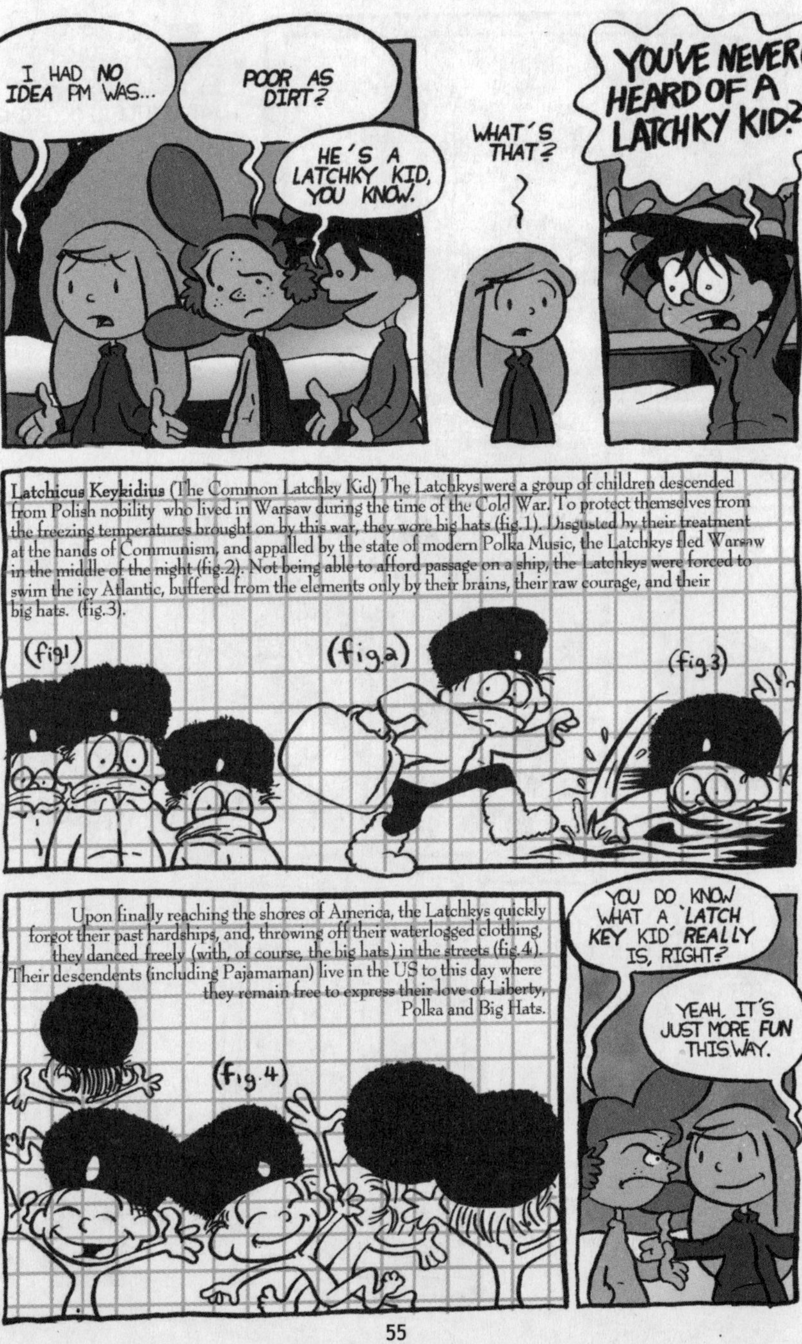
I HAD NO IDEA PM WAS...
POOR AS DIRT?
HE'S A LATCHKY KID, YOU KNOW.
WHAT'S THAT?
YOU'VE NEVER HEARD OF A LATCHKY KID?
Latchicus Keykidius (The Common Latchky Kid) The Latchkys were a group of children descended from Polish nobility who lived in Warsaw during the time of the Cold War. To protect themselves from the freezing temperatures brought on by this war, they wore big hats (fig.1). Disgusted by their treatment at the hands of Communism, and appalled by the state of modern Polka Music, the Latchkys fled Warsaw in the middle of the night (fig.2). Not being able to afford passage on a ship, the Latchkys were forced to swim the icy Atlantic, buffered from the elements only by their brains, their raw courage, and their big hats. (fig.3).
(fig.1)
(fig.2)
(fig.3)
Upon finally reaching the shores of America, the Latchkys quickly forgot their past hardships, and, throwing off their waterlogged clothing, they danced freely (with, of course, the big hats) in the streets (fig.4). Their descendents (including Pajamaman) live in the US to this day where they remain free to express their love of Liberty, Polka and Big Hats.
(fig.4)
YOU DO KNOW WHAT A 'LATCH KEY KID' REALLY IS, RIGHT?
YEAH, IT'S JUST MORE FUN THIS WAY.

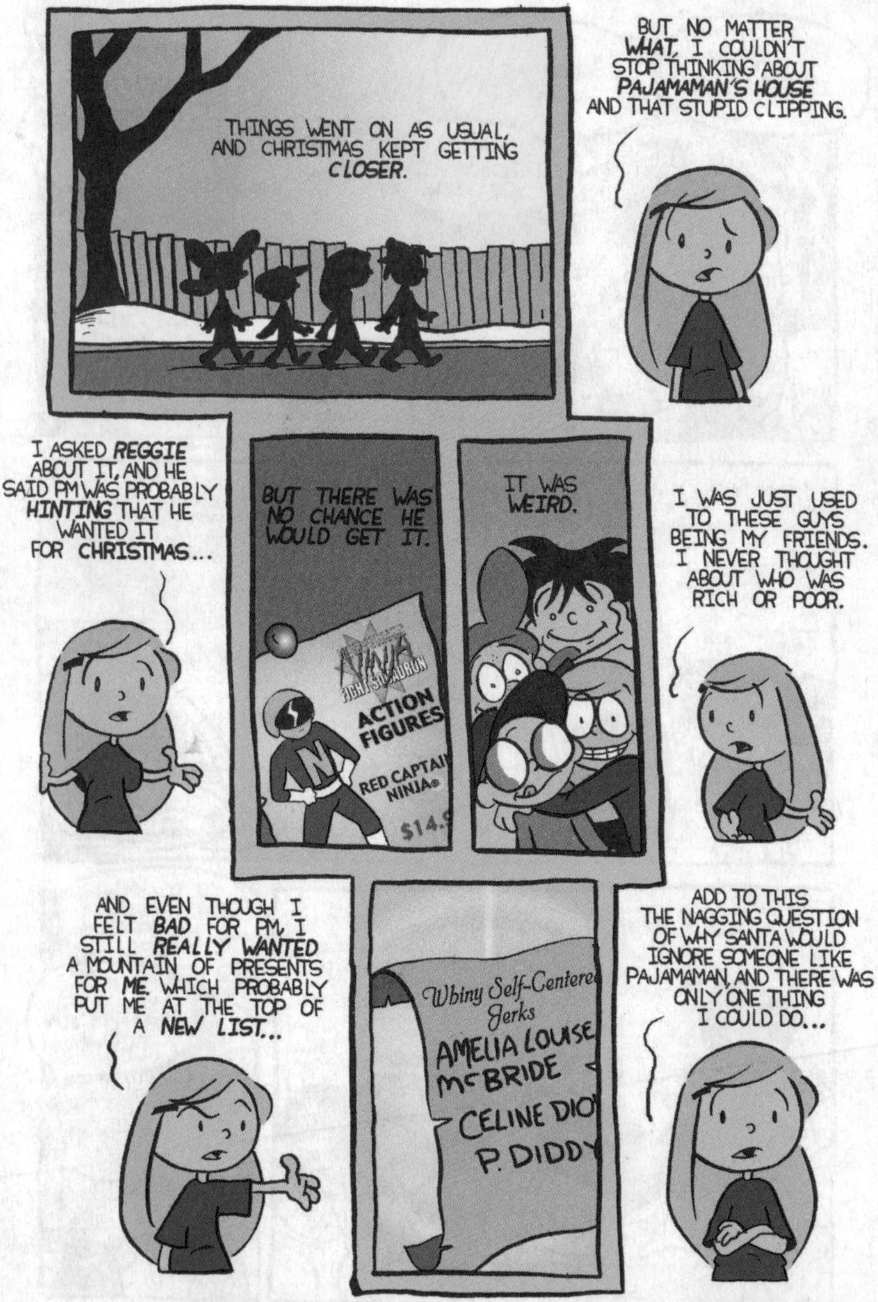

THINGS WENT ON AS USUAL, AND CHRISTMAS KEPT GETTING CLOSER.
BUT NO MATTER WHAT, I COULDN'T STOP THINKING ABOUT PAJAMAMAN'S HOUSE AND THAT STUPID CLIPPING.
I ASKED REGGIE ABOUT IT, AND HE SAID PM WAS PROBABLY HINTING THAT HE WANTED IT FOR CHRISTMAS...
BUT THERE WAS NO CHANCE HE WOULD GET IT.
NINJA
FIGHT SQUADRON
ACTION FIGURES
RED CAPTAIN NINJA®
$14.9
IT WAS WEIRD.
I WAS JUST USED TO THESE GUYS BEING MY FRIENDS. I NEVER THOUGHT ABOUT WHO WAS RICH OR POOR.
AND EVEN THOUGH I FELT BAD FOR PM, I STILL REALLY WANTED A MOUNTAIN OF PRESENTS FOR ME. WHICH PROBABLY PUT ME AT THE TOP OF A NEW LIST...
Whiny Self-Centere
Jerks
AMELIA LOUISE McBRIDE
CELINE DIO
P. DIDDY
ADD TO THIS THE NAGGING QUESTION OF WHY SANTA WOULD IGNORE SOMEONE LIKE PAJAMAMAN, AND THERE WAS ONLY ONE THING I COULD DO...

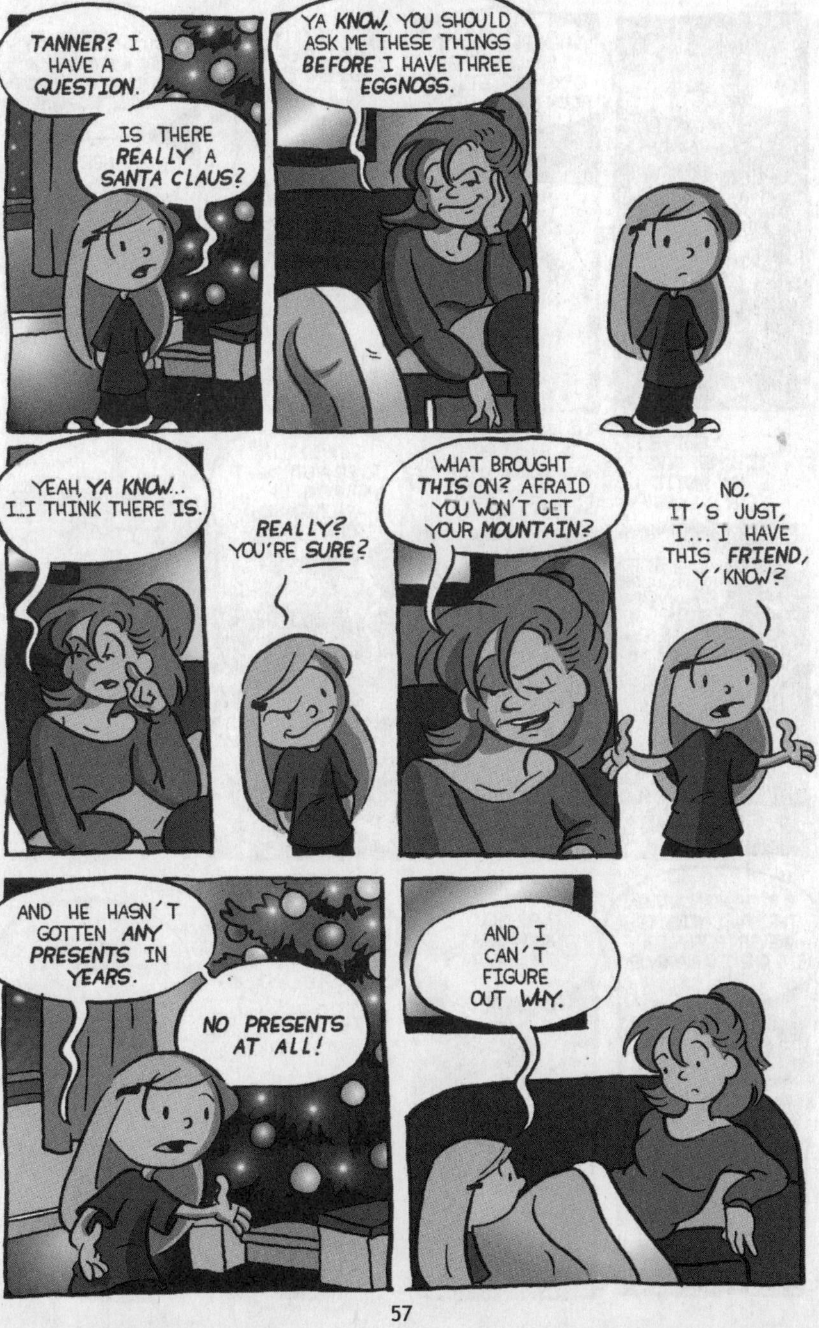
TANNER? I HAVE A QUESTION.
IS THERE REALLY A SANTA CLAUS?
YA KNOW, YOU SHOULD ASK ME THESE THINGS BEFORE I HAVE THREE EGGNOGS.
YEAH, YA KNOW... I...I THINK THERE IS.
REALLY? YOU'RE SURE?
WHAT BROUGHT THIS ON? AFRAID YOU WON'T GET YOUR MOUNTAIN?
NO. IT'S JUST, I... I HAVE THIS FRIEND, Y'KNOW?
AND HE HASN'T GOTTEN ANY PRESENTS IN YEARS.
NO PRESENTS AT ALL!
AND I CAN'T FIGURE OUT WHY.

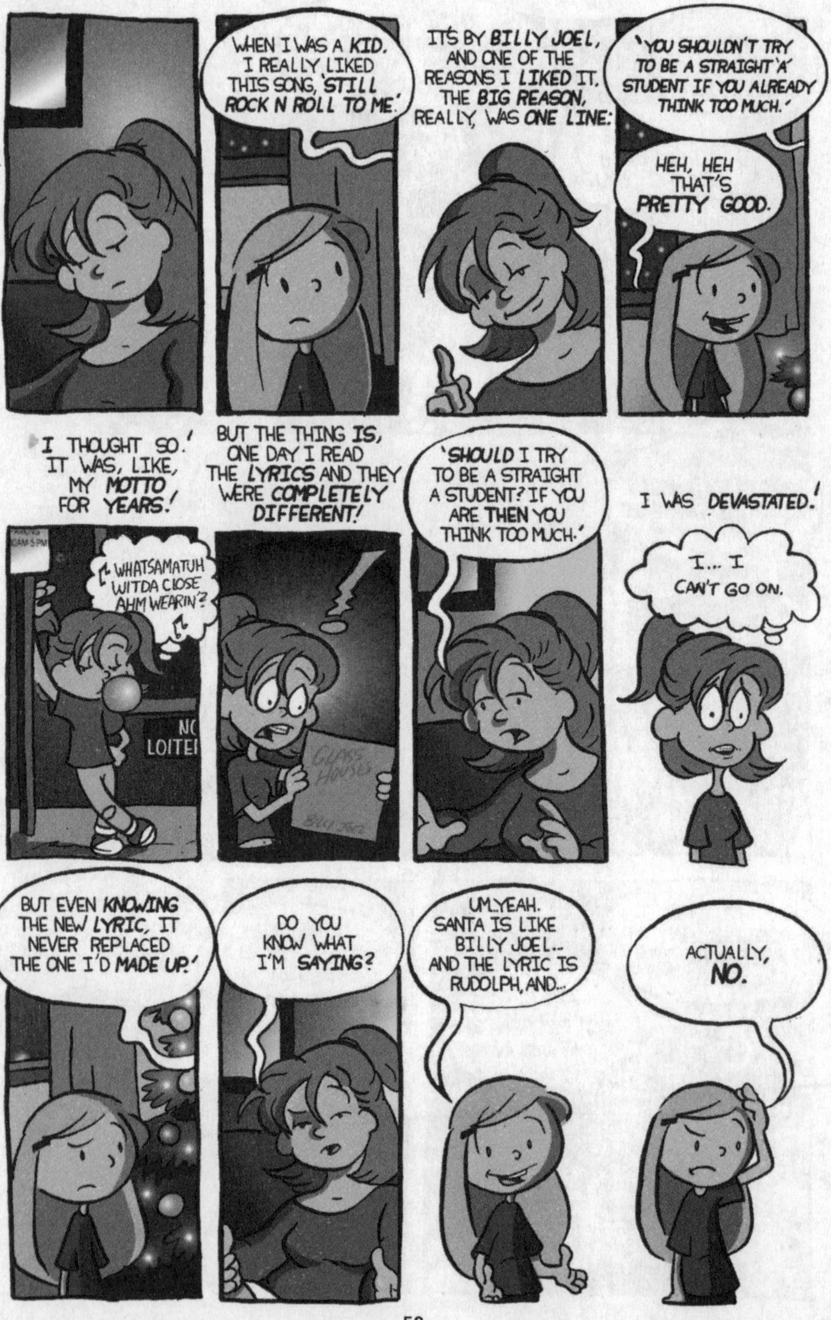
WHEN I WAS A KID, I REALLY LIKED THIS SONG, 'STILL ROCK N ROLL TO ME.'
IT'S BY BILLY JOEL, AND ONE OF THE REASONS I LIKED IT, THE BIG REASON, REALLY, WAS ONE LINE:
'YOU SHOULDN'T TRY TO BE A STRAIGHT 'A' STUDENT IF YOU ALREADY THINK TOO MUCH.'
HEH, HEH THAT'S PRETTY GOOD.
'I THOUGHT SO.' IT WAS, LIKE, MY MOTTO FOR YEARS!
WHATSAMATUH WITDA CLOSE AHM WEARIN'?
NO LOITER
BUT THE THING IS, ONE DAY I READ THE LYRICS AND THEY WERE COMPLETELY DIFFERENT!
'SHOULD I TRY TO BE A STRAIGHT A STUDENT? IF YOU ARE THEN YOU THINK TOO MUCH.'
I WAS DEVASTATED!
I... I CAN'T GO ON.
BUT EVEN KNOWING THE NEW LYRIC, IT NEVER REPLACED THE ONE I'D MADE UP.'
DO YOU KNOW WHAT I'M SAYING?
UM...YEAH. SANTA IS LIKE BILLY JOEL... AND THE LYRIC IS RUDOLPH, AND...
ACTUALLY, NO.

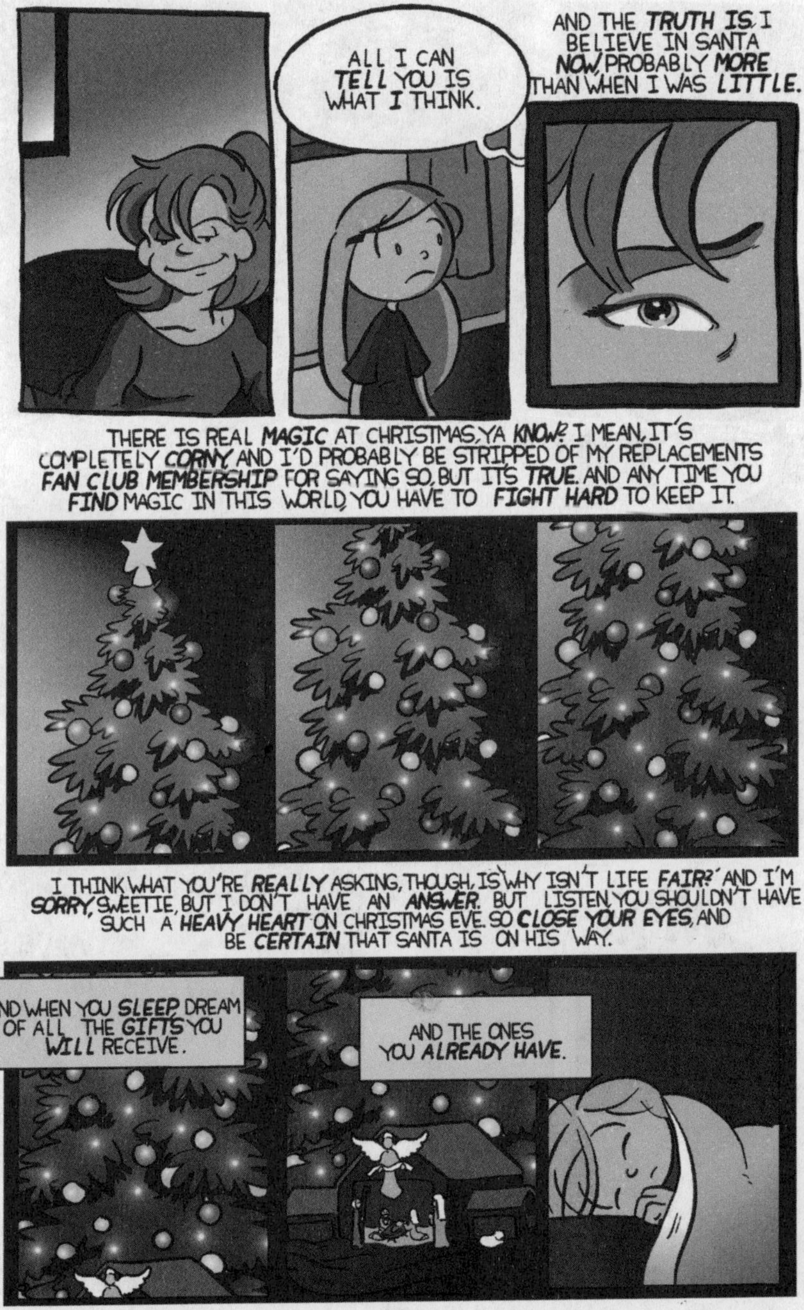
ALL I CAN TELL YOU IS WHAT I THINK.
AND THE TRUTH IS, I BELIEVE IN SANTA NOW, PROBABLY MORE THAN WHEN I WAS LITTLE.
THERE IS REAL MAGIC AT CHRISTMAS, YA KNOW? I MEAN, IT'S COMPLETELY CORNY, AND I'D PROBABLY BE STRIPPED OF MY REPLACEMENTS FAN CLUB MEMBERSHIP FOR SAYING SO, BUT IT'S TRUE. AND ANY TIME YOU FIND MAGIC IN THIS WORLD, YOU HAVE TO FIGHT HARD TO KEEP IT.
I THINK WHAT YOU'RE REALLY ASKING, THOUGH, IS 'WHY ISN'T LIFE FAIR?' AND I'M SORRY, SWEETIE, BUT I DON'T HAVE AN ANSWER. BUT LISTEN, YOU SHOULDN'T HAVE SUCH A HEAVY HEART ON CHRISTMAS EVE. SO CLOSE YOUR EYES, AND BE CERTAIN THAT SANTA IS ON HIS WAY.
AND WHEN YOU SLEEP, DREAM OF ALL THE GIFTS YOU WILL RECEIVE.
AND THE ONES YOU ALREADY HAVE.

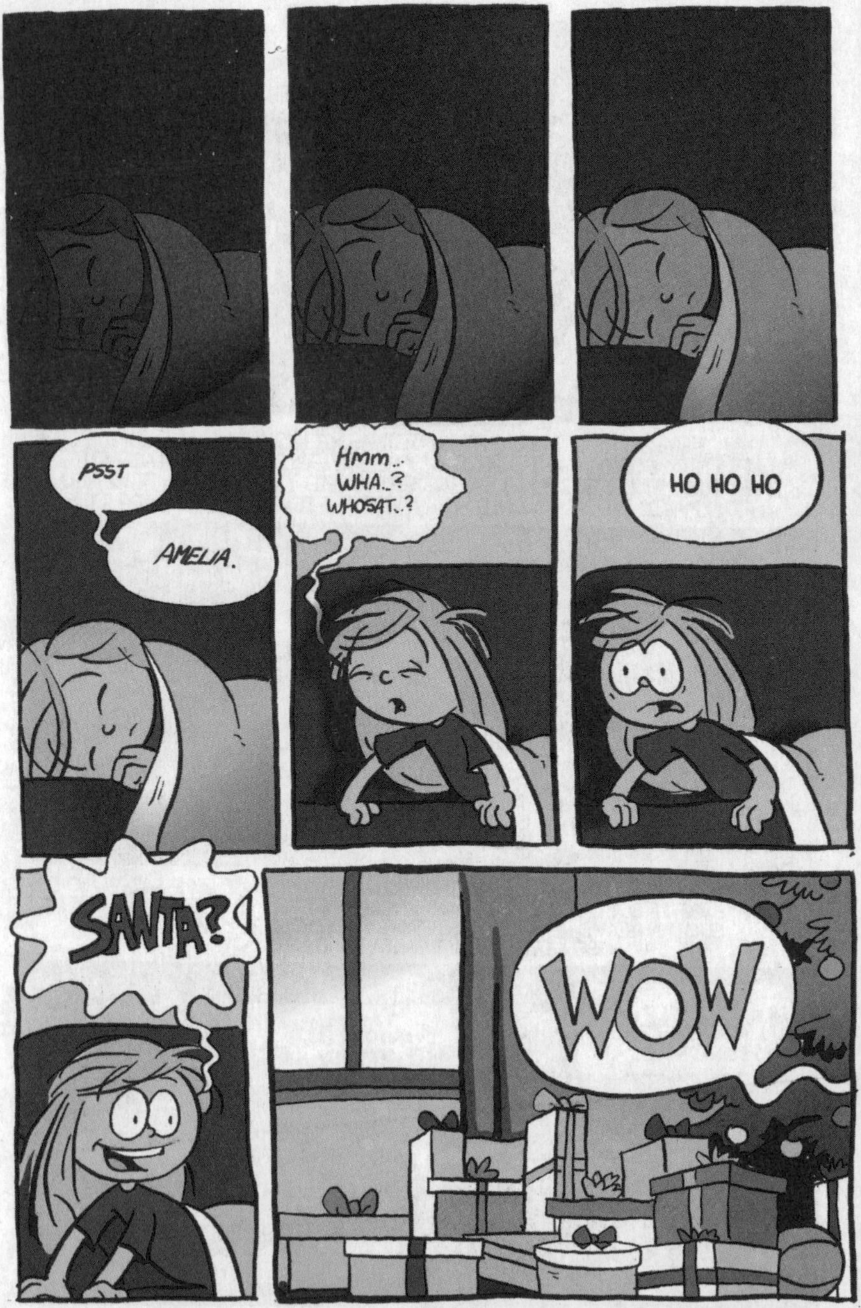
PSST
AMELIA.
Hmm..
WHA..?
WHOSAT..?
HO HO HO
SANTA?
WOW

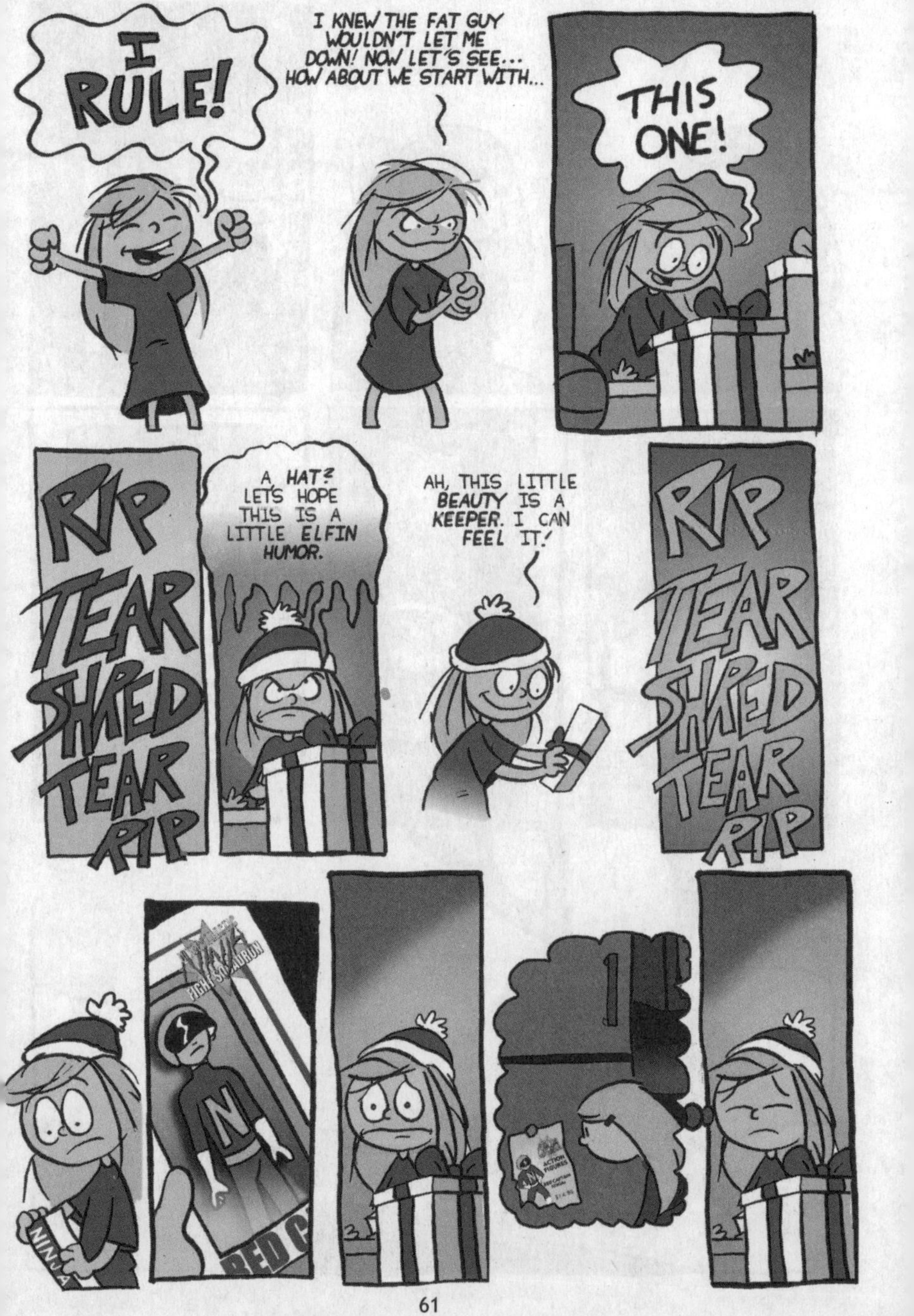
I RULE!
I KNEW THE FAT GUY WOULDN'T LET ME DOWN! NOW LET'S SEE... HOW ABOUT WE START WITH...
THIS ONE!
RIP TEAR SHRED TEAR RIP
A HAT? LET'S HOPE THIS IS A LITTLE ELFIN HUMOR.
AH, THIS LITTLE BEAUTY IS A KEEPER. I CAN FEEL IT!
RIP TEAR SHRED TEAR RIP
NINJA
ACTION FIGURES

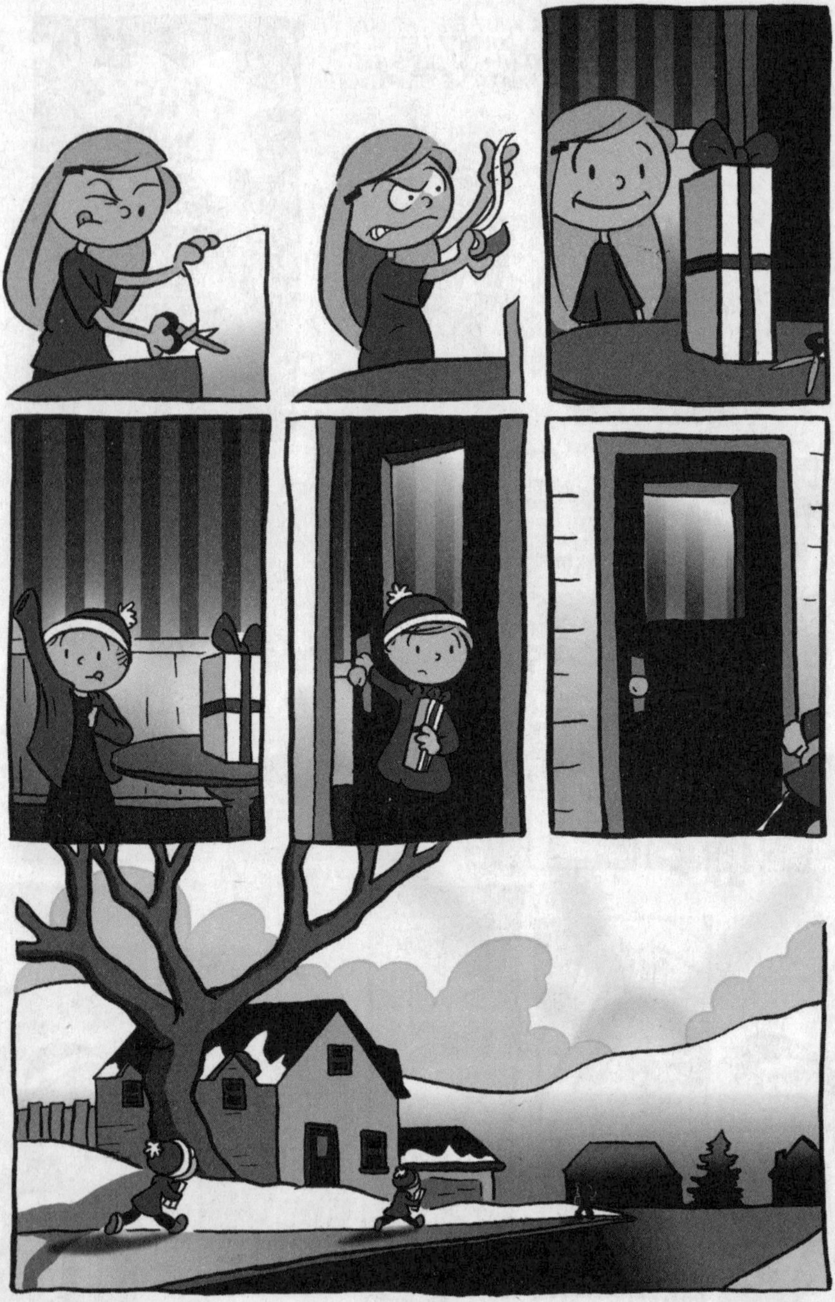

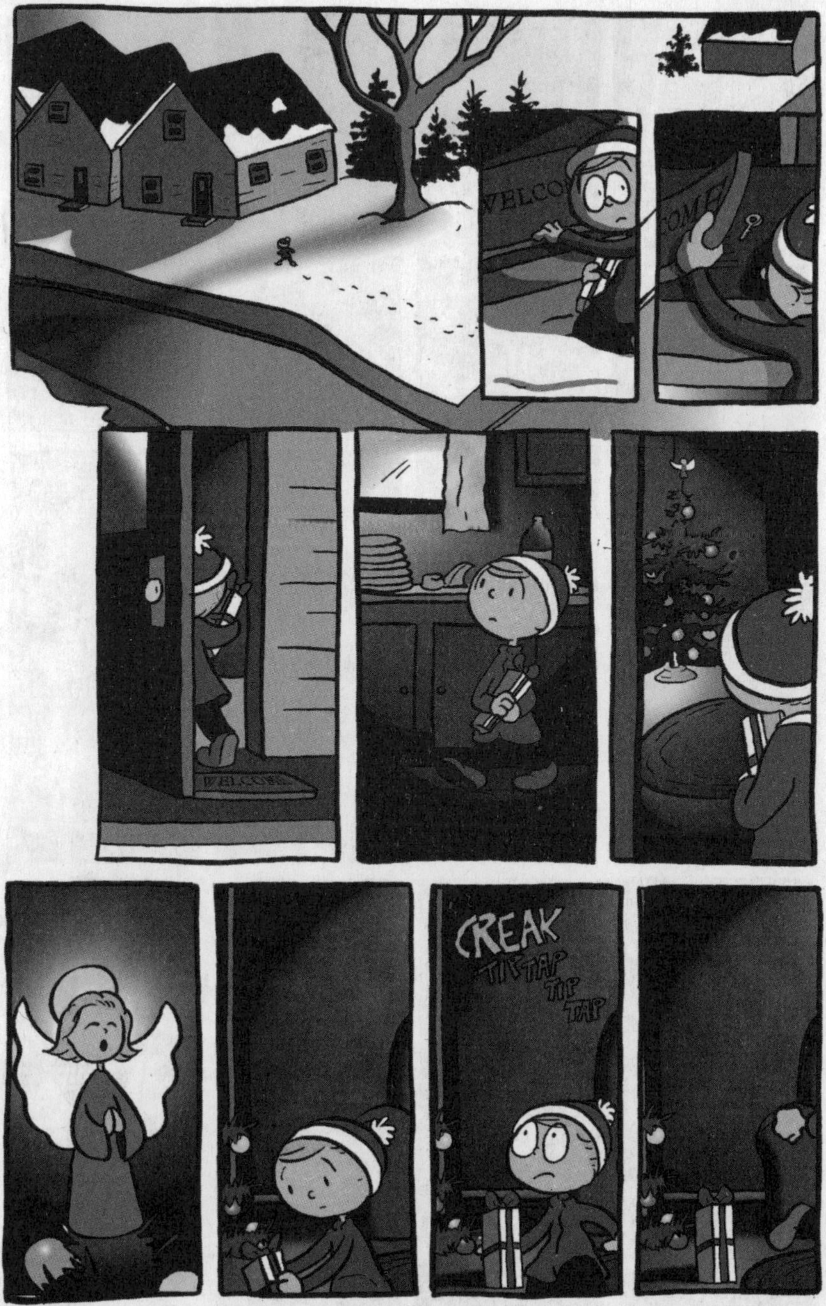
WELCOM
WELCOME
CREAK
TIP TAP
TIP
TAP

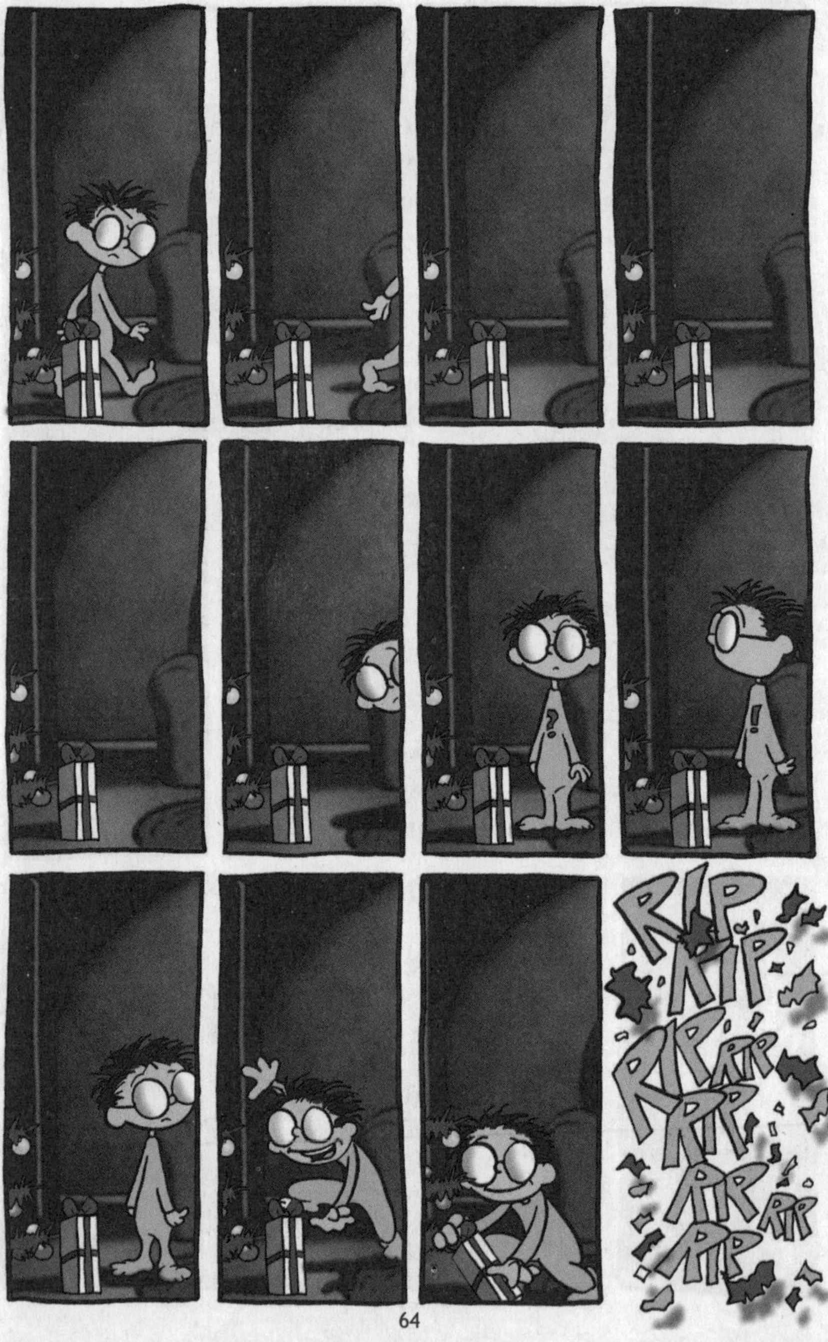
RIP
RIP
RIP
RIP
RIP
RIP
RIP
RIP
RIP

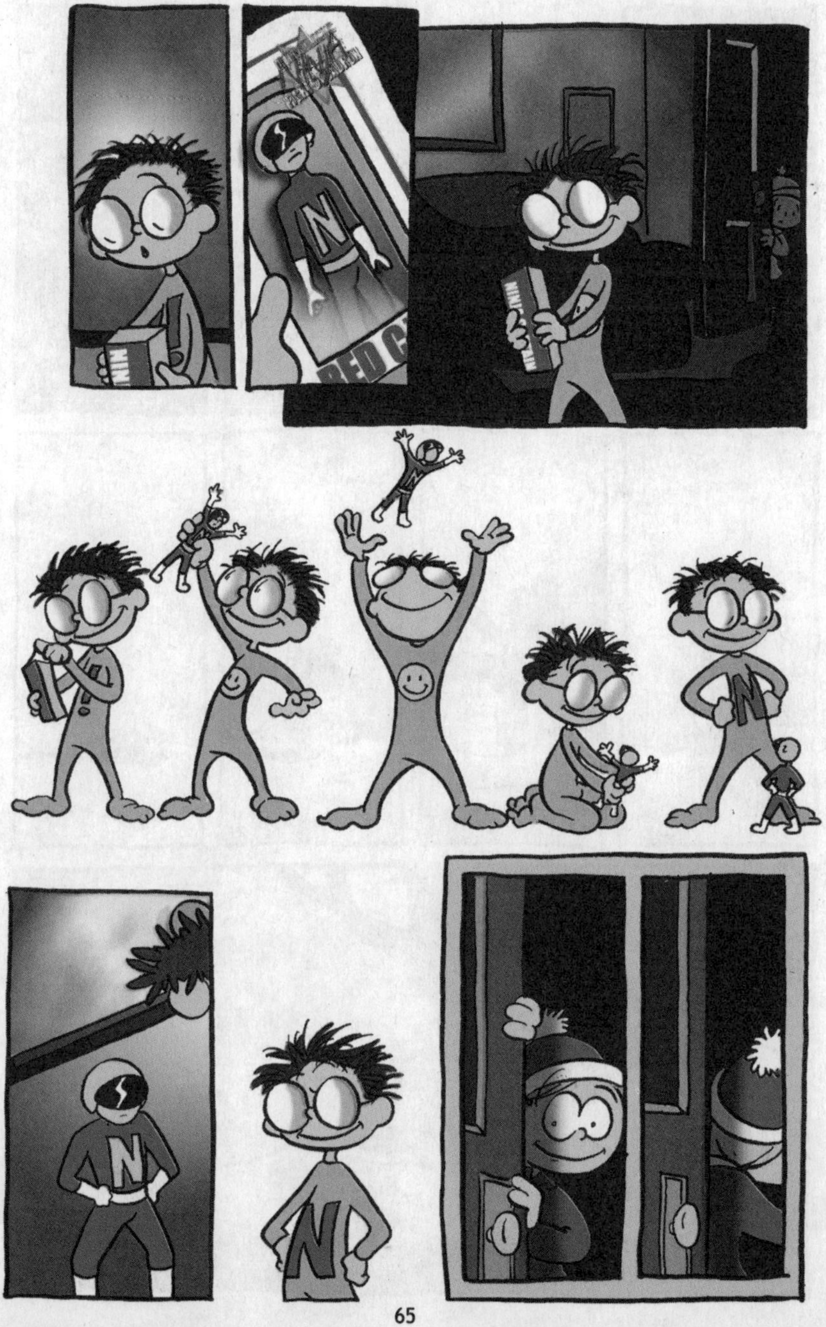

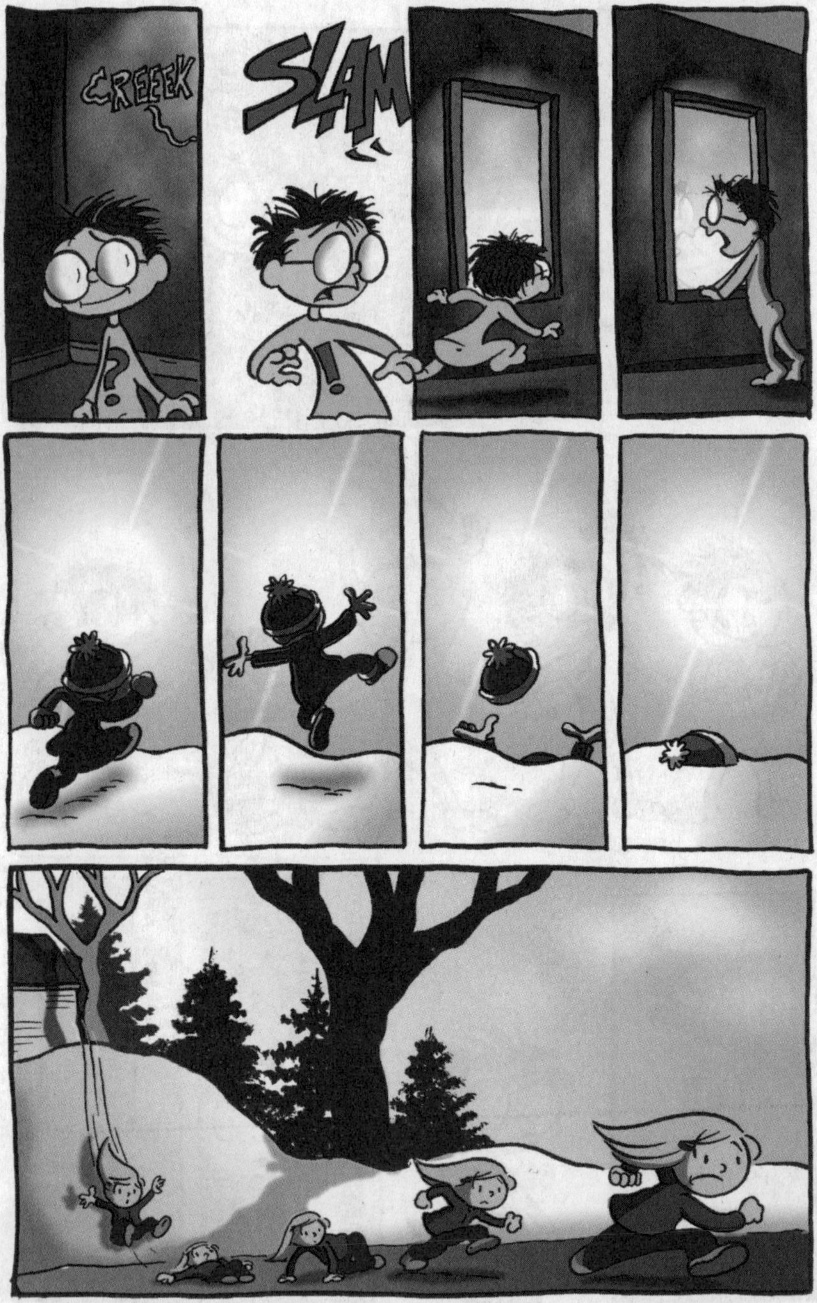
CREEEK
SLAM

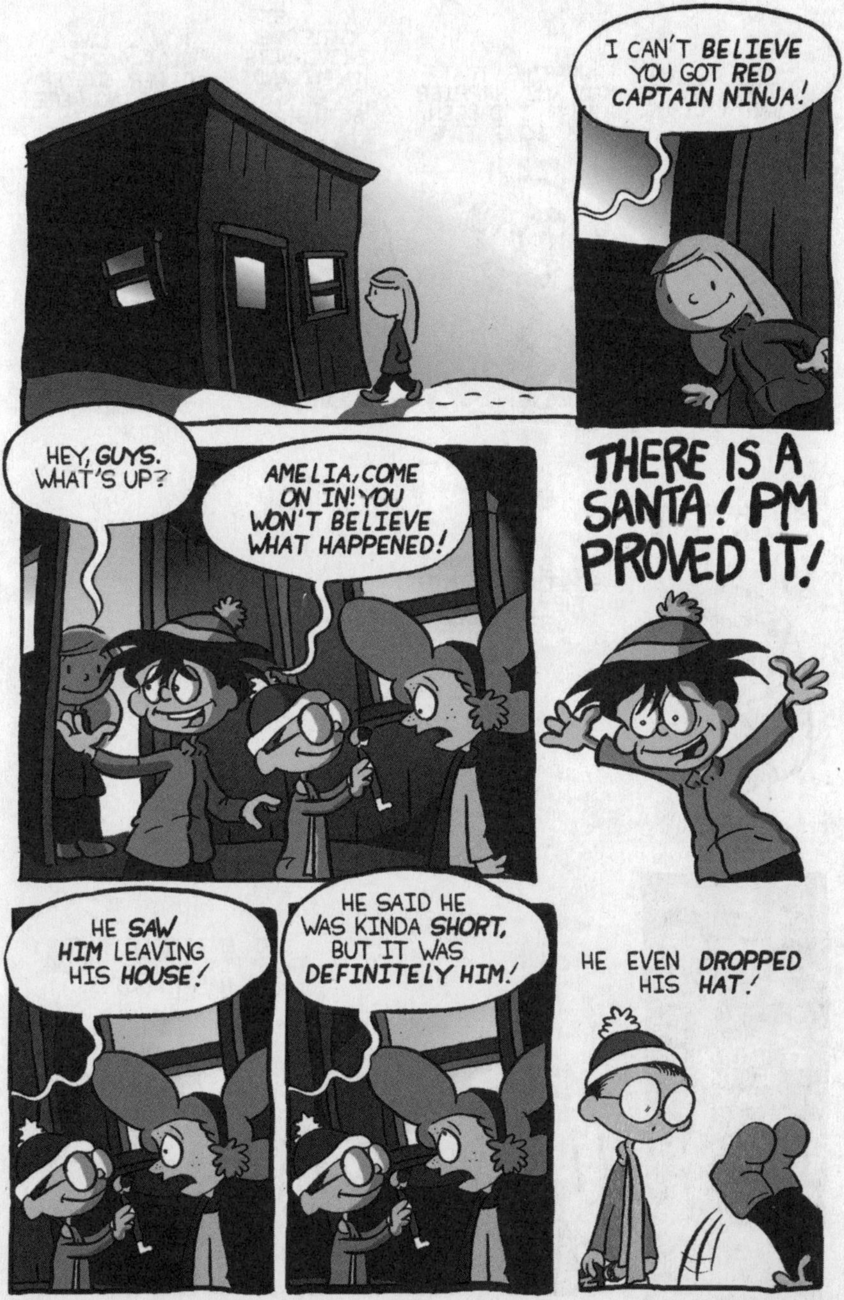
I CAN'T BELIEVE YOU GOT RED CAPTAIN NINJA!
HEY, GUYS. WHAT'S UP?
AMELIA, COME ON IN! YOU WON'T BELIEVE WHAT HAPPENED!
THERE IS A SANTA! PM PROVED IT!
HE SAW HIM LEAVING HIS HOUSE!
HE SAID HE WAS KINDA SHORT, BUT IT WAS DEFINITELY HIM!
HE EVEN DROPPED HIS HAT!

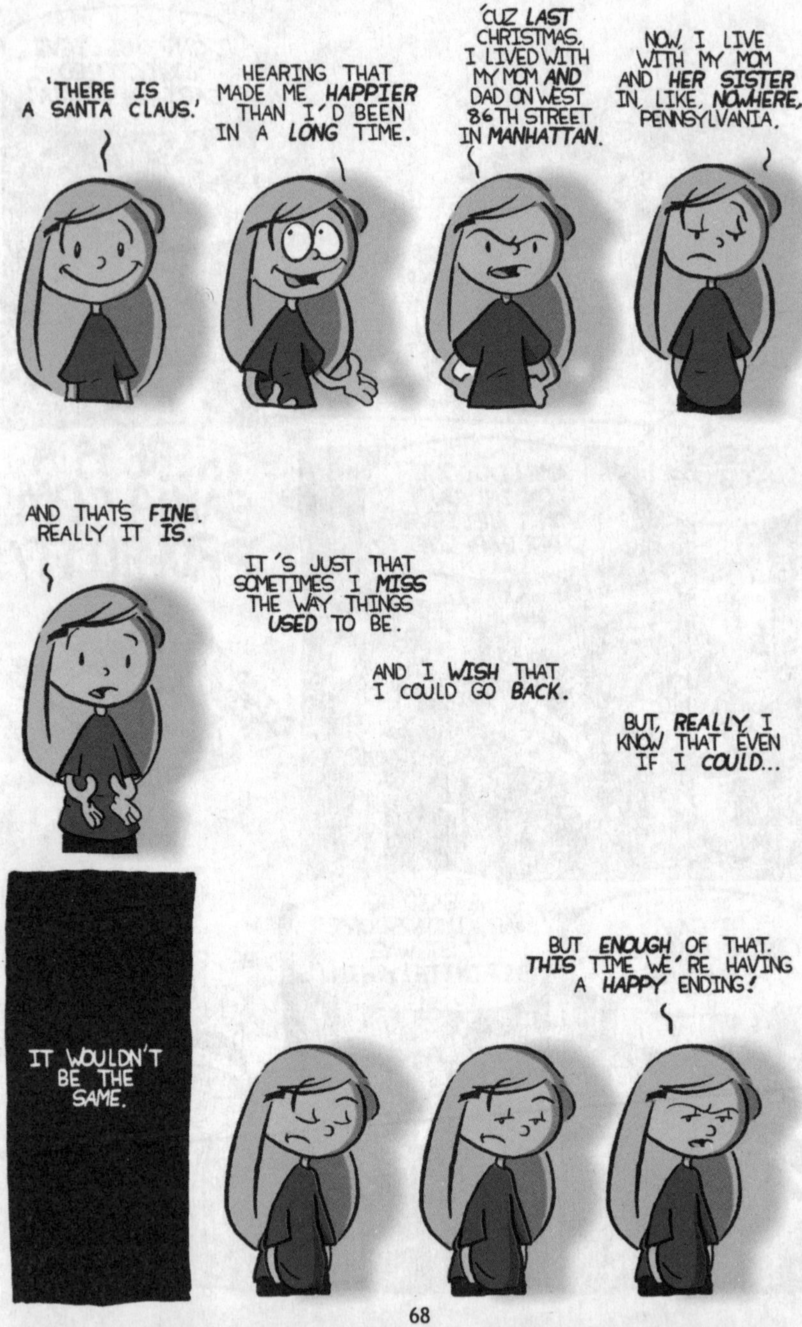
'THERE IS A SANTA CLAUS.'
HEARING THAT MADE ME HAPPIER THAN I'D BEEN IN A LONG TIME.
'CUZ LAST CHRISTMAS, I LIVED WITH MY MOM AND DAD ON WEST 86TH STREET IN MANHATTAN.
NOW, I LIVE WITH MY MOM AND HER SISTER IN, LIKE, NOWHERE, PENNSYLVANIA.
AND THAT'S FINE. REALLY IT IS.
IT'S JUST THAT SOMETIMES I MISS THE WAY THINGS USED TO BE.
AND I WISH THAT I COULD GO BACK.
BUT, REALLY, I KNOW THAT EVEN IF I COULD...
IT WOULDN'T BE THE SAME.
BUT ENOUGH OF THAT. THIS TIME WE'RE HAVING A HAPPY ENDING!

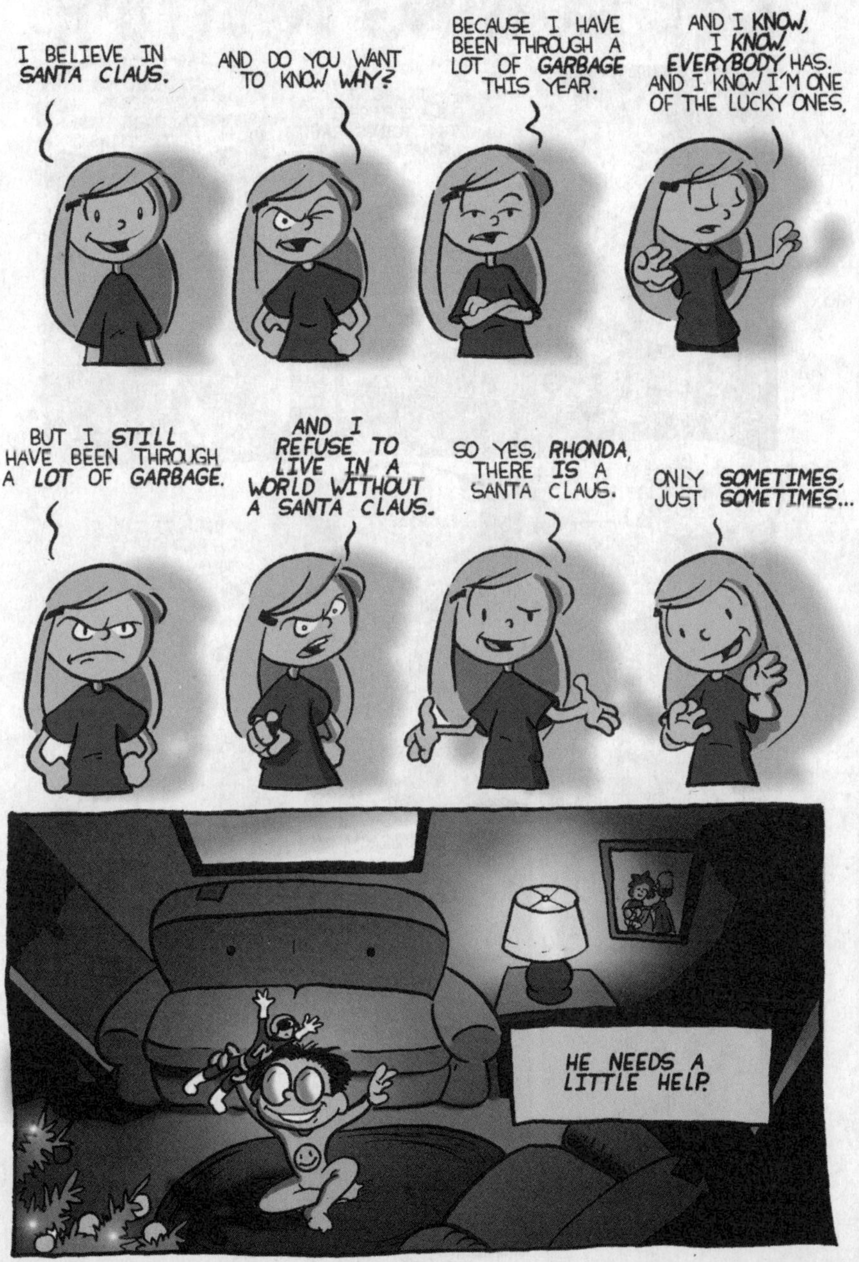
I BELIEVE IN SANTA CLAUS.
AND DO YOU WANT TO KNOW WHY?
BECAUSE I HAVE BEEN THROUGH A LOT OF GARBAGE THIS YEAR.
AND I KNOW, I KNOW, EVERYBODY HAS. AND I KNOW I'M ONE OF THE LUCKY ONES.
BUT I STILL HAVE BEEN THROUGH A LOT OF GARBAGE.
AND I REFUSE TO LIVE IN A WORLD WITHOUT A SANTA CLAUS.
SO YES, RHONDA, THERE IS A SANTA CLAUS.
ONLY SOMETIMES, JUST SOMETIMES...
HE NEEDS A LITTLE HELP.

LIFE DURING WARTIME

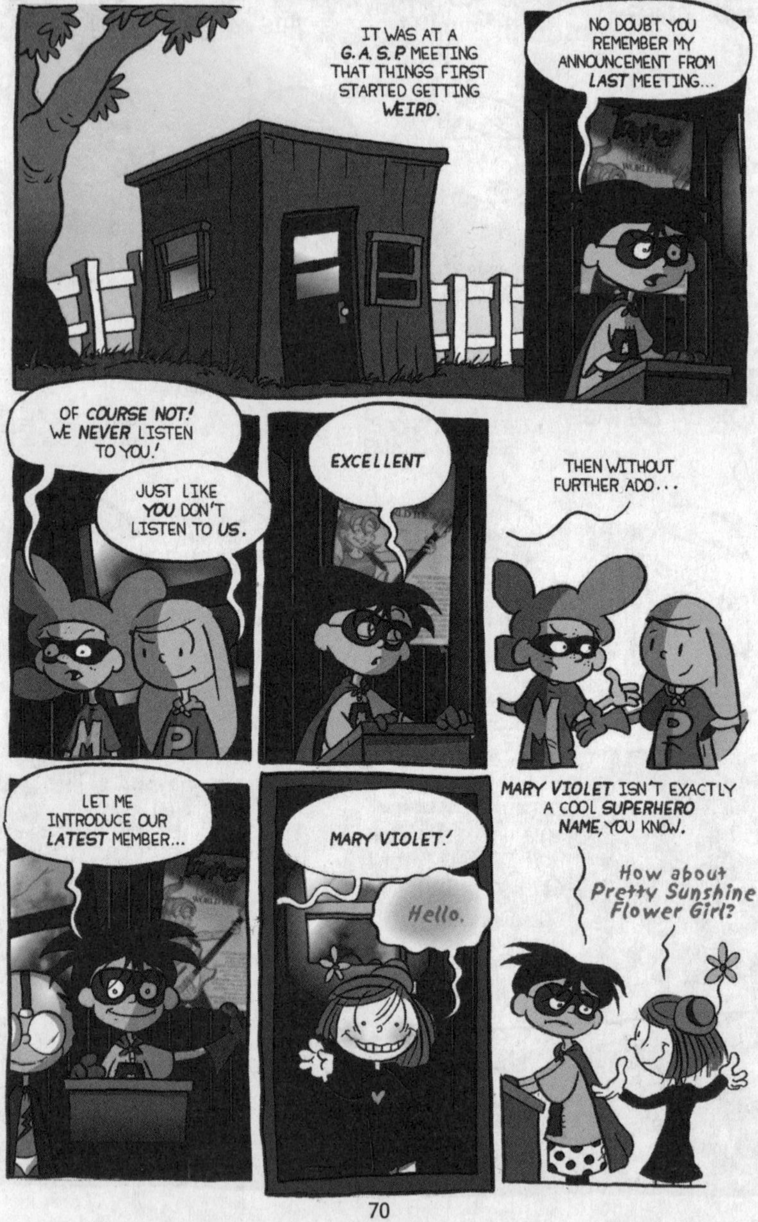
IT WAS AT A G. A. S. P. MEETING THAT THINGS FIRST STARTED GETTING WEIRD.
NO DOUBT YOU REMEMBER MY ANNOUNCEMENT FROM LAST MEETING...
OF COURSE NOT! WE NEVER LISTEN TO YOU!
JUST LIKE YOU DON'T LISTEN TO US.
EXCELLENT
THEN WITHOUT FURTHER ADO...
LET ME INTRODUCE OUR LATEST MEMBER...
MARY VIOLET!
Hello.
MARY VIOLET ISN'T EXACTLY A COOL SUPERHERO NAME, YOU KNOW.
How about Pretty Sunshine Flower Girl?

THAT WASN'T *EXACTLY* WHAT REGGIE HAD IN MIND *EITHER*.

I WAS PRETTY SURPRISED TO SEE *MARY VIOLET*.

SHE DIDN'T SEEM LIKE THE *MASKED AVENGER* TYPE.

HA! LITTLE DID I KNOW...

SO *ANYWAY*, REGGIE WANTED VIOLET TO BE IN THE CLUB.

BUT FIRST, SHE HAD TO PASS 'THE TRIALS'.

SO REGGIE DRAGGED US ALL THE WAY *ACROSS TOWN*...

TO THIS *PARK* HE AND *PAJAMAMAN* HAD FOUND.

I THINK HE LIKED IT 'CUZ HE COULD RUN AROUND WITH HIS UNDIES OUTSIDE HIS PANTS AND NO ONE KNEW HIM.

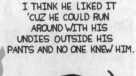

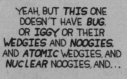

ISN'T THIS PLACE *GREAT?!*

IT'S A PARK.

LIKE THE ONE WE *ALWAYS* PLAY IN.

YEAH, BUT *THIS* ONE DOESN'T HAVE *BUG,* OR *IGGY* OR THEIR *WEDGIES* AND *NOOGIES,* AND *ATOMIC* WEDGIES, AND *NUCLEAR* NOOGIES, AND...

er.. uh...

ANYWAY... NOW IT'S TIME FOR THE *TRIALS!*

MARY VIOLET, TO BECOME A FULL FLEDGED MEMBER OF *G.A.S.P.*...

YOU MUST BEST 'KID *LIGHTNING*' AND ME IN A CONTEST OF *STRENGTH.*

'PRINCESS POWERFUL,' 'MISS MIRACULOUS,' YOU BE THE *LOOKOUTS.*

DO YOU THINK SHE'LL BE *OKAY?*

I DON'T THINK SHE EVER WAS 'OKAY.'

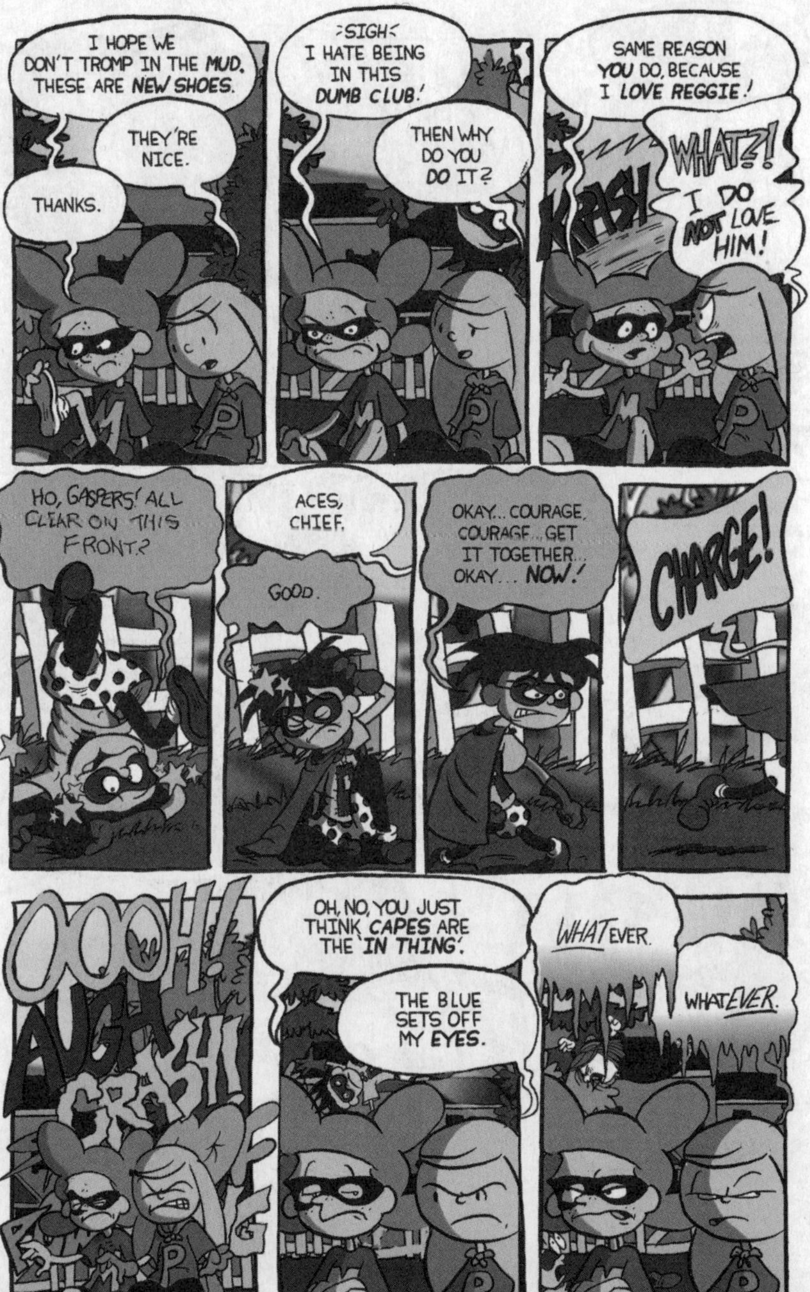
I HOPE WE DON'T TROMP IN THE MUD. THESE ARE NEW SHOES.
THEY'RE NICE.
THANKS.
>SIGH< I HATE BEING IN THIS DUMB CLUB!
THEN WHY DO YOU DO IT?
SAME REASON YOU DO, BECAUSE I LOVE REGGIE!
KRASH
WHAT?! I DO NOT LOVE HIM!
HO, GASPERS! ALL CLEAR ON THIS FRONT?
ACES, CHIEF.
GOOD.
OKAY... COURAGE, COURAGE... GET IT TOGETHER... OKAY... NOW!
CHARGE!
OOOH!
AUGH
CRASH!
OH, NO, YOU JUST THINK CAPES ARE THE 'IN THING'.
THE BLUE SETS OFF MY EYES.
WHATEVER.
WHATEVER.

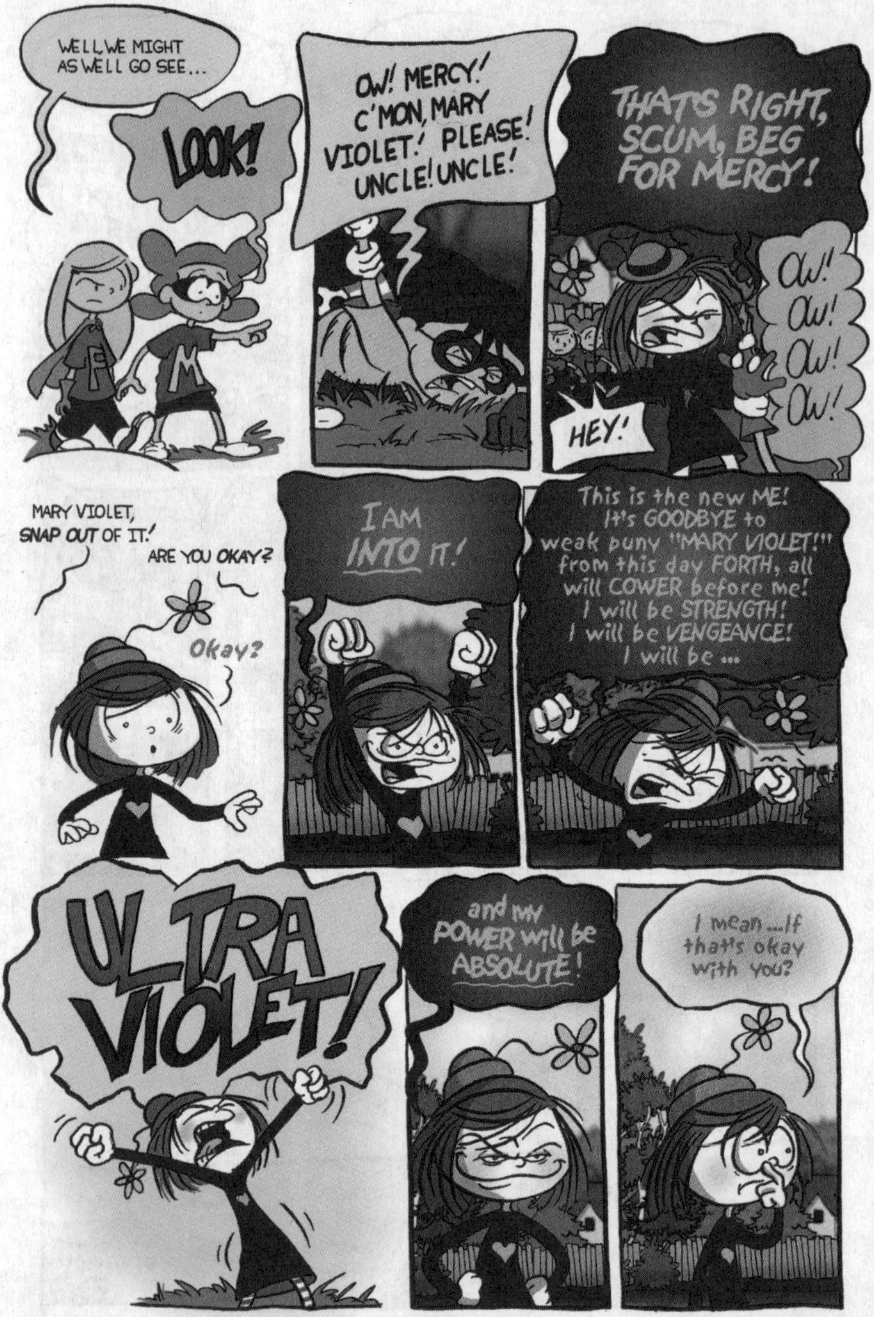
WELL, WE MIGHT AS WELL GO SEE...
LOOK!
OW! MERCY! C'MON, MARY VIOLET! PLEASE! UNCLE! UNCLE!
THAT'S RIGHT, SCUM, BEG FOR MERCY!
Ow! Ow! Ow! Ow!
HEY!
MARY VIOLET, SNAP OUT OF IT!
ARE YOU OKAY?
Okay?
I AM INTO IT!
This is the new ME! It's GOODBYE to weak puny "MARY VIOLET!" from this day FORTH, all will COWER before me! I will be STRENGTH! I will be VENGEANCE! I will be ...
ULTRA VIOLET!
and my POWER will be ABSOLUTE!
I mean ...If that's okay with you?

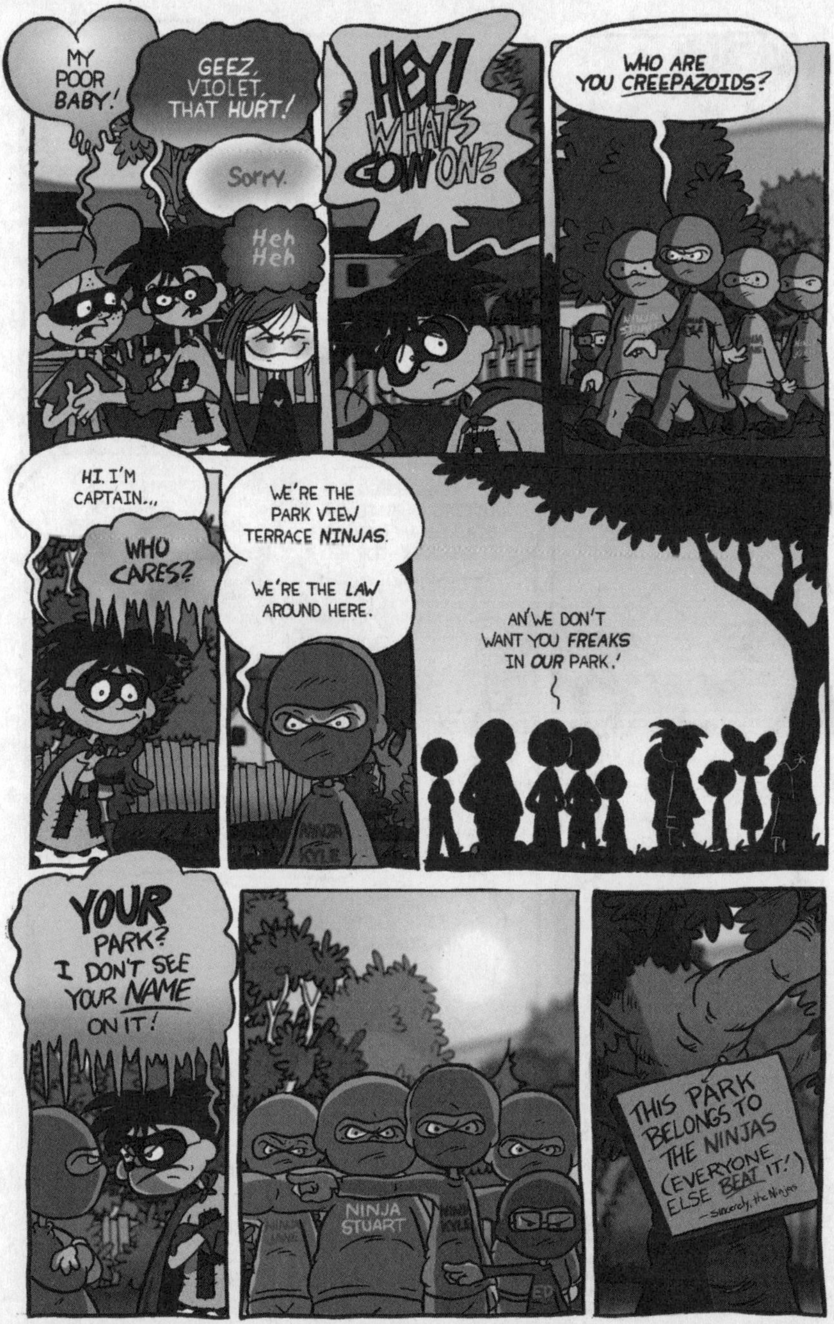
MY POOR BABY!
GEEZ, VIOLET, THAT HURT!
Sorry.
Heh Heh
HEY! WHAT'S GOIN ON?
WHO ARE YOU CREEPAZOIDS?
HI. I'M CAPTAIN...
WHO CARES?
WE'RE THE PARK VIEW TERRACE NINJAS.
WE'RE THE LAW AROUND HERE.
NINJA KYLE
AN' WE DON'T WANT YOU FREAKS IN OUR PARK!
YOUR PARK? I DON'T SEE YOUR NAME ON IT!
NINJA STUART
THIS PARK BELONGS TO THE NINJAS (EVERYONE ELSE BEAT IT!)
—sincerely, the Ninjas

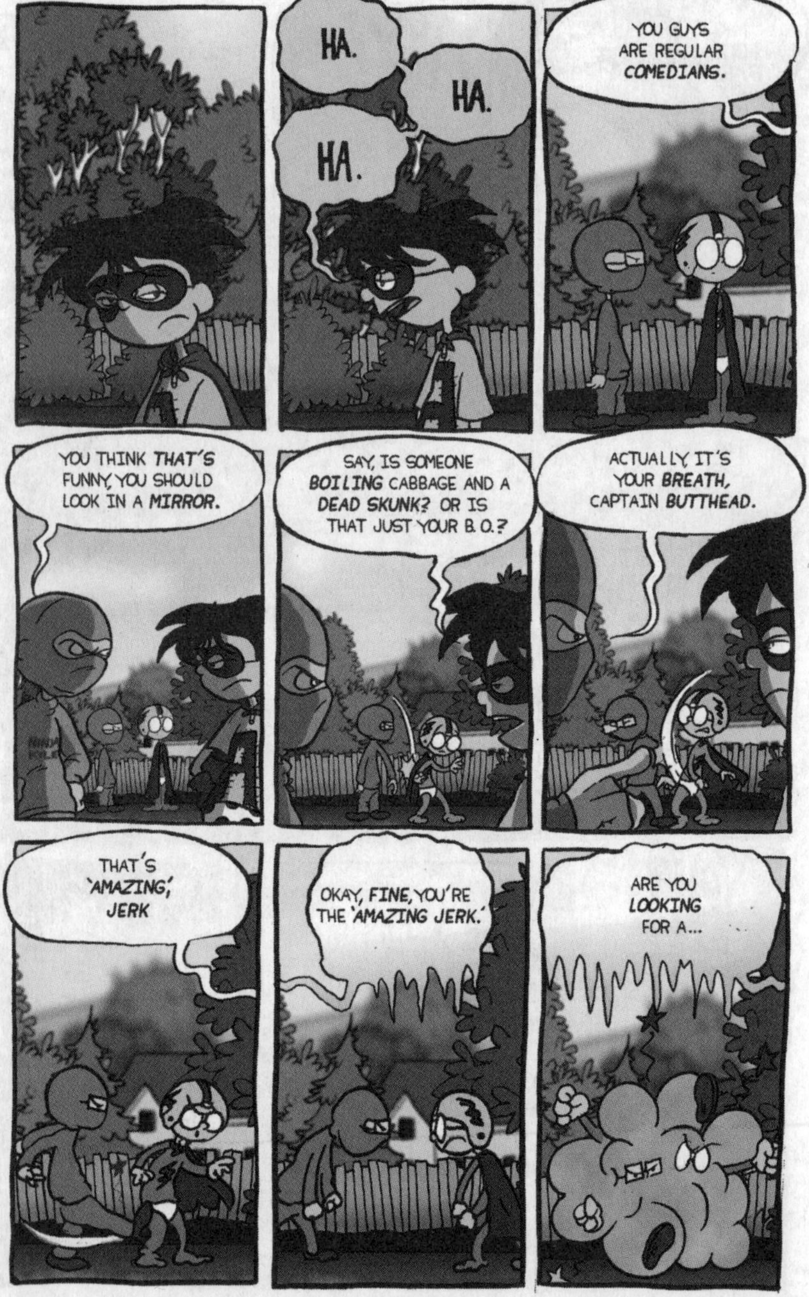
HA.
HA.
HA.
YOU GUYS ARE REGULAR COMEDIANS.
YOU THINK THAT'S FUNNY, YOU SHOULD LOOK IN A MIRROR.
SAY, IS SOMEONE BOILING CABBAGE AND A DEAD SKUNK? OR IS THAT JUST YOUR B. O.?
ACTUALLY, IT'S YOUR BREATH, CAPTAIN BUTTHEAD.
THAT'S 'AMAZING,' JERK
OKAY, FINE, YOU'RE THE 'AMAZING JERK.'
ARE YOU LOOKING FOR A...

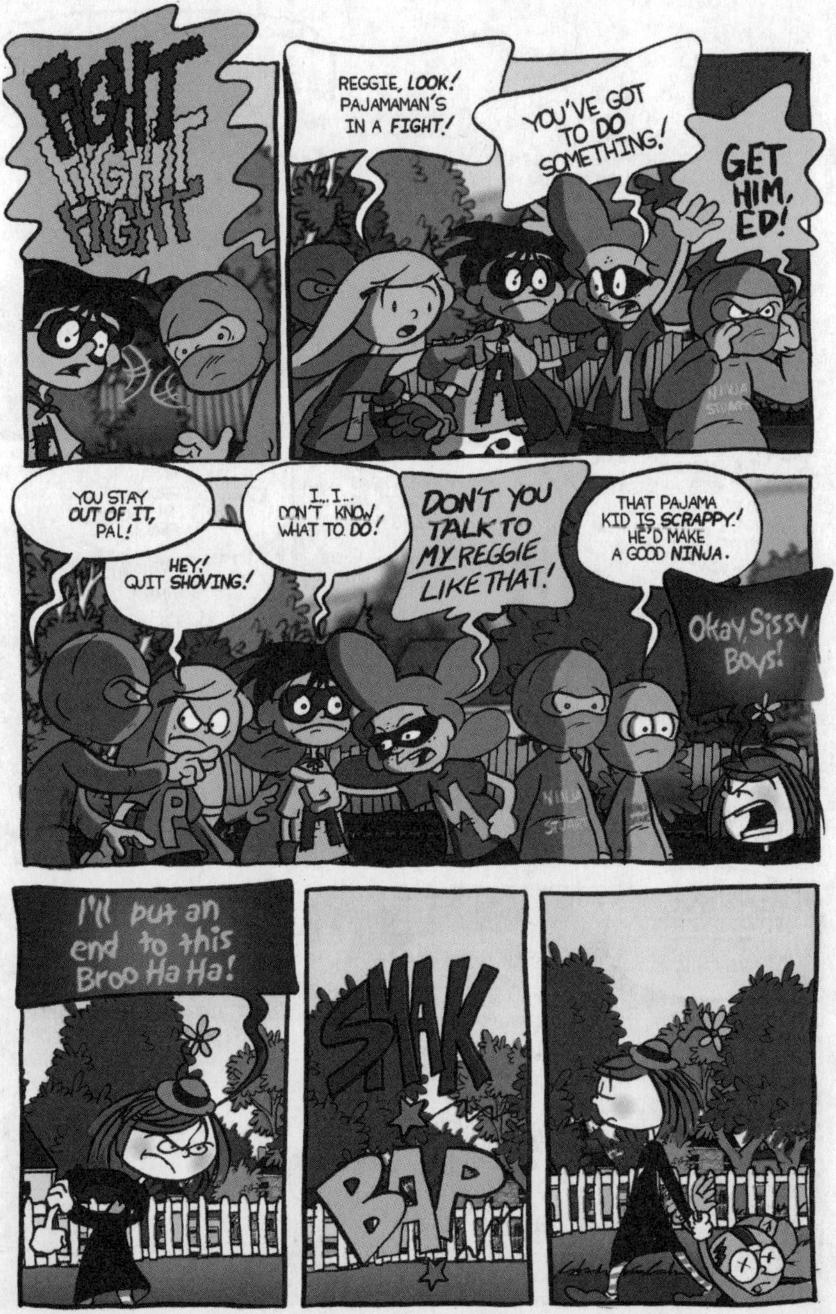
FIGHT FIGHT FIGHT
REGGIE, LOOK! PAJAMAMAN'S IN A FIGHT!
YOU'VE GOT TO DO SOMETHING!
GET HIM, ED!
YOU STAY OUT OF IT, PAL!
HEY! QUIT SHOVING!
I... I... DON'T KNOW WHAT TO DO!
DON'T YOU TALK TO MY REGGIE LIKE THAT!
THAT PAJAMA KID IS SCRAPPY! HE'D MAKE A GOOD NINJA.
Okay, Sissy Boys!
I'll put an end to this Broo Ha Ha!
SHAK
BAP

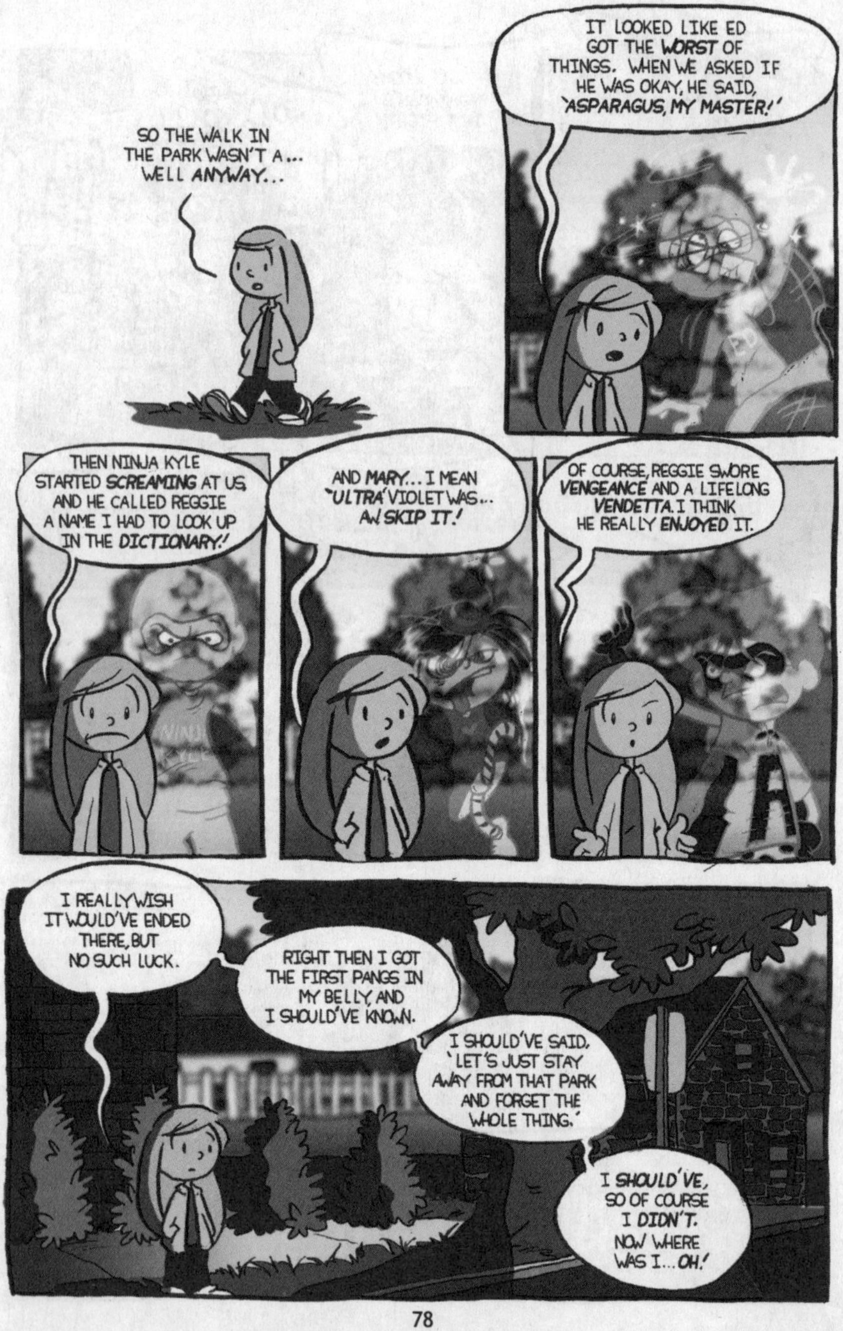
SO THE WALK IN THE PARK WASN'T A... WELL ANYWAY...
IT LOOKED LIKE ED GOT THE WORST OF THINGS. WHEN WE ASKED IF HE WAS OKAY, HE SAID, 'ASPARAGUS, MY MASTER!'
THEN NINJA KYLE STARTED SCREAMING AT US, AND HE CALLED REGGIE A NAME I HAD TO LOOK UP IN THE DICTIONARY!
AND MARY... I MEAN 'ULTRA' VIOLET WAS... AW SKIP IT!
OF COURSE, REGGIE SWORE VENGEANCE AND A LIFELONG VENDETTA. I THINK HE REALLY ENJOYED IT.
I REALLY WISH IT WOULD'VE ENDED THERE, BUT NO SUCH LUCK.
RIGHT THEN I GOT THE FIRST PANGS IN MY BELLY, AND I SHOULD'VE KNOWN.
I SHOULD'VE SAID, 'LET'S JUST STAY AWAY FROM THAT PARK AND FORGET THE WHOLE THING.'
I SHOULD'VE, SO OF COURSE I DIDN'T. NOW WHERE WAS I...OH!

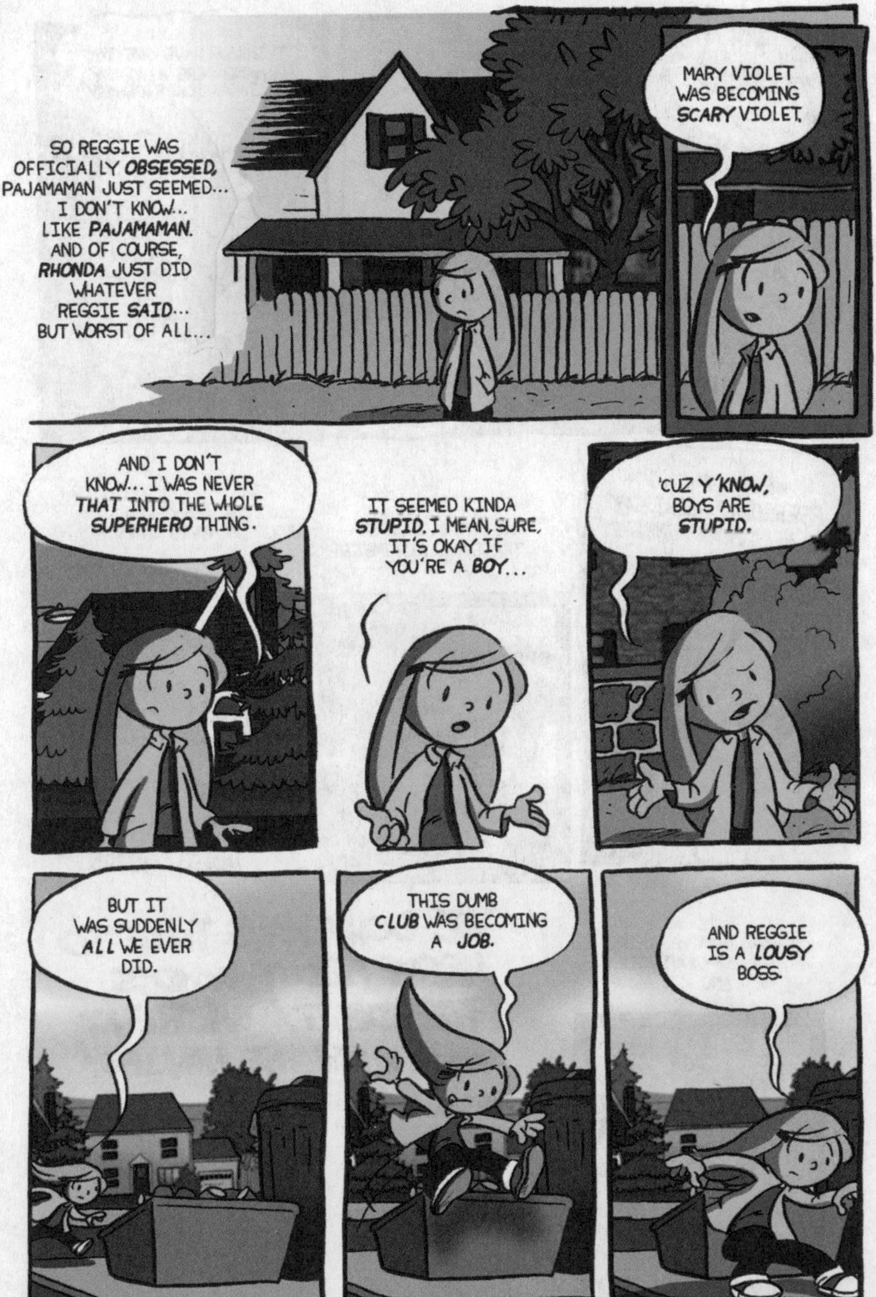
SO REGGIE WAS OFFICIALLY OBSESSED, PAJAMAMAN JUST SEEMED... I DON'T KNOW... LIKE PAJAMAMAN. AND OF COURSE, RHONDA JUST DID WHATEVER REGGIE SAID... BUT WORST OF ALL...
MARY VIOLET WAS BECOMING SCARY VIOLET.
AND I DON'T KNOW... I WAS NEVER THAT INTO THE WHOLE SUPERHERO THING.
IT SEEMED KINDA STUPID. I MEAN, SURE, IT'S OKAY IF YOU'RE A BOY...
'CUZ Y'KNOW, BOYS ARE STUPID.
BUT IT WAS SUDDENLY ALL WE EVER DID.
THIS DUMB CLUB WAS BECOMING A JOB.
AND REGGIE IS A LOUSY BOSS.

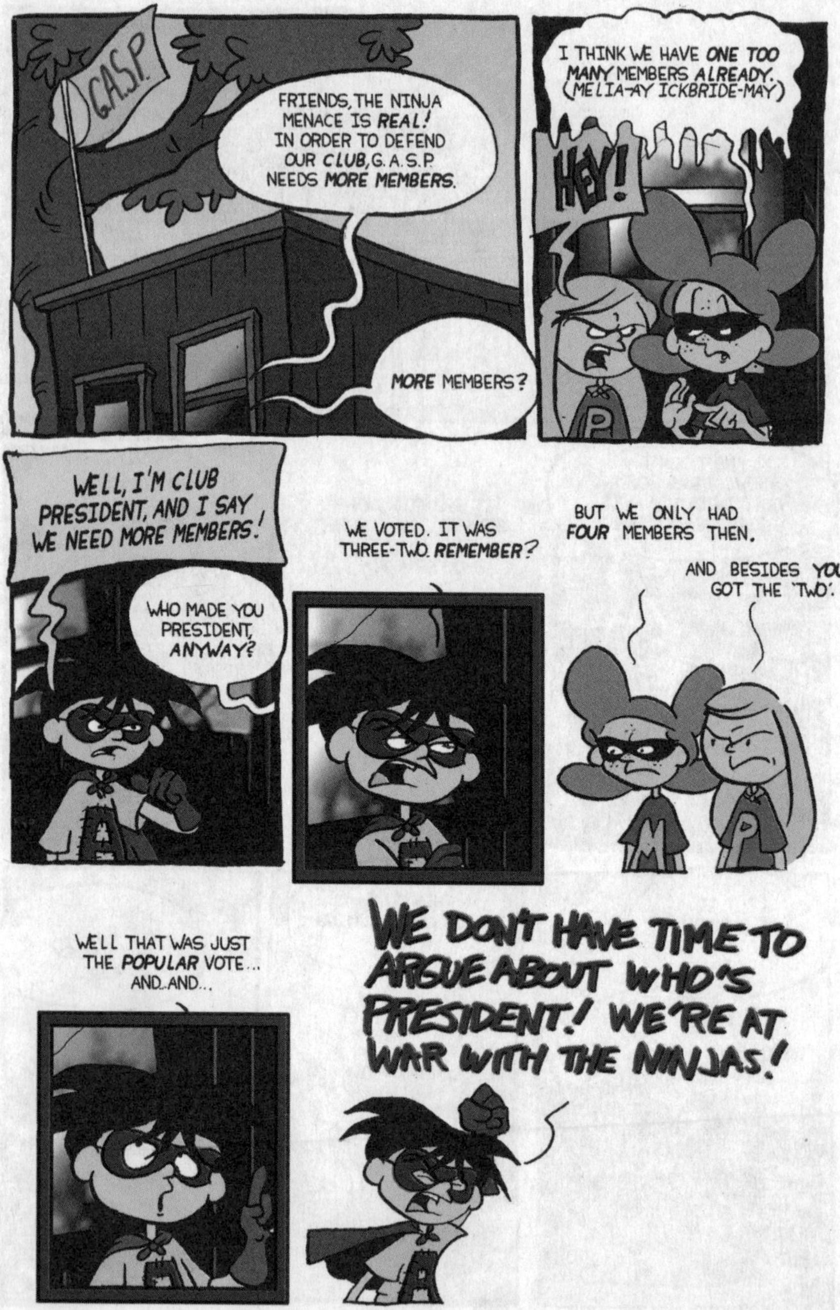
G.A.S.P.
FRIENDS, THE NINJA MENACE IS REAL! IN ORDER TO DEFEND OUR CLUB, G.A.S.P. NEEDS MORE MEMBERS.
MORE MEMBERS?
I THINK WE HAVE ONE TOO MANY MEMBERS ALREADY. (MELIA-AY ICKBRIDE-MAY)
HEY!
WELL, I'M CLUB PRESIDENT, AND I SAY WE NEED MORE MEMBERS!
WHO MADE YOU PRESIDENT, ANYWAY?
WE VOTED. IT WAS THREE-TWO. REMEMBER?
BUT WE ONLY HAD FOUR MEMBERS THEN.
AND BESIDES YOU GOT THE 'TWO'.
WELL THAT WAS JUST THE POPULAR VOTE... AND..AND...
WE DON'T HAVE TIME TO ARGUE ABOUT WHO'S PRESIDENT! WE'RE AT WAR WITH THE NINJAS!

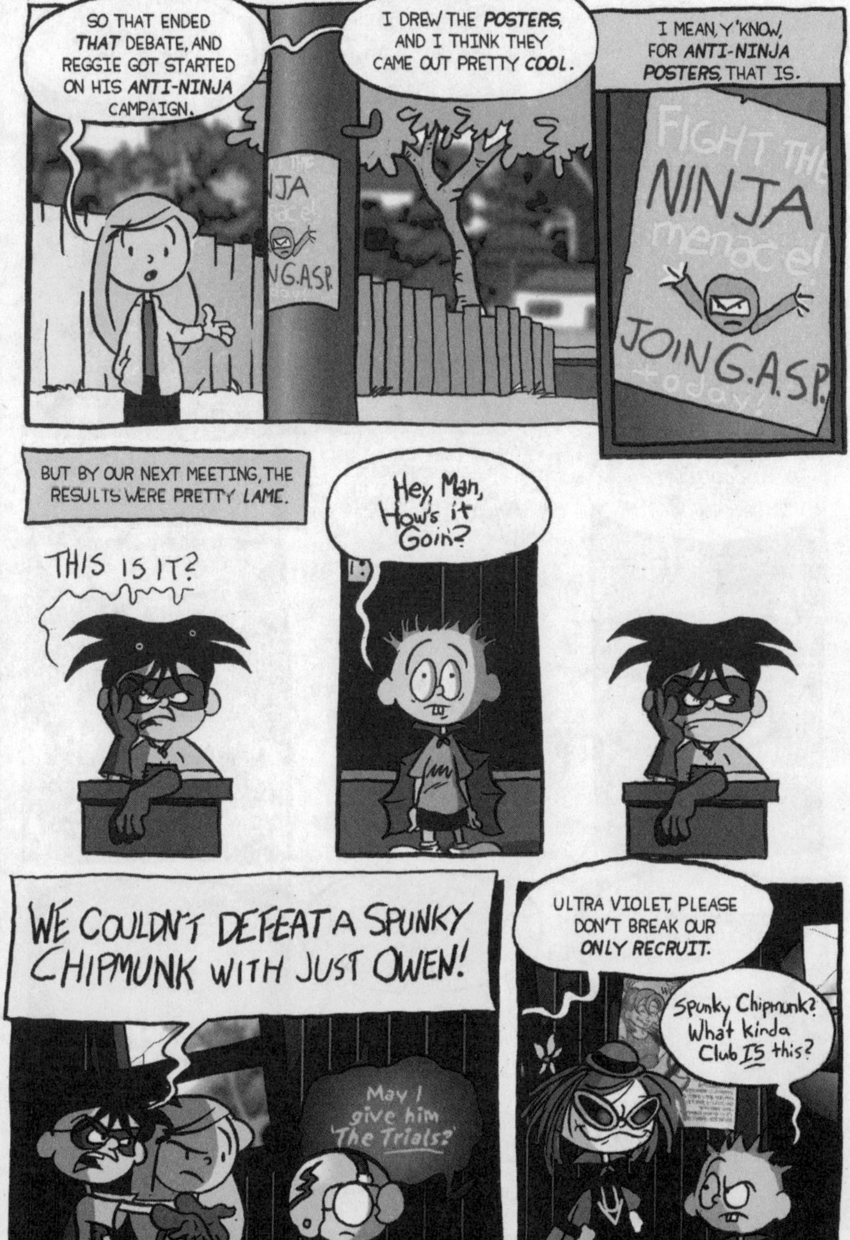
SO THAT ENDED THAT DEBATE, AND REGGIE GOT STARTED ON HIS ANTI-NINJA CAMPAIGN.
I DREW THE POSTERS, AND I THINK THEY CAME OUT PRETTY COOL.
I MEAN, Y'KNOW, FOR ANTI-NINJA POSTERS, THAT IS.
FIGHT THE NINJA menace! JOIN G.A.S.P. today!
BUT BY OUR NEXT MEETING, THE RESULTS WERE PRETTY LAME.
THIS IS IT?
Hey, Man, How's it Goin?
WE COULDN'T DEFEAT A SPUNKY CHIPMUNK WITH JUST OWEN!
May I give him 'The Trials?'
ULTRA VIOLET, PLEASE DON'T BREAK OUR ONLY RECRUIT.
Spunky Chipmunk? What kinda Club IS this?

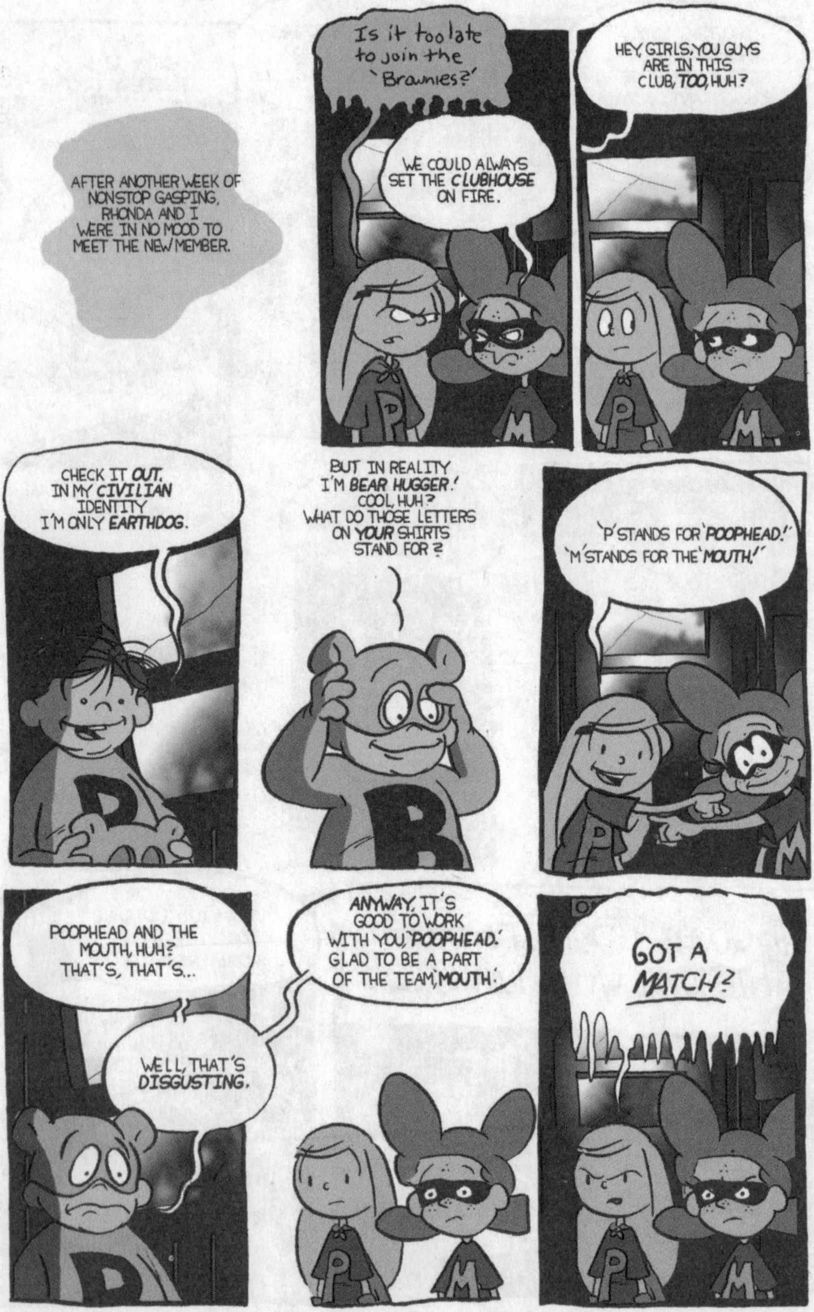
AFTER ANOTHER WEEK OF NONSTOP GASPING, RHONDA AND I WERE IN NO MOOD TO MEET THE NEW MEMBER.
Is it too late to join the 'Brownies?'
WE COULD ALWAYS SET THE CLUBHOUSE ON FIRE.
HEY, GIRLS, YOU GUYS ARE IN THIS CLUB, TOO, HUH?
CHECK IT OUT. IN MY CIVILIAN IDENTITY I'M ONLY EARTHDOG.
BUT IN REALITY I'M BEAR HUGGER! COOL, HUH? WHAT DO THOSE LETTERS ON YOUR SHIRTS STAND FOR?
'P' STANDS FOR 'POOPHEAD!' 'M' STANDS FOR THE 'MOUTH!'
POOPHEAD AND THE MOUTH, HUH? THAT'S, THAT'S...
WELL, THAT'S DISGUSTING.
ANYWAY, IT'S GOOD TO WORK WITH YOU, 'POOPHEAD!' GLAD TO BE A PART OF THE TEAM, 'MOUTH!'
GOT A MATCH?

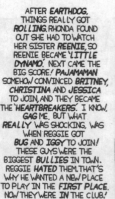

AFTER *EARTHDOG,* THINGS REALLY GOT *ROLLING.* RHONDA FOUND OUT SHE HAD TO WATCH HER SISTER *REENIE,* SO REENIE BECAME *"LITTLE DYNAMO."* NEXT CAME THE BIG SCORE! PAJAMAMAN SOMEHOW CONVINCED *BRITNEY, CHRISTINA* AND *JESSICA* TO JOIN, AND THEY BECAME THE *"HEARTBREAKERS."* I KNOW. *GAG* ME. BUT WHAT *REALLY* WAS SHOCKING, WAS WHEN REGGIE GOT *BUG* AND *IGGY* TO JOIN! THESE GUYS WERE THE BIGGEST *BULLIES* IN TOWN. REGGIE *HATED* THEM. THAT'S WHY HE WANTED A NEW PLACE TO PLAY IN THE *FIRST PLACE.* NOW THEY WERE *IN* THE CLUB! THE ONLY *GOOD* PART WAS WATCHING *"ULTRA VIOLET"* PUT THEM THROUGH THE *"TRIALS."* ::HEH HEH::

OF COURSE, NO ONE WHO JOINED THE CLUB KNEW ABOUT THE *NINJAS,* OR REGGIE'S PLAN TO *FIGHT* THEM. EVEN *OWEN* PRETTY MUCH THOUGHT HE WAS KIDDING.

AND I REALLY COULDN'T FIGURE OUT WHY I WAS GOING *ALONG* WITH IT.

BUT THEN I *REALIZED* SOMETHING...

PAJAMAMAN BROUGHT THE *DEVIL TRIPLETS.*

REGGIE GOT *MARY VIOLET* AND *BUG* AND *IGGY.* AND OWEN BROUGHT IN *EARTHDOG.*

WHICH MAY BE *LAME,* BUT AT LEAST IT'S *SOMETHING.*

I THINK I WENT ALONG WITH ALL OF THIS, 'CUZ IF I HAD *MY OWN* CLUB...

I MIGHT BE THE *ONLY* MEMBER.

ONE WAY

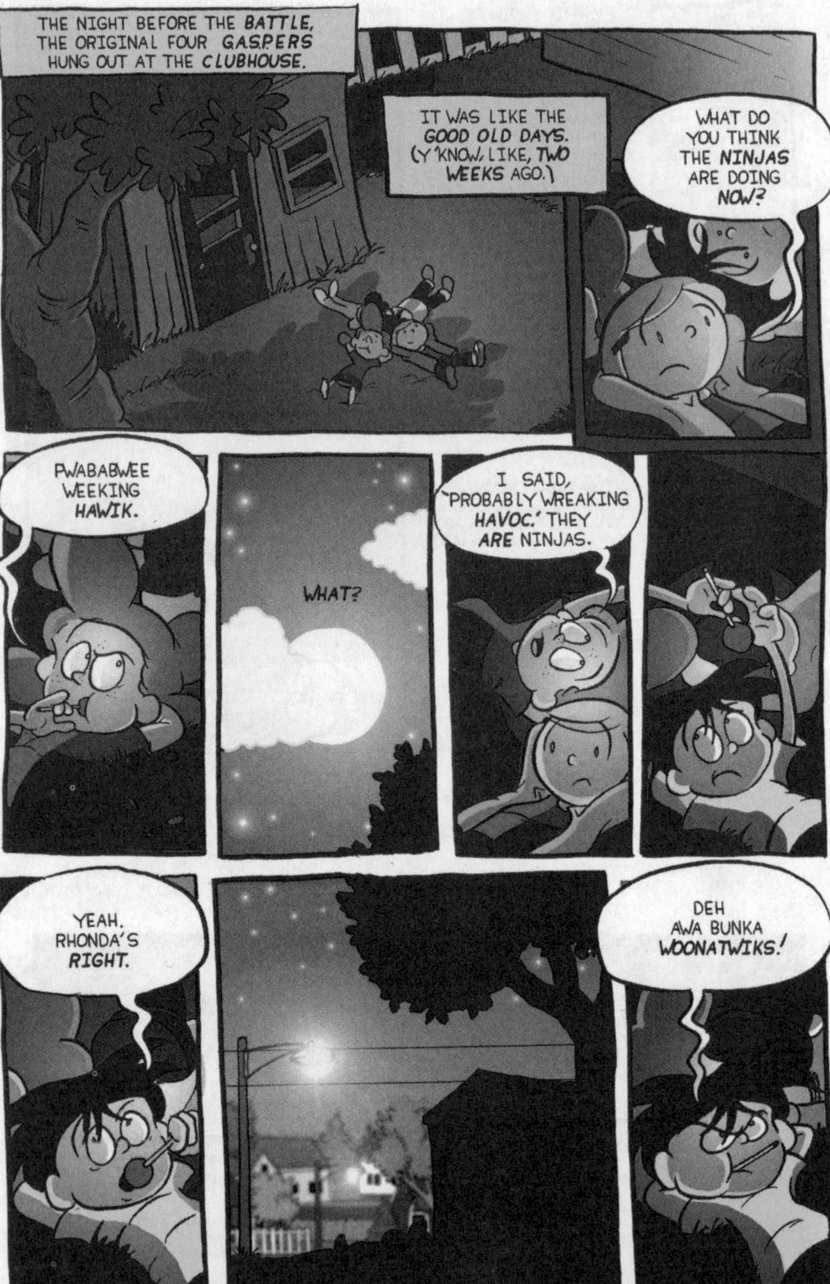
THE NIGHT BEFORE THE BATTLE, THE ORIGINAL FOUR GASPERS HUNG OUT AT THE CLUBHOUSE.
IT WAS LIKE THE GOOD OLD DAYS. (Y'KNOW, LIKE, TWO WEEKS AGO.)
WHAT DO YOU THINK THE NINJAS ARE DOING NOW?
PWABABWEE WEEKING HAWIK.
WHAT?
I SAID, 'PROBABLY WREAKING HAVOC.' THEY ARE NINJAS.
YEAH. RHONDA'S RIGHT.
DEH AWA BUNKA WOONATWIKS!

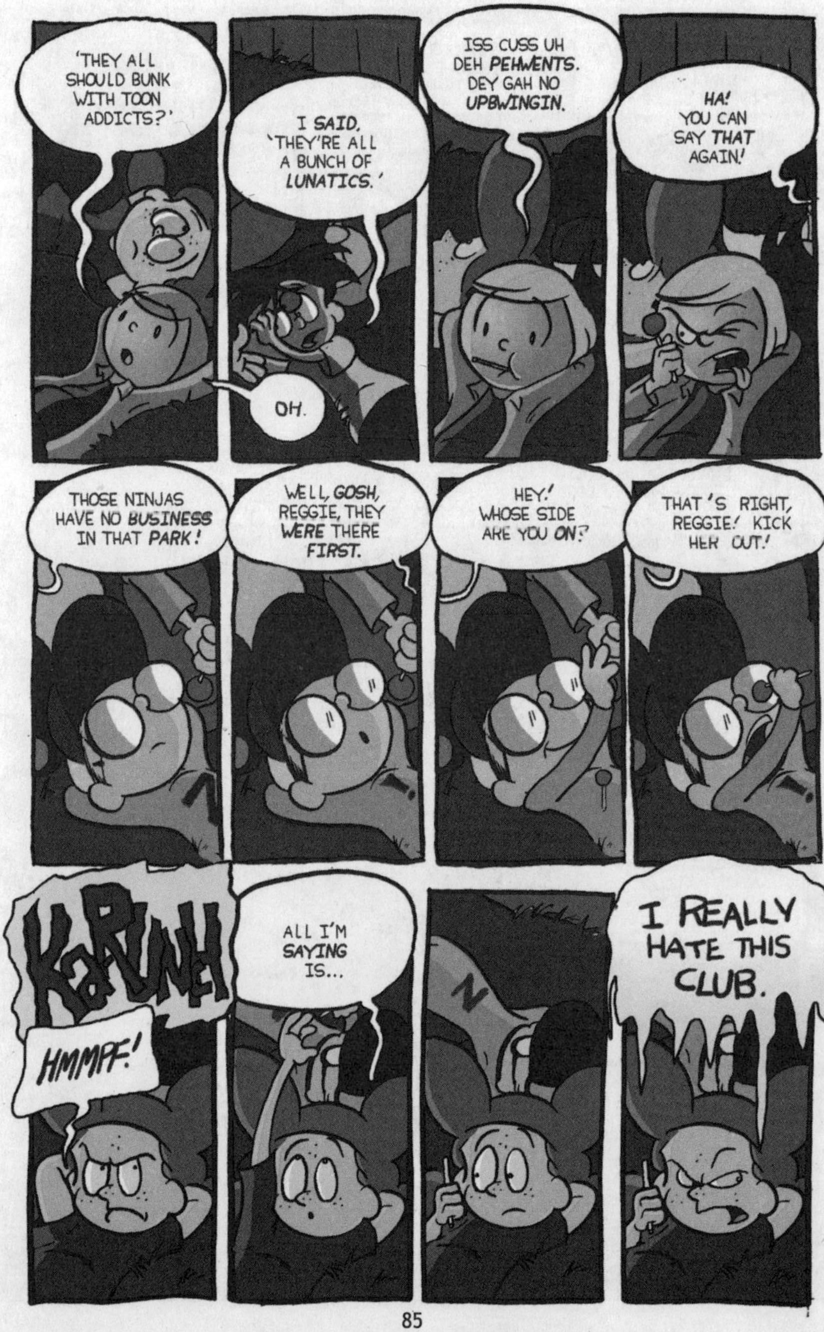
'THEY ALL SHOULD BUNK WITH TOON ADDICTS?'
I SAID, 'THEY'RE ALL A BUNCH OF LUNATICS.'
OH.
ISS CUSS UH DEH PEHWENTS. DEY GAH NO UPBWINGIN.
HA! YOU CAN SAY THAT AGAIN!
THOSE NINJAS HAVE NO BUSINESS IN THAT PARK!
WELL, GOSH, REGGIE, THEY WERE THERE FIRST.
HEY! WHOSE SIDE ARE YOU ON?
THAT'S RIGHT, REGGIE! KICK HER OUT!
KaRUNCH
HMMPF!
ALL I'M SAYING IS...
I REALLY HATE THIS CLUB.

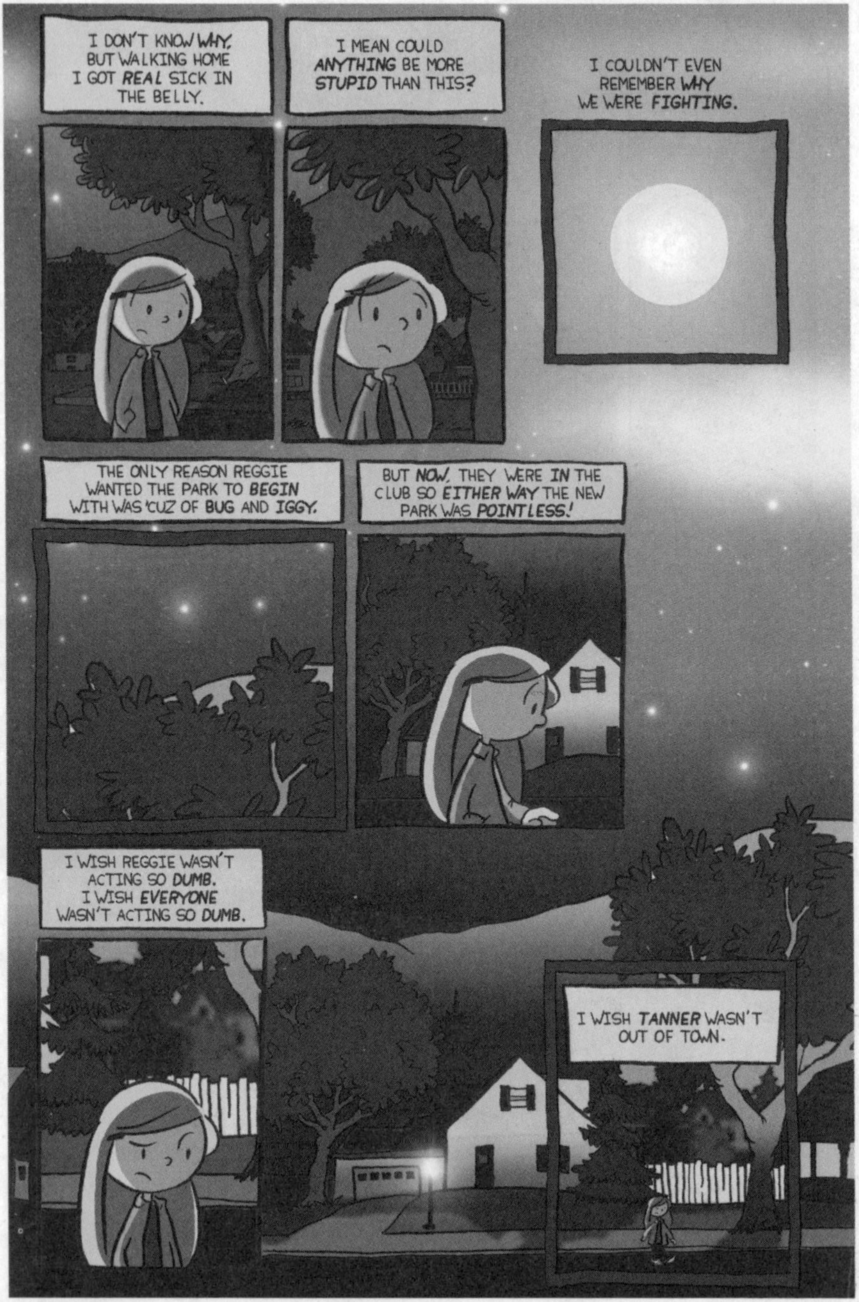
I DON'T KNOW WHY, BUT WALKING HOME I GOT REAL SICK IN THE BELLY.
I MEAN COULD ANYTHING BE MORE STUPID THAN THIS?
I COULDN'T EVEN REMEMBER WHY WE WERE FIGHTING.
THE ONLY REASON REGGIE WANTED THE PARK TO BEGIN WITH WAS 'CUZ OF BUG AND IGGY.
BUT NOW, THEY WERE IN THE CLUB SO EITHER WAY THE NEW PARK WAS POINTLESS!
I WISH REGGIE WASN'T ACTING SO DUMB. I WISH EVERYONE WASN'T ACTING SO DUMB.
I WISH TANNER WASN'T OUT OF TOWN.

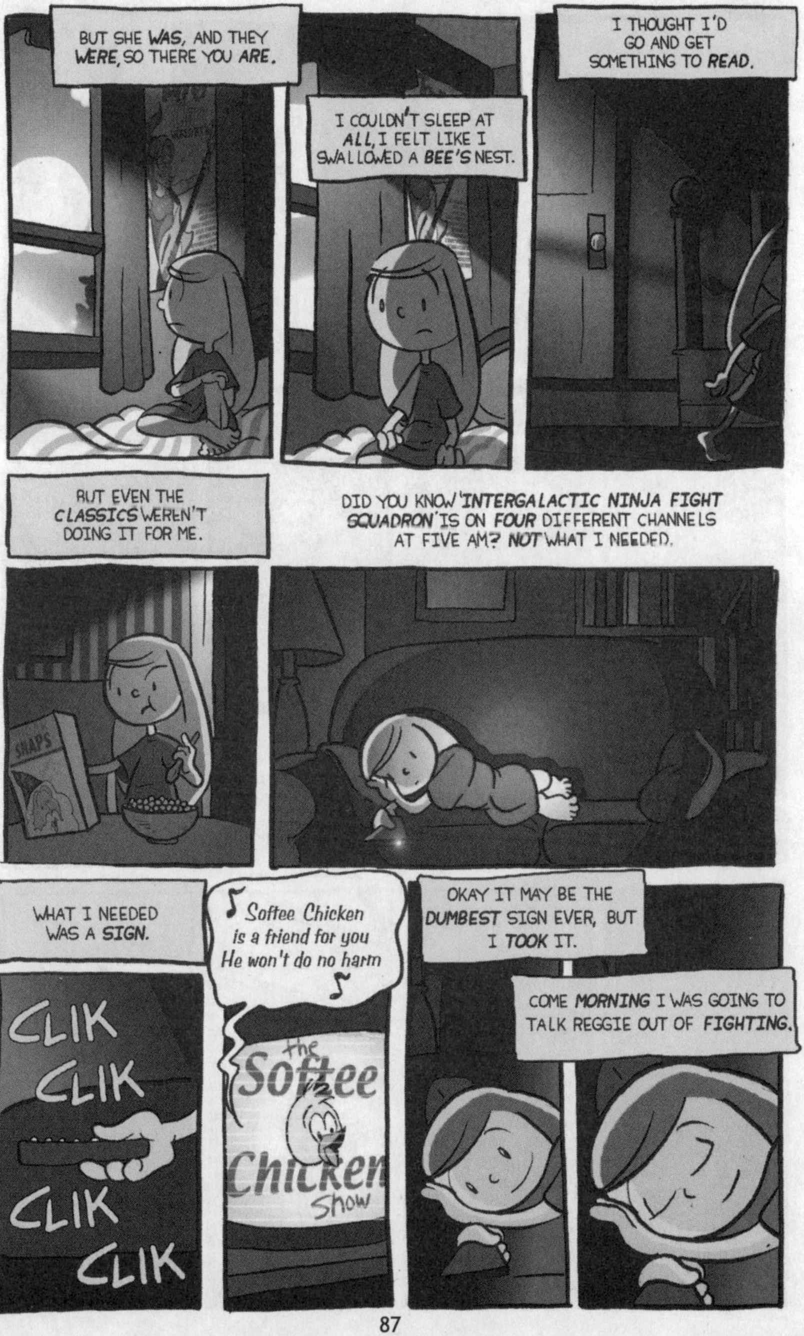

BUT SHE WAS, AND THEY WERE, SO THERE YOU ARE.
I COULDN'T SLEEP AT ALL, I FELT LIKE I SWALLOWED A BEE'S NEST.
I THOUGHT I'D GO AND GET SOMETHING TO READ.
BUT EVEN THE CLASSICS WEREN'T DOING IT FOR ME.
DID YOU KNOW 'INTERGALACTIC NINJA FIGHT SQUADRON' IS ON FOUR DIFFERENT CHANNELS AT FIVE AM? NOT WHAT I NEEDED.
SNAPS
WHAT I NEEDED WAS A SIGN.
CLIK
CLIK
CLIK
CLIK
Softee Chicken is a friend for you He won't do no harm
the Softee Chicken Show
OKAY IT MAY BE THE DUMBEST SIGN EVER, BUT I TOOK IT.
COME MORNING I WAS GOING TO TALK REGGIE OUT OF FIGHTING.

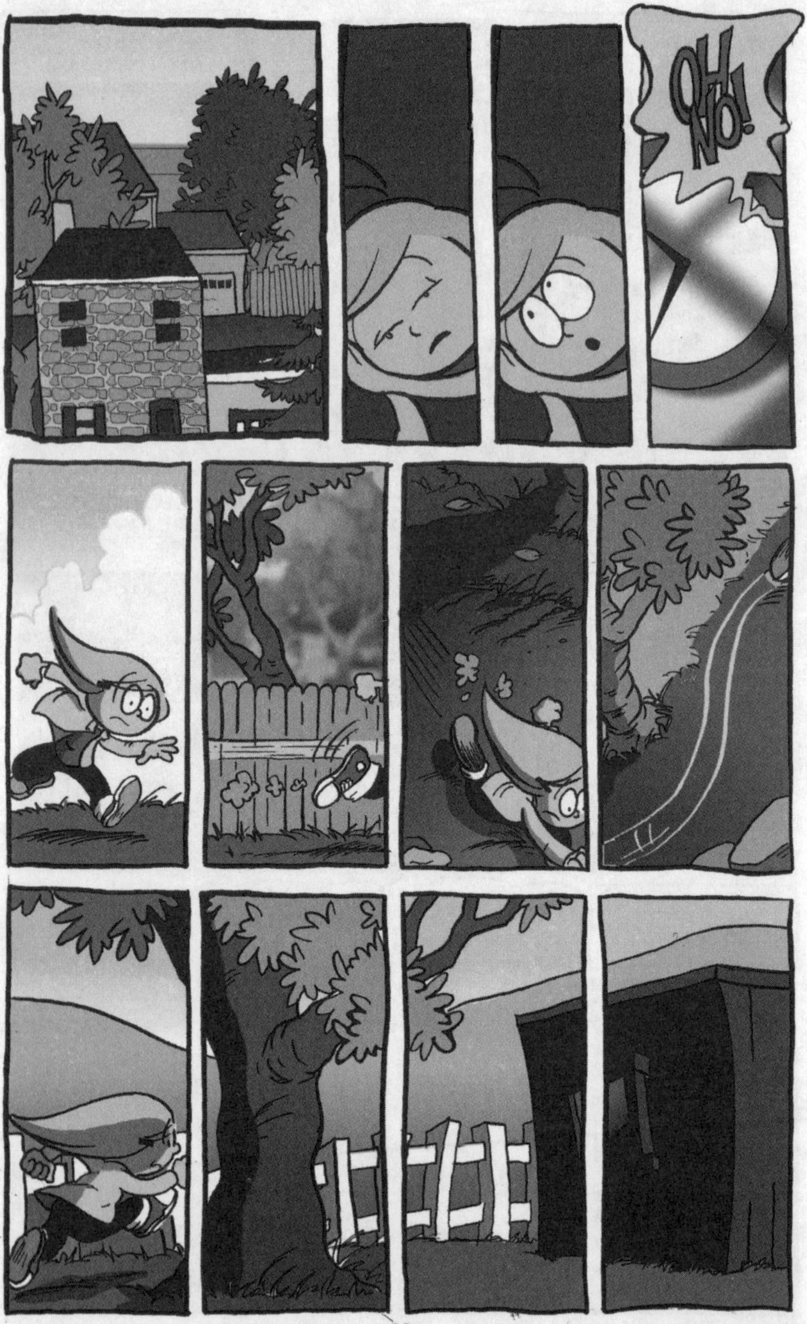
OH NO!

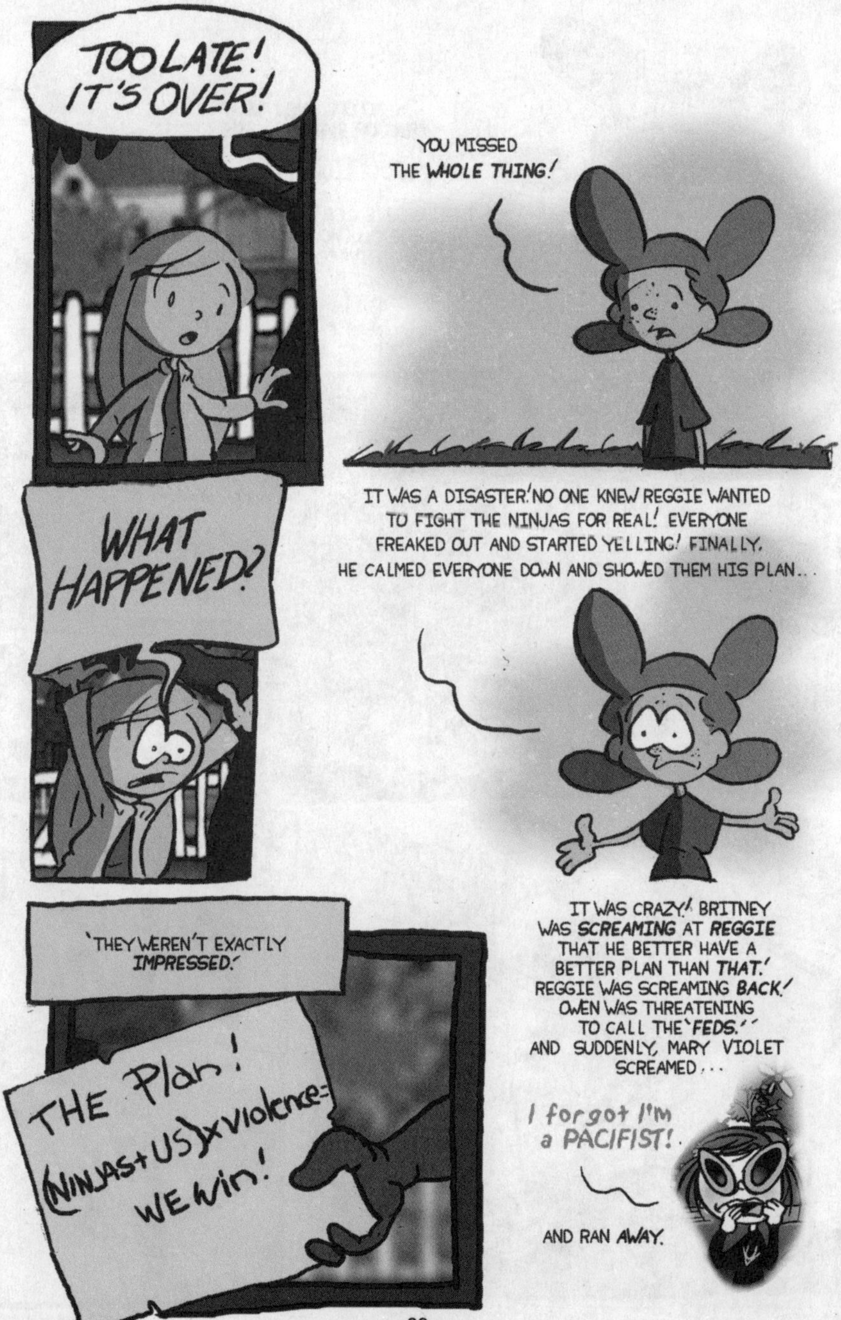
TOO LATE! IT'S OVER!
YOU MISSED THE WHOLE THING!
WHAT HAPPENED?
IT WAS A DISASTER! NO ONE KNEW REGGIE WANTED TO FIGHT THE NINJAS FOR REAL! EVERYONE FREAKED OUT AND STARTED YELLING! FINALLY, HE CALMED EVERYONE DOWN AND SHOWED THEM HIS PLAN...
THEY WEREN'T EXACTLY IMPRESSED.
THE Plan!
(NINJAS+US)x violence= WE win!
IT WAS CRAZY! BRITNEY WAS SCREAMING AT REGGIE THAT HE BETTER HAVE A BETTER PLAN THAN THAT! REGGIE WAS SCREAMING BACK! OWEN WAS THREATENING TO CALL THE "FEDS." AND SUDDENLY, MARY VIOLET SCREAMED...
I forgot I'm a PACIFIST!
AND RAN AWAY.

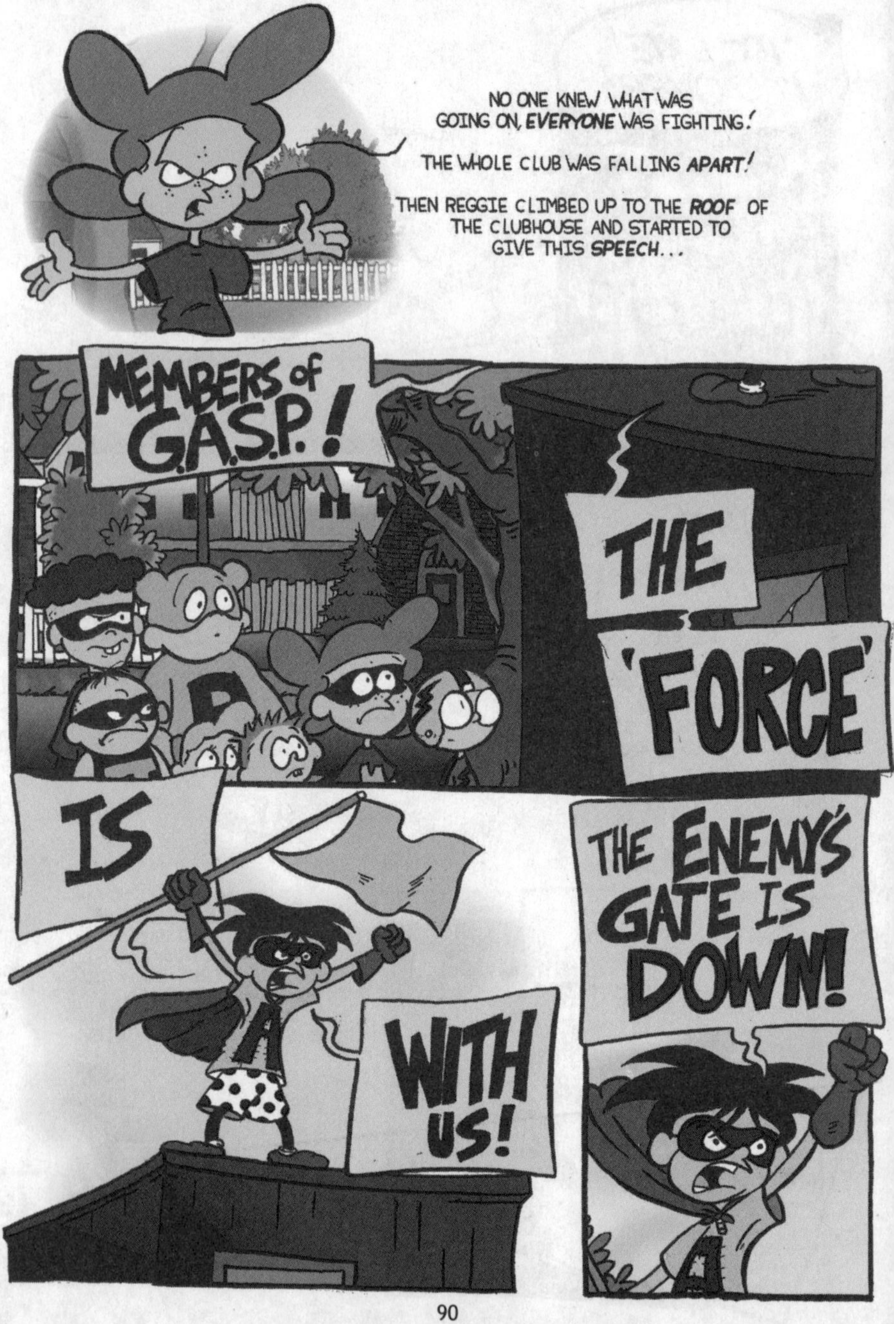
NO ONE KNEW WHAT WAS GOING ON, EVERYONE WAS FIGHTING!
THE WHOLE CLUB WAS FALLING APART!
THEN REGGIE CLIMBED UP TO THE ROOF OF THE CLUBHOUSE AND STARTED TO GIVE THIS SPEECH...
MEMBERS of G.A.S.P.!
THE
'FORCE'
IS
WITH US!
THE ENEMY'S GATE IS DOWN!

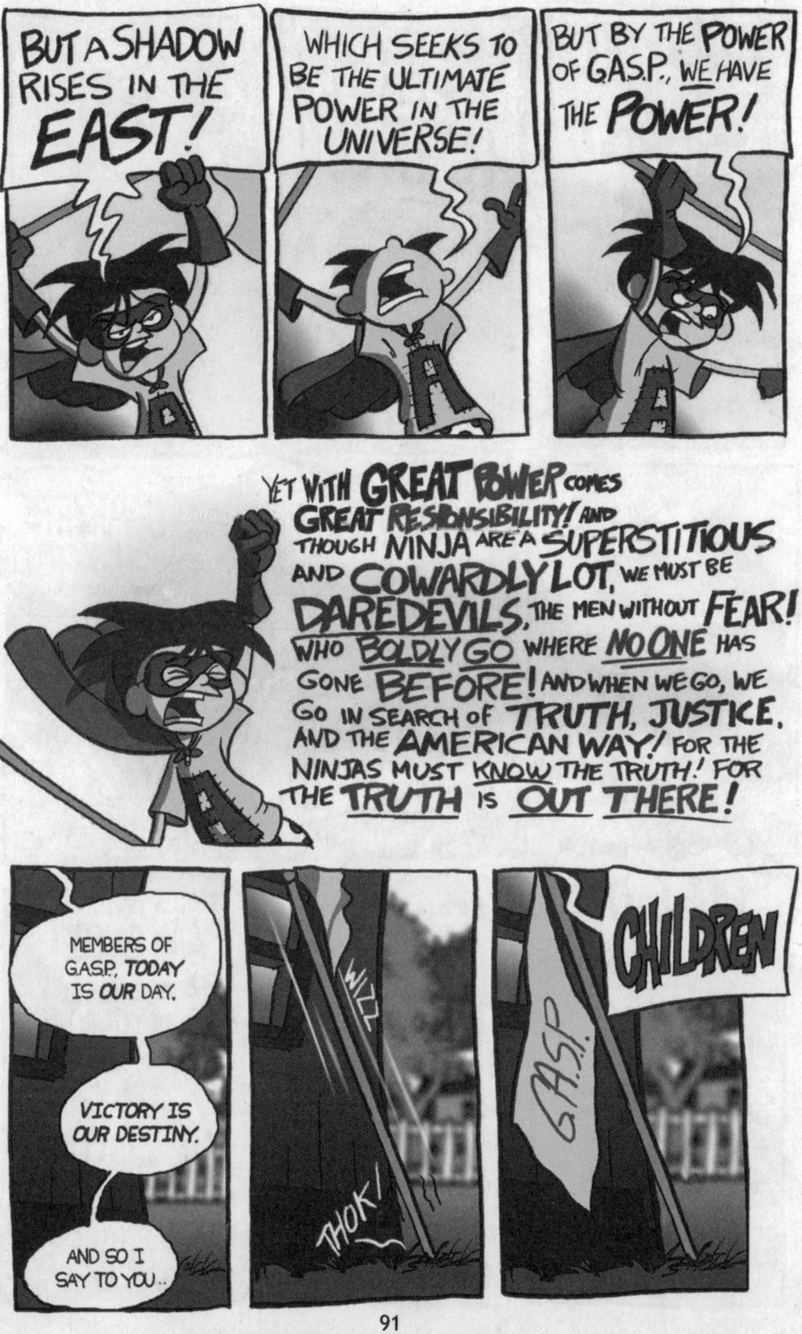

BUT A SHADOW RISES IN THE EAST!
WHICH SEEKS TO BE THE ULTIMATE POWER IN THE UNIVERSE!
BUT BY THE POWER OF G.A.S.P., WE HAVE THE POWER!
YET WITH GREAT POWER COMES GREAT RESPONSIBILITY! AND THOUGH NINJA ARE A SUPERSTITIOUS AND COWARDLY LOT, WE MUST BE DAREDEVILS, THE MEN WITHOUT FEAR! WHO BOLDLY GO WHERE NO ONE HAS GONE BEFORE! AND WHEN WE GO, WE GO IN SEARCH OF TRUTH, JUSTICE, AND THE AMERICAN WAY! FOR THE NINJAS MUST KNOW THE TRUTH! FOR THE TRUTH IS OUT THERE!
MEMBERS OF G.A.S.P., TODAY IS OUR DAY.
VICTORY IS OUR DESTINY.
AND SO I SAY TO YOU...
WIZZ
THOK!
G.A.S.P.
CHILDREN

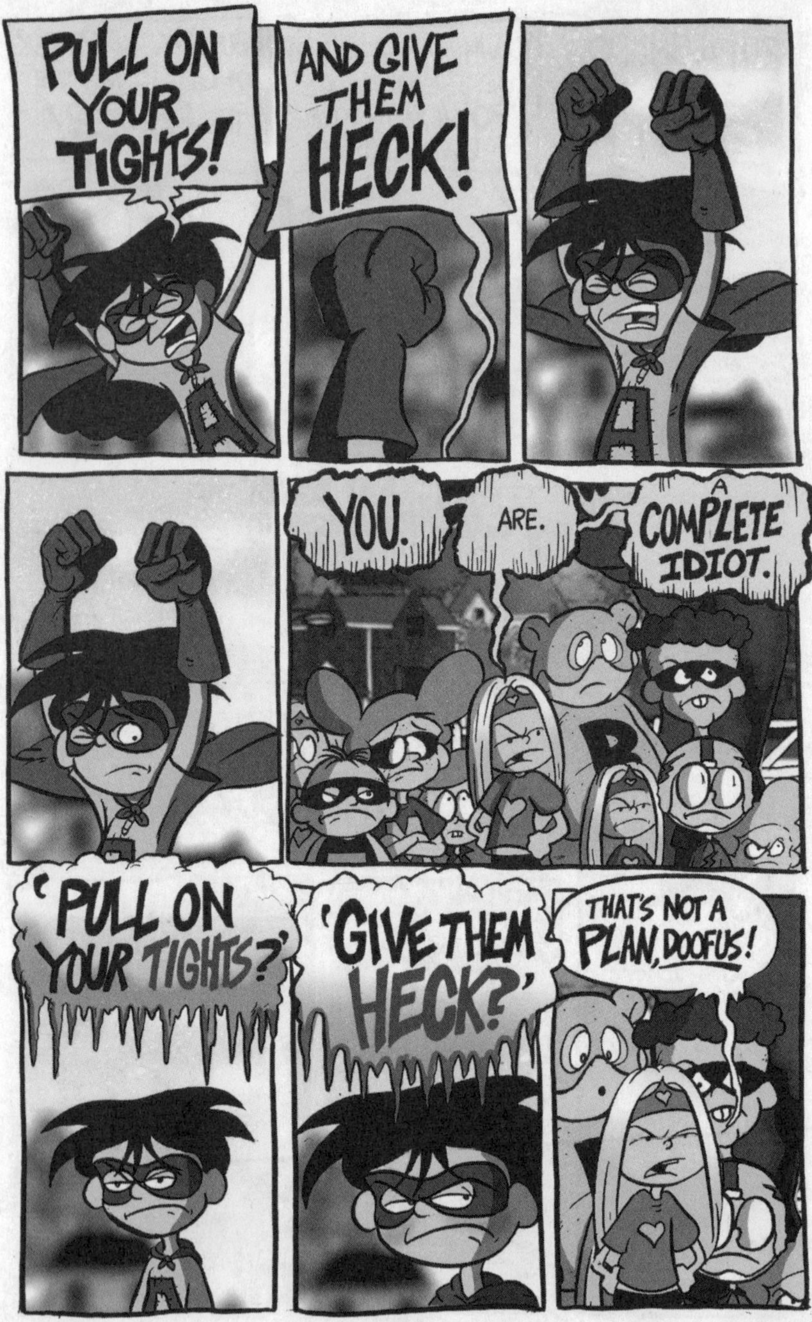
PULL ON YOUR TIGHTS!
AND GIVE THEM HECK!
YOU.
ARE.
A COMPLETE IDIOT.
'PULL ON YOUR TIGHTS?'
'GIVE THEM HECK?'
THAT'S NOT A PLAN, DOOFUS!

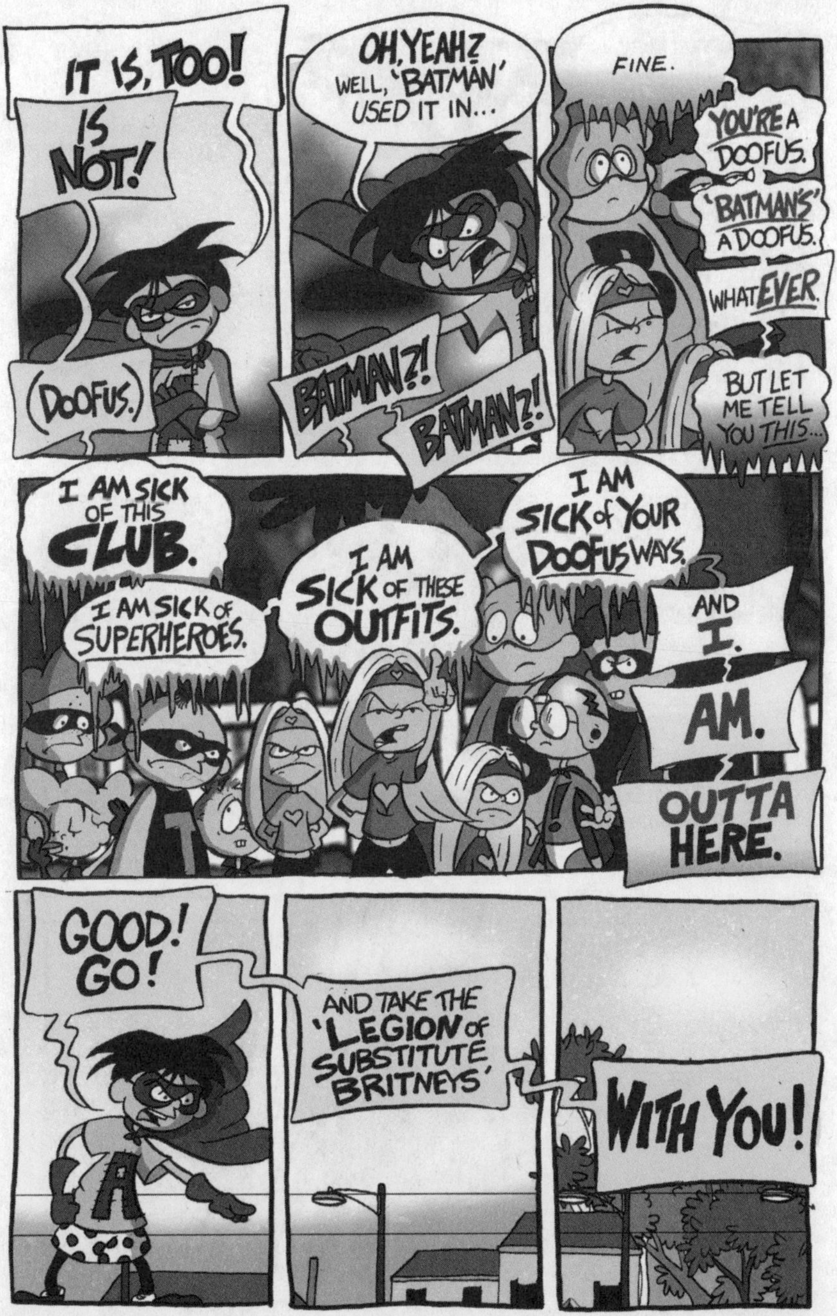
IT IS, TOO!
IS NOT!
(DOOFUS.)
OH, YEAH? WELL, 'BATMAN' USED IT IN...
BATMAN?!
BATMAN?!
FINE.
YOU'RE A DOOFUS.
'BATMAN'S' A DOOFUS.
WHATEVER.
BUT LET ME TELL YOU THIS...
I AM SICK OF THIS CLUB.
I AM SICK OF SUPERHEROES.
I AM SICK OF THESE OUTFITS.
I AM SICK OF YOUR DOOFUS WAYS.
AND I.
AM.
OUTTA HERE.
GOOD! GO!
AND TAKE THE 'LEGION OF SUBSTITUTE BRITNEYS'
WITH YOU!

AND THAT WAS IT! THEY LEFT.
BUT THE REST OF US DECIDED TO STICK IT OUT.
SO WE HEADED OVER TO THE PARK.

THERE WAS **NO SIGN** OF THE NINJAS WHEN WE GOT THERE, SO WE DECIDED TO TRY AN **AMBUSH.**

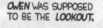

OWEN WAS SUPPOSED TO BE THE ***LOOKOUT.***

NO ONE'S REALLY SURE WHAT **HAPPENED.**

MAYBE OWEN DECIDED TO ***JUMP.***

MAYBE HE ***REALLY THOUGHT*** HE COULD ***FLY.***

OR MAYBE HE JUST ***FELL.***

ALL WE KNOW IS...

ONE MINUTE HE WAS ***IN*** THE TREE...

AND THE ***NEXT...***

FLAP
FLAP
FLAP
FLAP
FLAP
FLAP
FLAP
FLAP
FLAP
FLAP
FLAP
FLAP
WHAM

I REALLY DIDN'T WANT TO HEAR WHAT RHONDA WAS *SAYING*, BUT I HAD TO KNOW WHAT *HAPPENED*.

SO *EARTHDOG* RUNS AND GETS OWEN'S *MOM* RIGHT. AND SHE'S SCREAMING, *"MY BABY, MY BABY!"* AN' *OWEN'S* BAWLING LIKE A *LOON,* RIGHT, 'CUZ IT'S PRETTY *OBVIOUS* HE'S HURT, AND THE WHOLE TIME THE *NINJAS* ARE WAITIN' AROUND, SEE, 'CUZ *NOW* THEY'RE NOT *SURPRISED,* AND THEY FIGURE THEY CAN *POUND* US. SO AS SOON AS OWEN'S MOM *LEAVES* THEY GET READY TO MAKE THEIR *MOVE.*

OH, NO!

BUT THEN EARTHDOG'S DAD SHOWS UP! AND STARTS SCREAMIN' AT EVERYBODY FOR FIGHTING! AND THOSE NINJAS TOOK OFF.

THAT'S GREAT! THERE WAS NO FIGHT!

WELL, NOT *EXACTLY.*

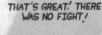

BUG AND *IGGY* GOT SO MAD WE WASTED THEIR SATURDAY THAT THEY BEAT THE SNOT OUT OF *EVERYONE.*

THE GOOD NEWS IS THAT REGGIE WAS SO MAD YOU DIDN'T SHOW UP THAT HE'S NO LONGER SPEAKING TO YOU.

OH.

THE WHOLE THING WAS A BIG *DISASTER.* I GUESS *EARTHDOG* SUMMED IT UP IN THE FOLLOWING *POEM.*

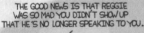

95

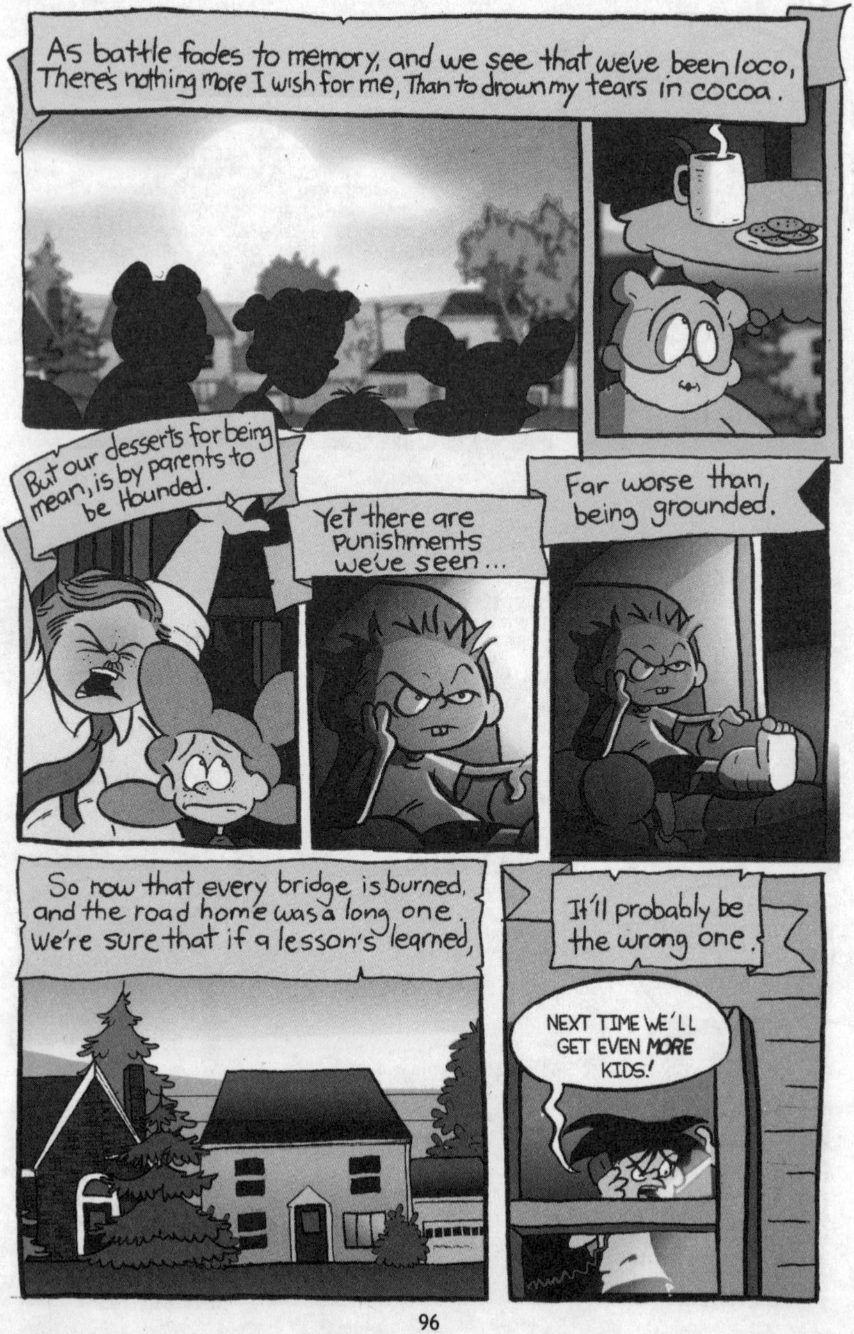

As battle fades to memory, and we see that we've been loco,
There's nothing more I wish for me, Than to drown my tears in cocoa.
But our desserts for being mean, is by parents to be Hounded.
Yet there are punishments we've seen...
Far worse than, being grounded.
So now that every bridge is burned, and the road home was a long one. We're sure that if a lesson's learned,
It'll probably be the wrong one.
NEXT TIME WE'LL GET EVEN MORE KIDS!

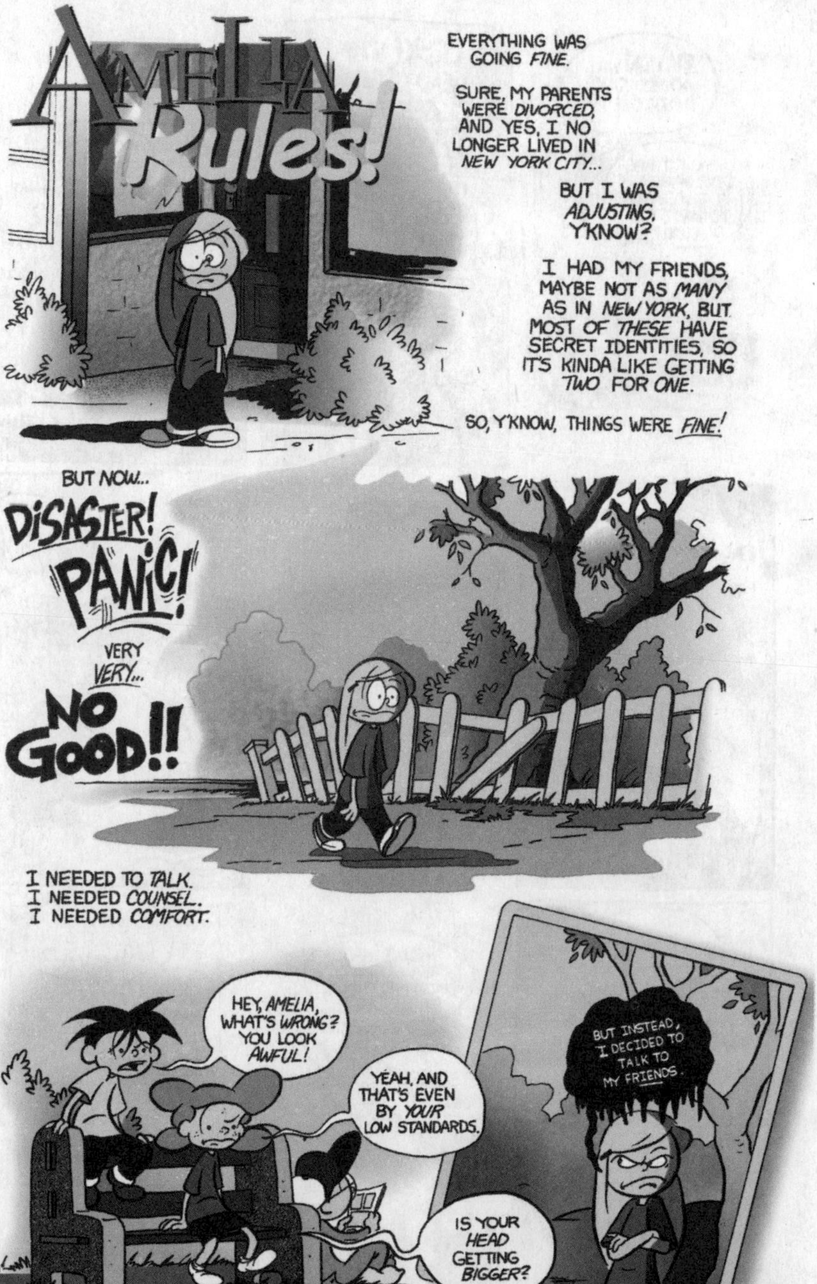
AMELIA Rules!
EVERYTHING WAS GOING FINE.
SURE, MY PARENTS WERE DIVORCED, AND YES, I NO LONGER LIVED IN NEW YORK CITY...
BUT I WAS ADJUSTING, Y'KNOW?
I HAD MY FRIENDS, MAYBE NOT AS MANY AS IN NEW YORK, BUT MOST OF THESE HAVE SECRET IDENTITIES, SO IT'S KINDA LIKE GETTING TWO FOR ONE.
SO, Y'KNOW, THINGS WERE FINE!
BUT NOW...
DISASTER!
PANIC!
VERY VERY...
NO GOOD!!
I NEEDED TO TALK.
I NEEDED COUNSEL.
I NEEDED COMFORT.
BUT INSTEAD, I DECIDED TO TALK TO MY FRIENDS.
HEY, AMELIA, WHAT'S WRONG? YOU LOOK AWFUL!
YEAH, AND THAT'S EVEN BY YOUR LOW STANDARDS.
IS YOUR HEAD GETTING BIGGER?

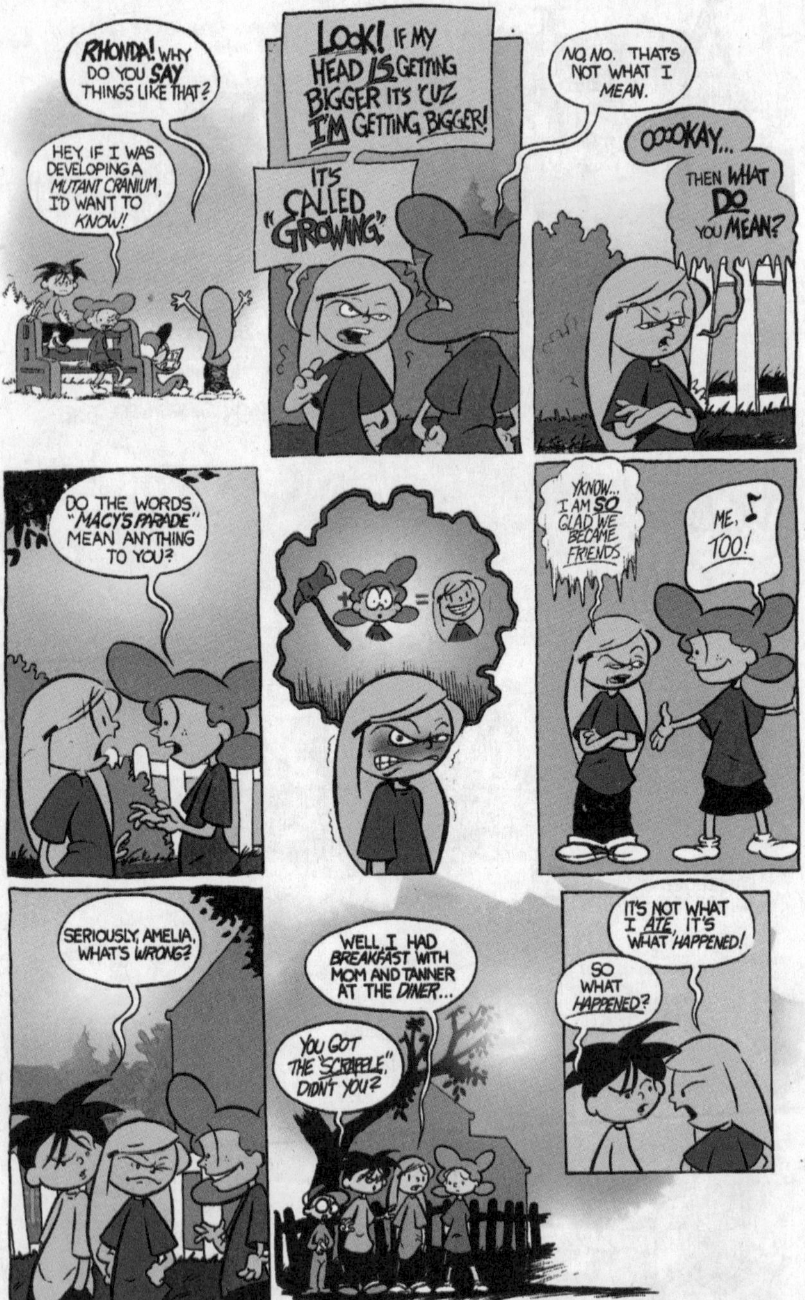
RHONDA! WHY DO YOU SAY THINGS LIKE THAT?
HEY, IF I WAS DEVELOPING A MUTANT CRANIUM, I'D WANT TO KNOW!
LOOK! IF MY HEAD IS GETTING BIGGER IT'S 'CUZ I'M GETTING BIGGER!
IT'S CALLED "GROWING."
NO, NO. THAT'S NOT WHAT I MEAN.
OOOOKAY...
THEN WHAT DO YOU MEAN?
DO THE WORDS "MACY'S PARADE" MEAN ANYTHING TO YOU?
Y'KNOW... I AM SO GLAD WE BECAME FRIENDS
ME, TOO!
SERIOUSLY, AMELIA, WHAT'S WRONG?
WELL, I HAD BREAKFAST WITH MOM AND TANNER AT THE DINER...
YOU GOT THE "SCRAPPLE," DIDN'T YOU?
SO WHAT HAPPENED?
IT'S NOT WHAT I ATE, IT'S WHAT HAPPENED!

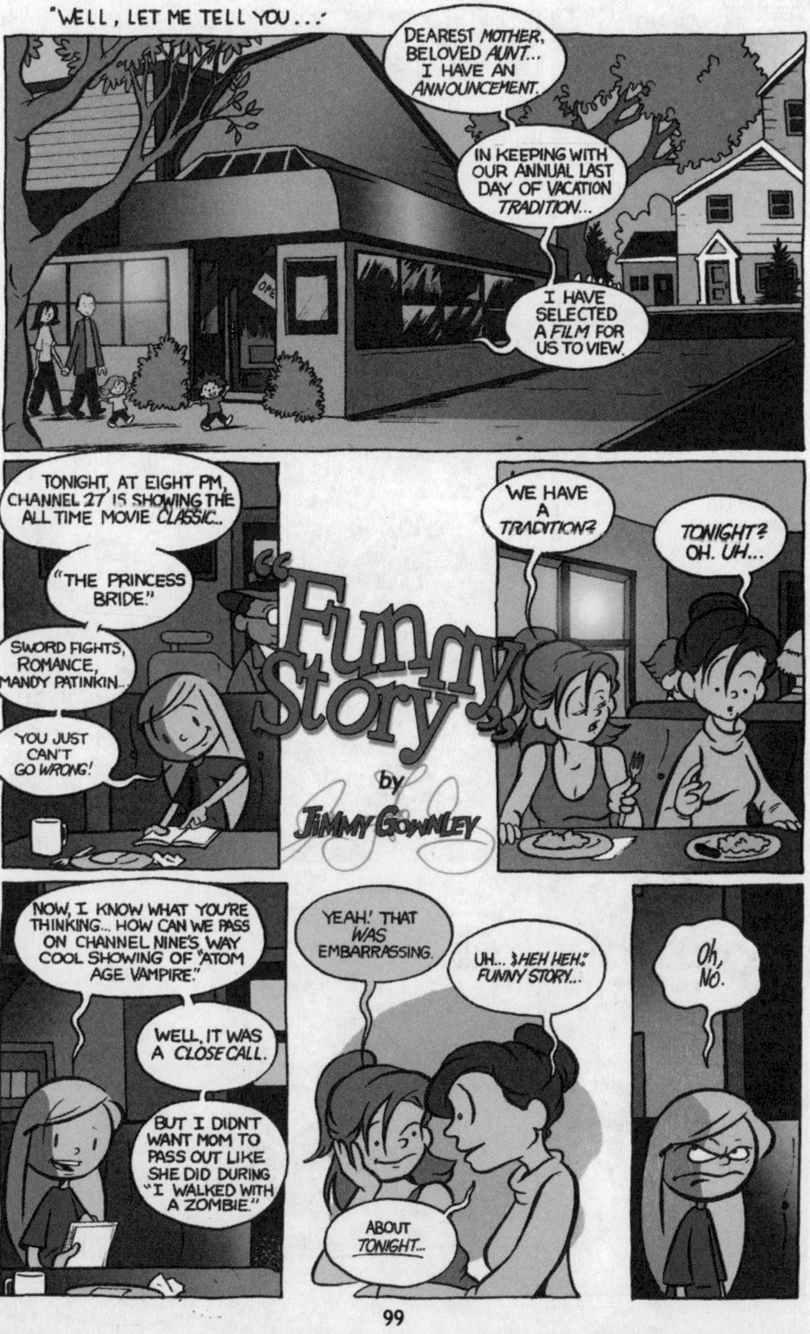
"WELL, LET ME TELL YOU..."
DEAREST *MOTHER*, BELOVED *AUNT*... I HAVE AN *ANNOUNCEMENT*.
IN KEEPING WITH OUR ANNUAL LAST DAY OF VACATION *TRADITION*...
I HAVE SELECTED A *FILM* FOR US TO VIEW.
OPE
TONIGHT, AT EIGHT PM, CHANNEL 27 IS SHOWING THE ALL TIME MOVIE *CLASSIC*...
"THE PRINCESS BRIDE."
SWORD FIGHTS, ROMANCE, MANDY PATINKIN...
YOU JUST CAN'T GO *WRONG*!
"Funny Story"
by
JIMMY GOWNLEY
WE HAVE A *TRADITION*?
TONIGHT? OH. UH...
NOW, I KNOW WHAT YOU'RE THINKING... HOW CAN WE PASS ON CHANNEL NINE'S WAY COOL SHOWING OF "ATOM AGE VAMPIRE."
WELL, IT WAS A *CLOSE CALL*.
BUT I DIDN'T WANT MOM TO PASS OUT LIKE SHE DID DURING "I WALKED WITH A ZOMBIE."
YEAH! THAT *WAS* EMBARRASSING.
UH... *HEH HEH.* *FUNNY STORY*...
ABOUT *TONIGHT*...
Oh, NO.

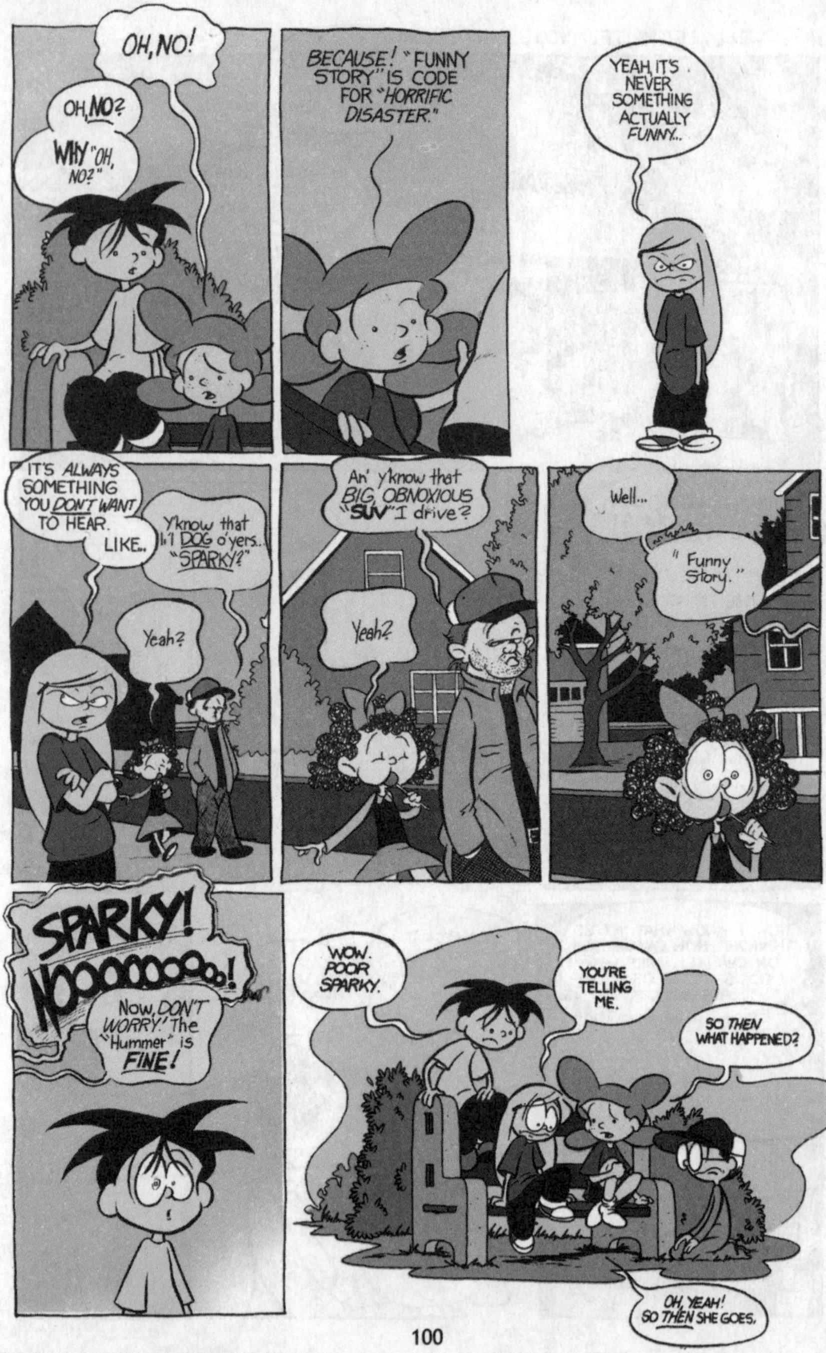

OH, NO!
OH, NO?
WHY "OH, NO?"
BECAUSE! "FUNNY STORY" IS CODE FOR "HORRIFIC DISASTER."
YEAH, IT'S NEVER SOMETHING ACTUALLY FUNNY...
IT'S ALWAYS SOMETHING YOU DON'T WANT TO HEAR.
LIKE..
Y'know that li'l DOG o'yers.. "SPARKY?"
Yeah?
An' y'know that BIG, OBNOXIOUS "SUV" I drive?
Yeah?
Well...
"Funny Story."
SPARKY! NOOOOOOOoo!
Now, DON'T WORRY! The "Hummer" is FINE!
WOW. POOR SPARKY.
YOU'RE TELLING ME.
SO THEN WHAT HAPPENED?
OH, YEAH! SO THEN SHE GOES,

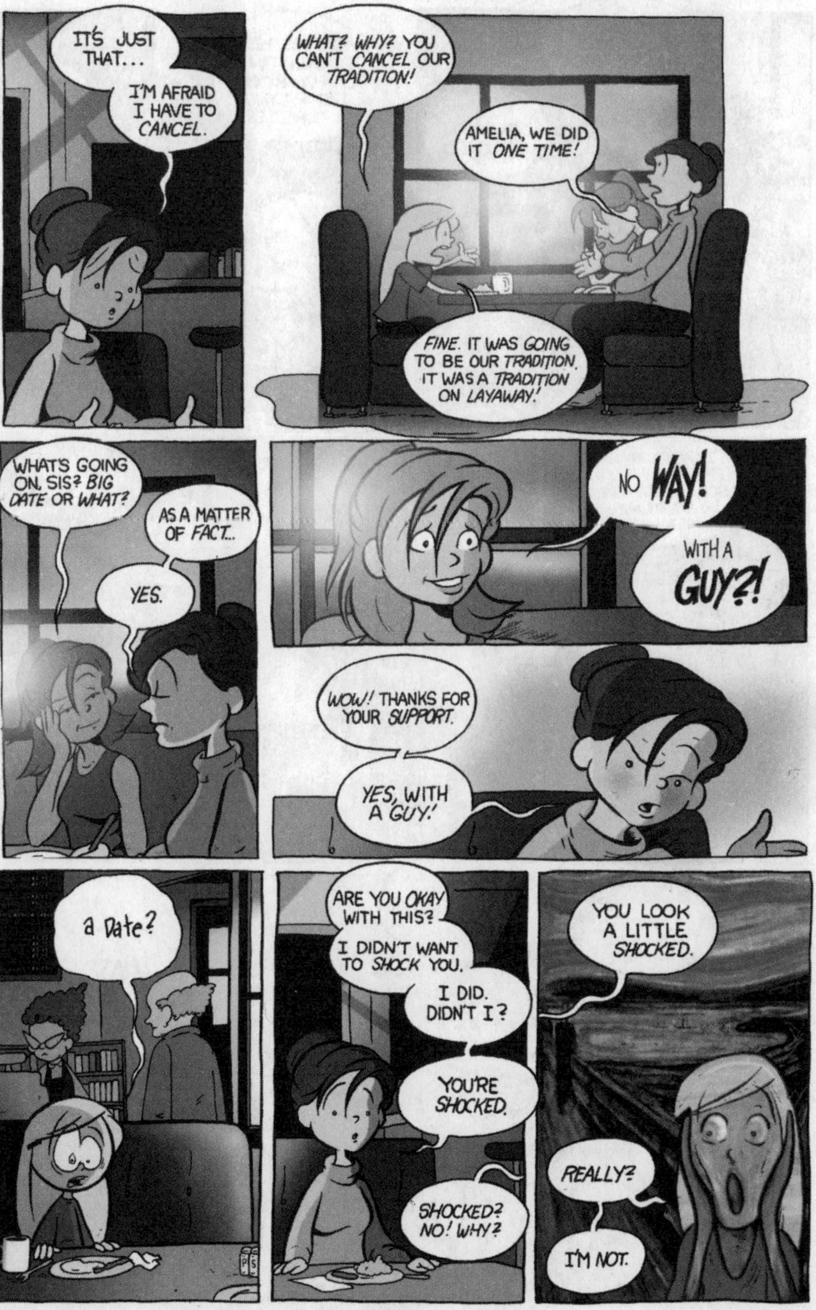
IT'S JUST THAT...
I'M AFRAID I HAVE TO CANCEL.
WHAT? WHY? YOU CAN'T CANCEL OUR TRADITION!
AMELIA, WE DID IT ONE TIME!
FINE. IT WAS GOING TO BE OUR TRADITION. IT WAS A TRADITION ON LAYAWAY!
WHAT'S GOING ON, SIS? BIG DATE OR WHAT?
AS A MATTER OF FACT...
YES.
NO WAY!
WITH A GUY?!
WOW! THANKS FOR YOUR SUPPORT.
YES, WITH A GUY!
a Date?
ARE YOU OKAY WITH THIS?
I DIDN'T WANT TO SHOCK YOU.
I DID. DIDN'T I?
YOU'RE SHOCKED.
SHOCKED? NO! WHY?
YOU LOOK A LITTLE SHOCKED.
REALLY?
I'M NOT.

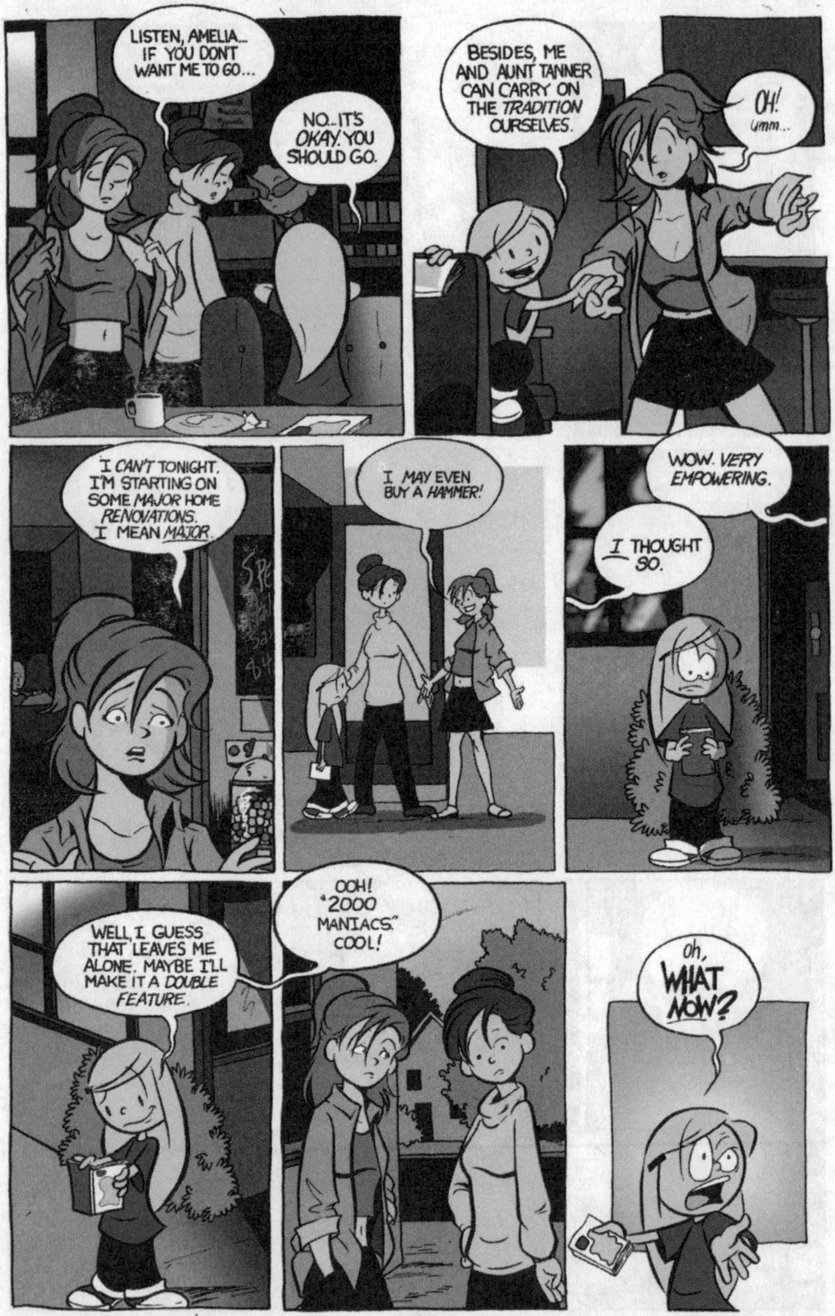
LISTEN, AMELIA... IF YOU DON'T WANT ME TO GO...
NO...IT'S OKAY. YOU SHOULD GO.
BESIDES, ME AND AUNT TANNER CAN CARRY ON THE TRADITION OURSELVES.
OH! umm...
I CAN'T TONIGHT. I'M STARTING ON SOME MAJOR HOME RENOVATIONS. I MEAN MAJOR.
I MAY EVEN BUY A HAMMER!
WOW. VERY EMPOWERING.
I THOUGHT SO.
WELL, I GUESS THAT LEAVES ME ALONE. MAYBE I'LL MAKE IT A DOUBLE FEATURE.
OOH! "2000 MANIACS." COOL!
oh, WHAT NOW?

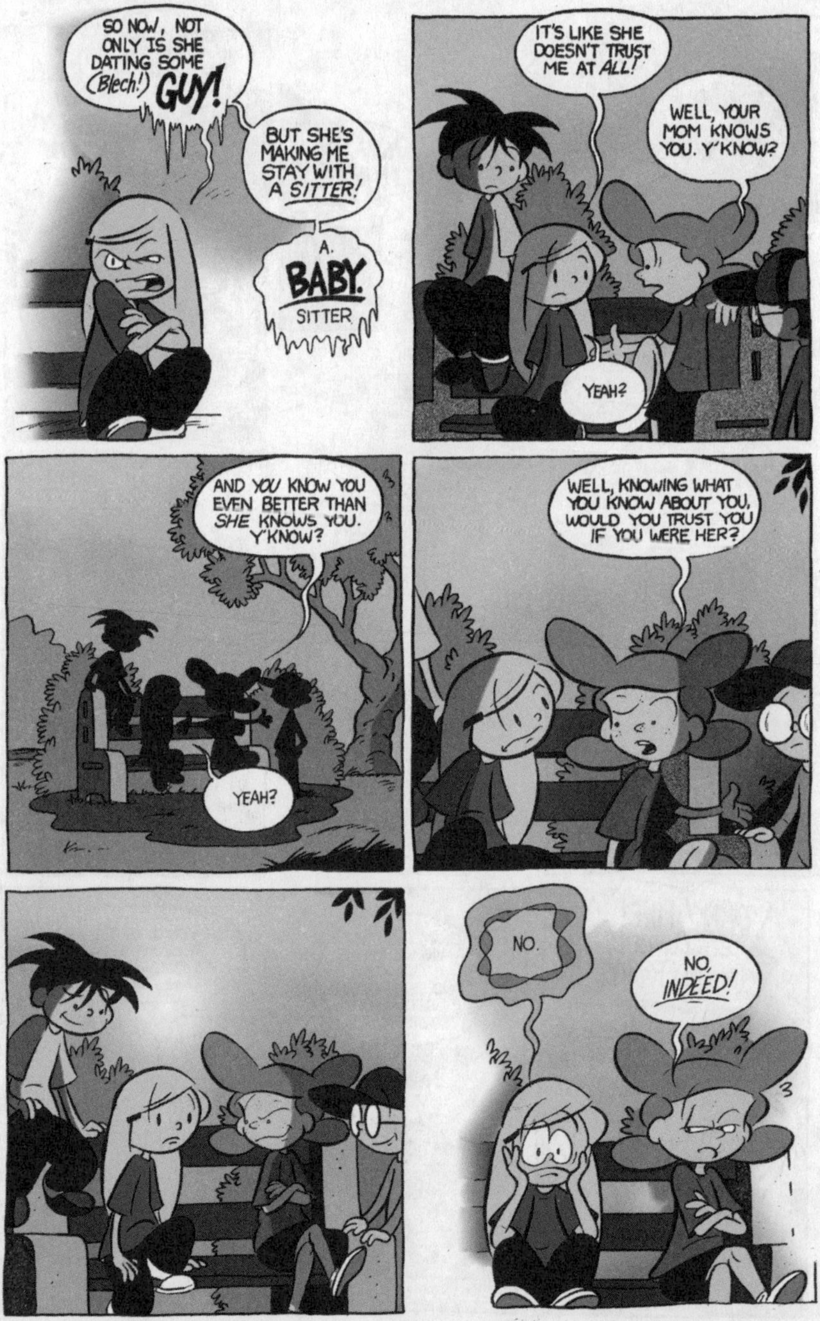
SO NOW, NOT ONLY IS SHE DATING SOME (Blech!) GUY!
BUT SHE'S MAKING ME STAY WITH A SITTER!
A. BABY. SITTER
IT'S LIKE SHE DOESN'T TRUST ME AT ALL!
WELL, YOUR MOM KNOWS YOU. Y'KNOW?
YEAH?
AND YOU KNOW YOU EVEN BETTER THAN SHE KNOWS YOU. Y'KNOW?
YEAH?
WELL, KNOWING WHAT YOU KNOW ABOUT YOU, WOULD YOU TRUST YOU IF YOU WERE HER?
NO.
NO, INDEED!

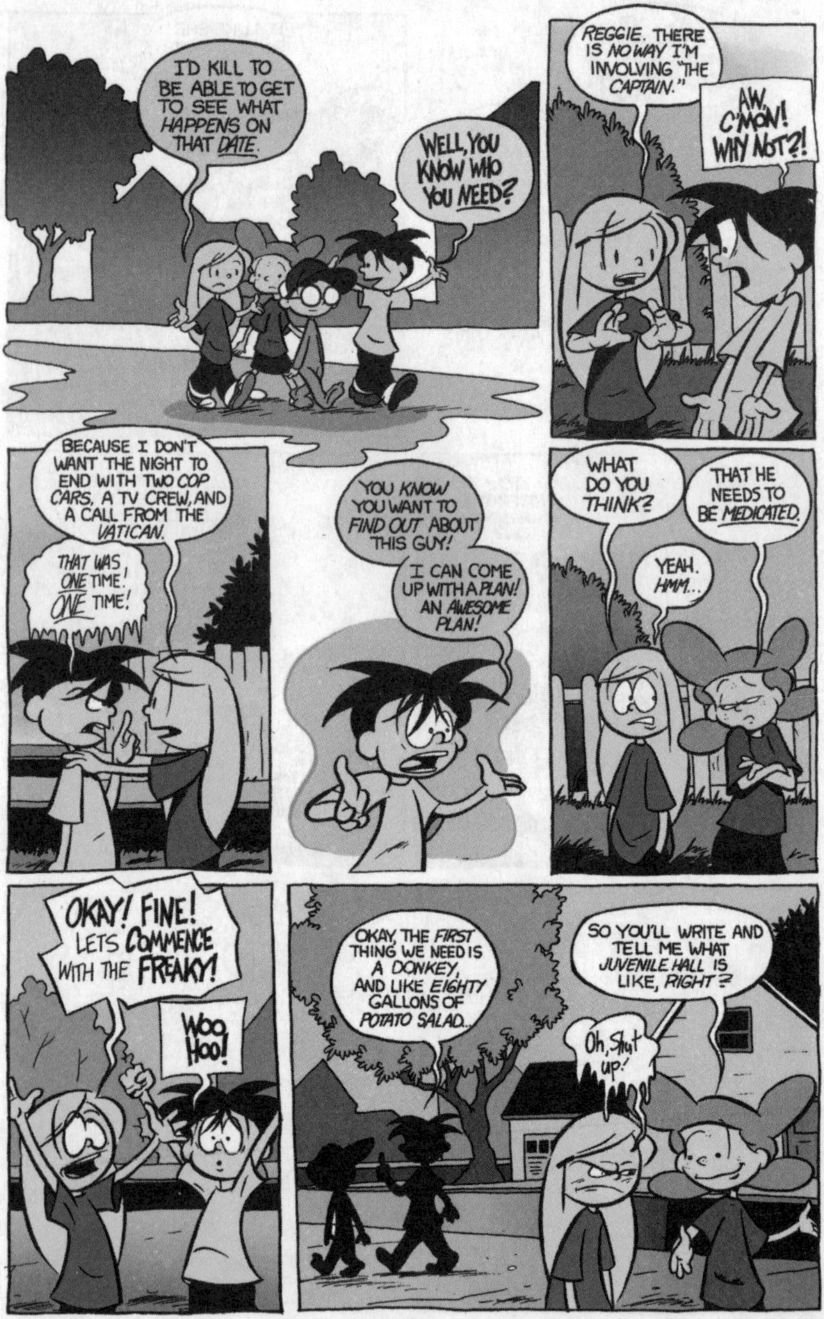
I'D KILL TO BE ABLE TO GET TO SEE WHAT HAPPENS ON THAT DATE.
WELL, YOU KNOW WHO YOU NEED?
REGGIE. THERE IS NO WAY I'M INVOLVING "THE CAPTAIN."
AW, C'MON! WHY NOT?!
BECAUSE I DON'T WANT THE NIGHT TO END WITH TWO COP CARS, A TV CREW, AND A CALL FROM THE VATICAN.
THAT WAS ONE TIME! ONE TIME!
YOU KNOW YOU WANT TO FIND OUT ABOUT THIS GUY!
I CAN COME UP WITH A PLAN! AN AWESOME PLAN!
WHAT DO YOU THINK?
THAT HE NEEDS TO BE MEDICATED.
YEAH. HMM...
OKAY! FINE! LETS COMMENCE WITH THE FREAKY!
WOO HOO!
OKAY, THE FIRST THING WE NEED IS A DONKEY, AND LIKE EIGHTY GALLONS OF POTATO SALAD...
SO YOU'LL WRITE AND TELL ME WHAT JUVENILE HALL IS LIKE, RIGHT?
Oh, Shut up!

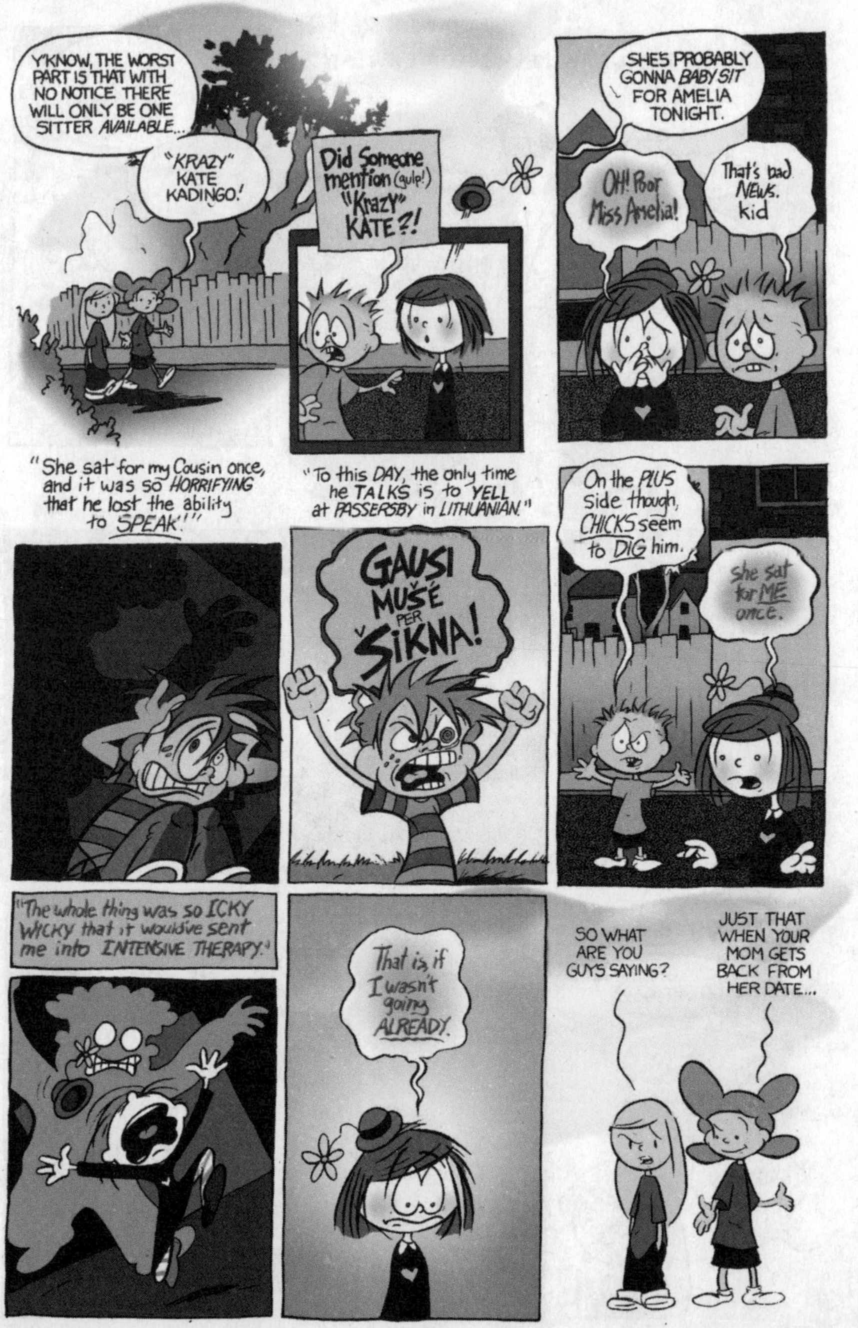

Y'KNOW, THE WORST PART IS THAT WITH NO NOTICE THERE WILL ONLY BE ONE SITTER AVAILABLE...
"KRAZY" KATE KADINGO!
Did Someone mention (gulp!) "Krazy" KATE?!
SHE'S PROBABLY GONNA BABY SIT FOR AMELIA TONIGHT.
OH! Poor Miss Amelia!
That's bad NEWS. kid
"She sat for my Cousin once, and it was so HORRIFYING that he lost the ability to SPEAK!"
"To this DAY, the only time he TALKS is to YELL at PASSERSBY in LITHUANIAN."
On the PLUS side though, CHICKS seem to DIG him.
She sat for ME once.
GAUSI MUŠĖ PER ŠIKNA!
"The whole thing was so ICKY WICKY that it would've sent me into INTENSIVE THERAPY."
That is, if I wasn't going ALREADY.
SO WHAT ARE YOU GUYS SAYING?
JUST THAT WHEN YOUR MOM GETS BACK FROM HER DATE...

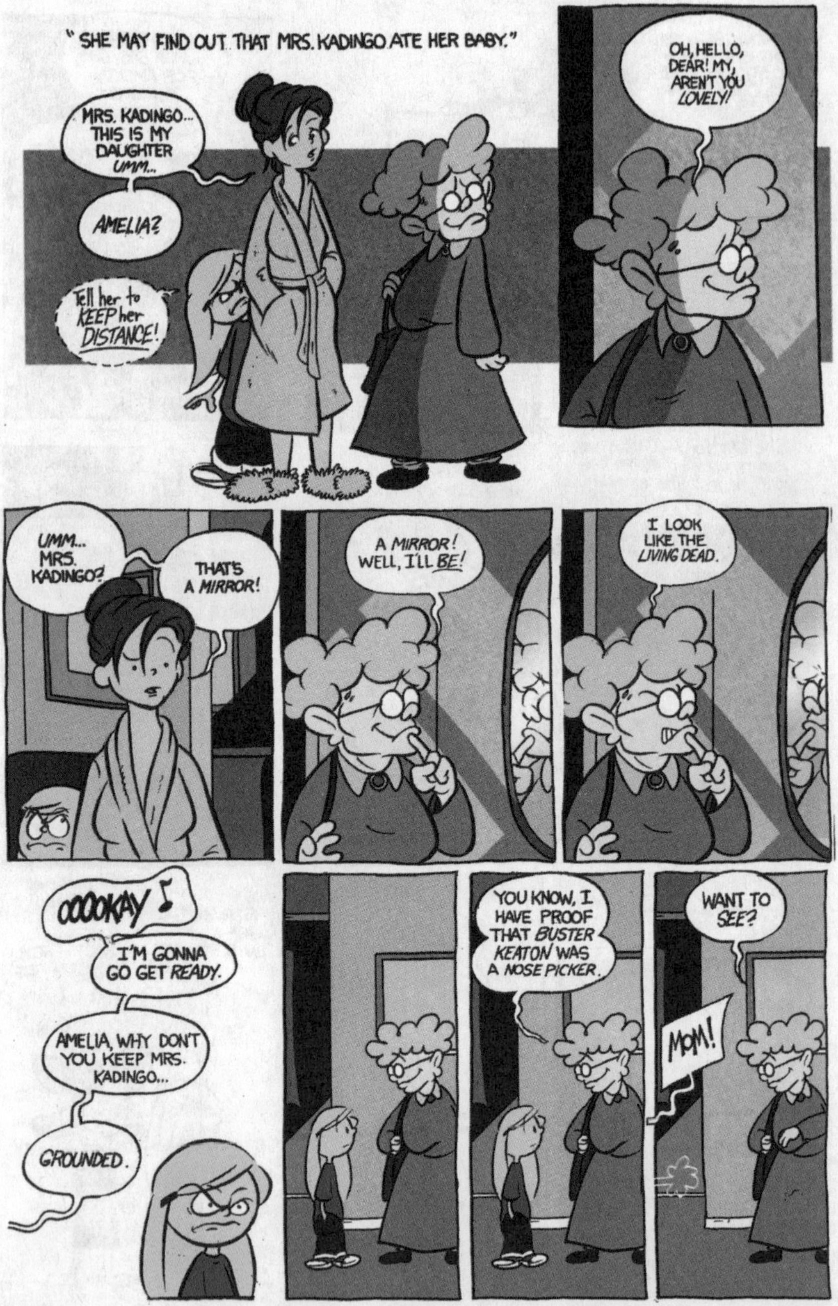
" SHE MAY FIND OUT THAT MRS. KADINGO ATE HER BABY."
MRS. KADINGO... THIS IS MY DAUGHTER UMM...
AMELIA?
Tell her to KEEP her DISTANCE!
OH, HELLO, DEAR! MY, AREN'T YOU LOVELY!
UMM... MRS. KADINGO?
THAT'S A MIRROR!
A MIRROR! WELL, I'LL BE!
I LOOK LIKE THE LIVING DEAD.
OOOOKAY
I'M GONNA GO GET READY.
AMELIA, WHY DON'T YOU KEEP MRS. KADINGO...
GROUNDED.
YOU KNOW, I HAVE PROOF THAT BUSTER KEATON WAS A NOSE PICKER.
WANT TO SEE?
MOM!

SO, BEING TOTALLY ***GROSSED OUT***, I WENT UPSTAIRS TO WATCH MOM GET READY. LOOKING IN THE MIRROR, I DIDN'T SEE THE ***LIVING DEAD***, BUT I FELT LIKE THE ***WALKING WOUNDED***.

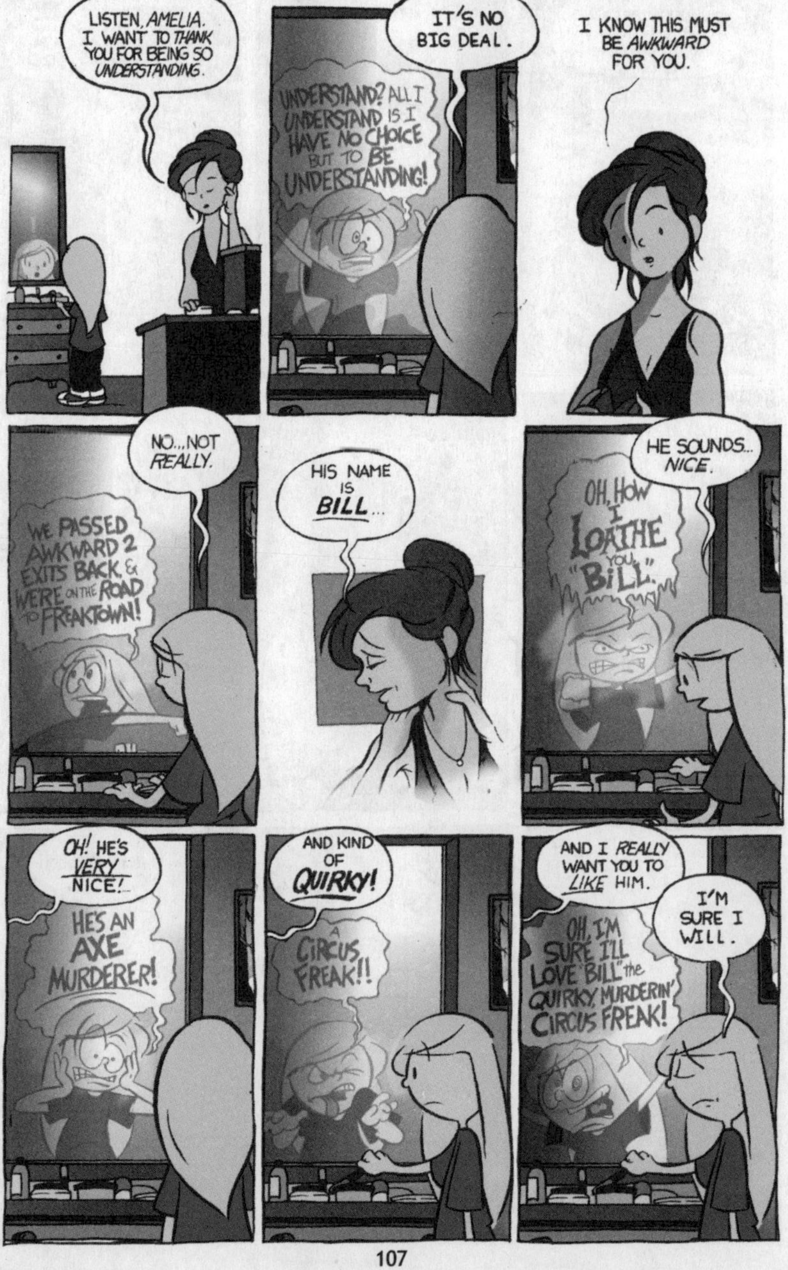

LISTEN, AMELIA. I WANT TO THANK YOU FOR BEING SO UNDERSTANDING.
IT'S NO BIG DEAL.
UNDERSTAND? ALL I UNDERSTAND IS I HAVE NO CHOICE BUT TO BE UNDERSTANDING!
I KNOW THIS MUST BE AWKWARD FOR YOU.
NO...NOT REALLY.
WE PASSED AWKWARD 2 EXITS BACK, & WE'RE ON THE ROAD TO FREAKTOWN!
HIS NAME IS BILL...
HE SOUNDS... NICE.
OH, HOW I LOATHE YOU, "BILL."
OH! HE'S VERY NICE!
HE'S AN AXE MURDERER!
AND KIND OF QUIRKY!
A CIRCUS FREAK!!
AND I REALLY WANT YOU TO LIKE HIM.
I'M SURE I WILL.
OH, I'M SURE I'LL LOVE "BILL" the QUIRKY, MURDERIN' CIRCUS FREAK!

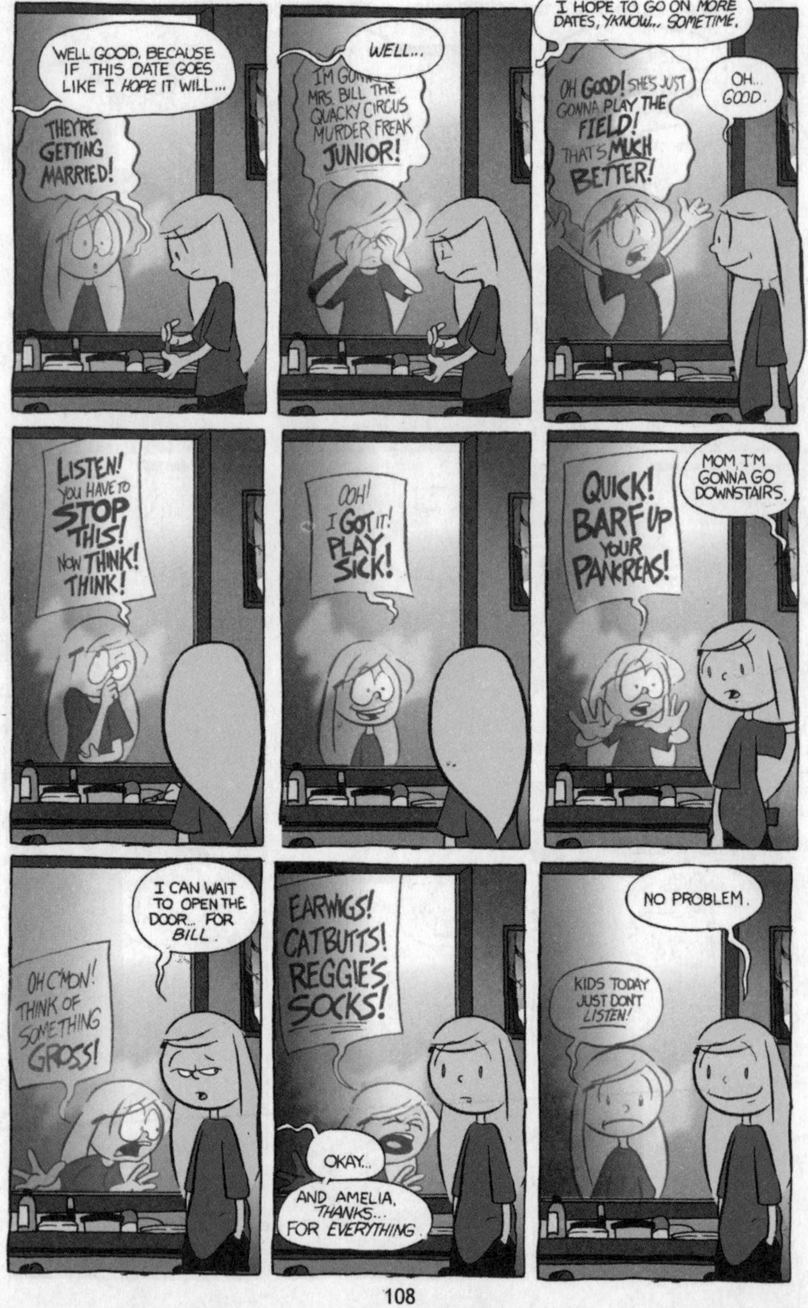
WELL GOOD, BECAUSE IF THIS DATE GOES LIKE I HOPE IT WILL...
THEY'RE GETTING MARRIED!
WELL...
I'M GONNA BE MRS. BILL THE QUACKY CIRCUS MURDER FREAK JUNIOR!
I HOPE TO GO ON MORE DATES, Y'KNOW... SOMETIME.
OH GOOD! SHE'S JUST GONNA PLAY THE FIELD! THAT'S MUCH BETTER!
OH... GOOD.
LISTEN! YOU HAVE TO STOP THIS! NOW THINK! THINK!
OOH! I GOT IT! PLAY SICK!
QUICK! BARF UP YOUR PANCREAS!
MOM, I'M GONNA GO DOWNSTAIRS.
I CAN WAIT TO OPEN THE DOOR... FOR BILL.
OH C'MON! THINK OF SOMETHING GROSS!
EARWIGS! CATBUTTS! REGGIE'S SOCKS!
OKAY...
AND AMELIA, THANKS... FOR EVERYTHING.
NO PROBLEM.
KIDS TODAY JUST DON'T LISTEN!

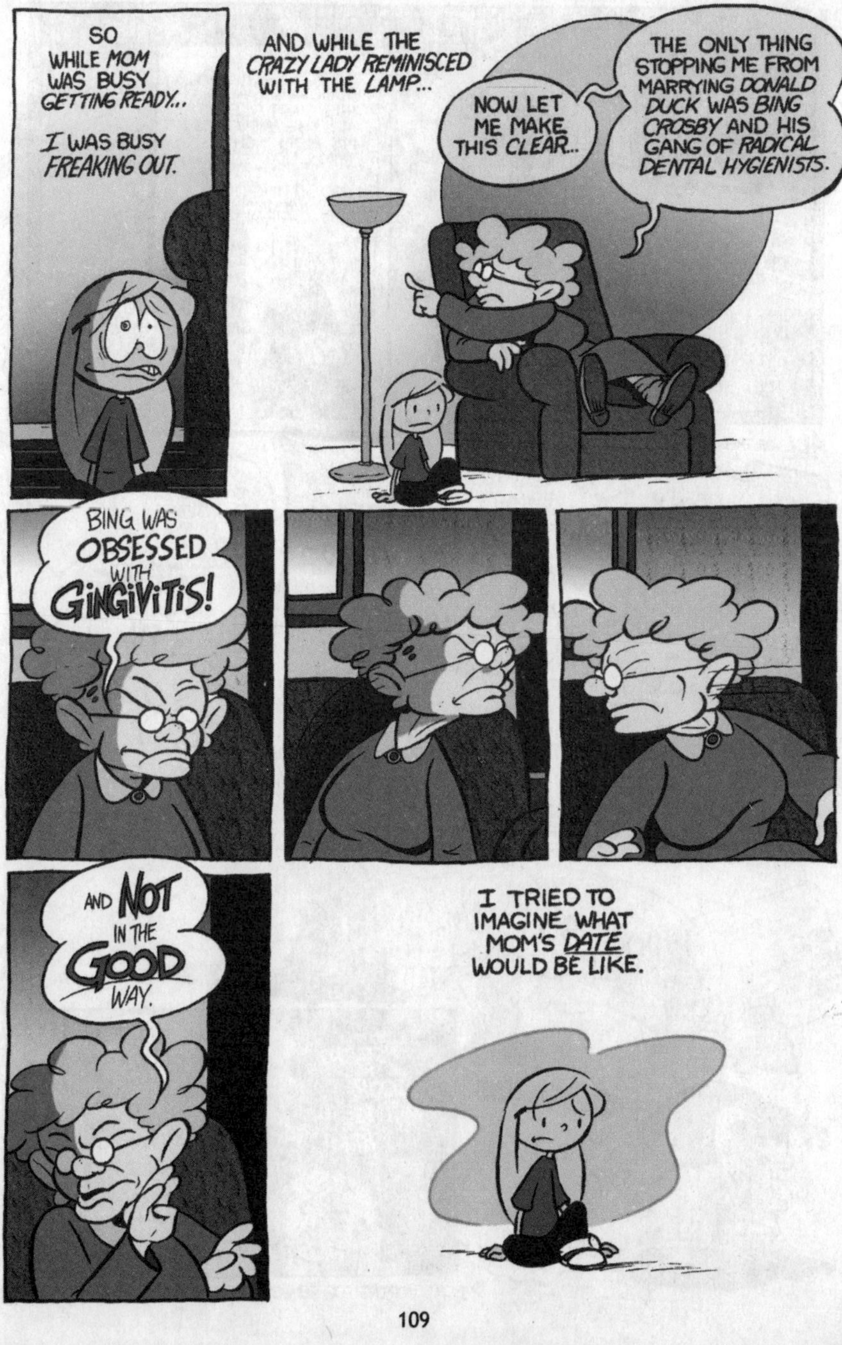

SO WHILE MOM WAS BUSY GETTING READY...
I WAS BUSY FREAKING OUT.
AND WHILE THE CRAZY LADY REMINISCED WITH THE LAMP...
NOW LET ME MAKE THIS CLEAR...
THE ONLY THING STOPPING ME FROM MARRYING DONALD DUCK WAS BING CROSBY AND HIS GANG OF RADICAL DENTAL HYGIENISTS.
BING WAS OBSESSED WITH GINGIVITIS!
AND NOT IN THE GOOD WAY.
I TRIED TO IMAGINE WHAT MOM'S DATE WOULD BE LIKE.

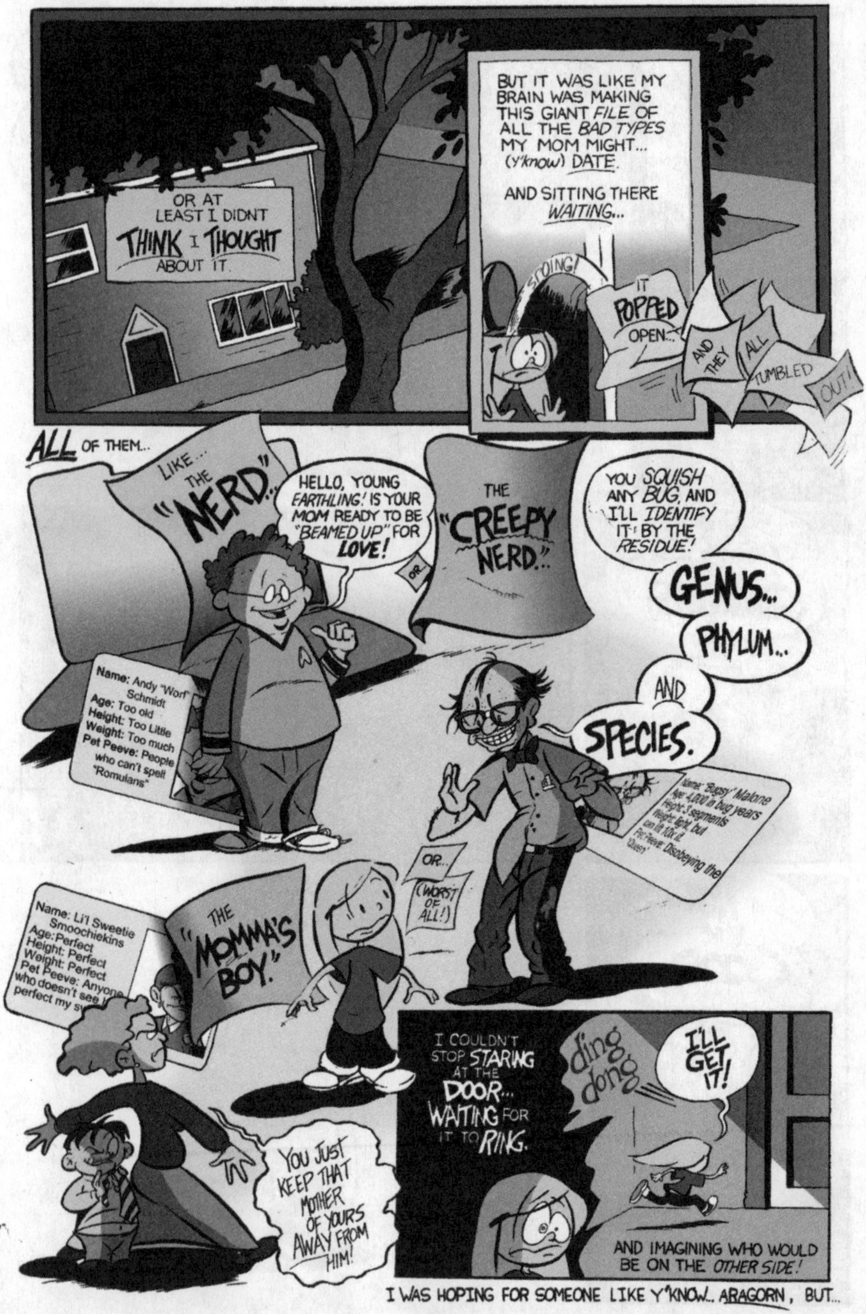
OR AT LEAST I DIDNT THINK I THOUGHT ABOUT IT.
BUT IT WAS LIKE MY BRAIN WAS MAKING THIS GIANT FILE OF ALL THE BAD TYPES MY MOM MIGHT... (y'know) DATE.
AND SITTING THERE WAITING...
SPOING!
IT POPPED OPEN...
AND THEY ALL TUMBLED OUT!
ALL OF THEM...
LIKE... THE "NERD"...
HELLO, YOUNG EARTHLING! IS YOUR MOM READY TO BE "BEAMED UP" FOR LOVE!
Name: Andy "Worf" Schmidt
Age: Too old
Height: Too Little
Weight: Too much
Pet Peeve: People who can't spell "Romulans"
OR...
THE "CREEPY NERD"...
YOU SQUISH ANY BUG, AND I'LL IDENTIFY IT BY THE RESIDUE!
GENUS...
PHYLUM...
AND
SPECIES.
Name: "Bugsy" Malone
Age: 4,000 in bug years
Height: 3 segments
Weight: light, but can lift 10x it.
Pet Peeve: Disobeying the "Queen"
OR...
(WORST OF ALL!)
THE "MOMMA'S BOY."
Name: Li'l Sweetie Smoochiekins
Age: Perfect
Height: Perfect
Weight: Perfect
Pet Peeve: Anyone who doesn't see perfect my sw
YOU JUST KEEP THAT MOTHER OF YOURS AWAY FROM HIM!
I COULDN'T STOP STARING AT THE DOOR... WAITING FOR IT TO RING.
ding dong
I'LL GET IT!
AND IMAGINING WHO WOULD BE ON THE OTHER SIDE!
I WAS HOPING FOR SOMEONE LIKE Y'KNOW... ARAGORN, BUT...

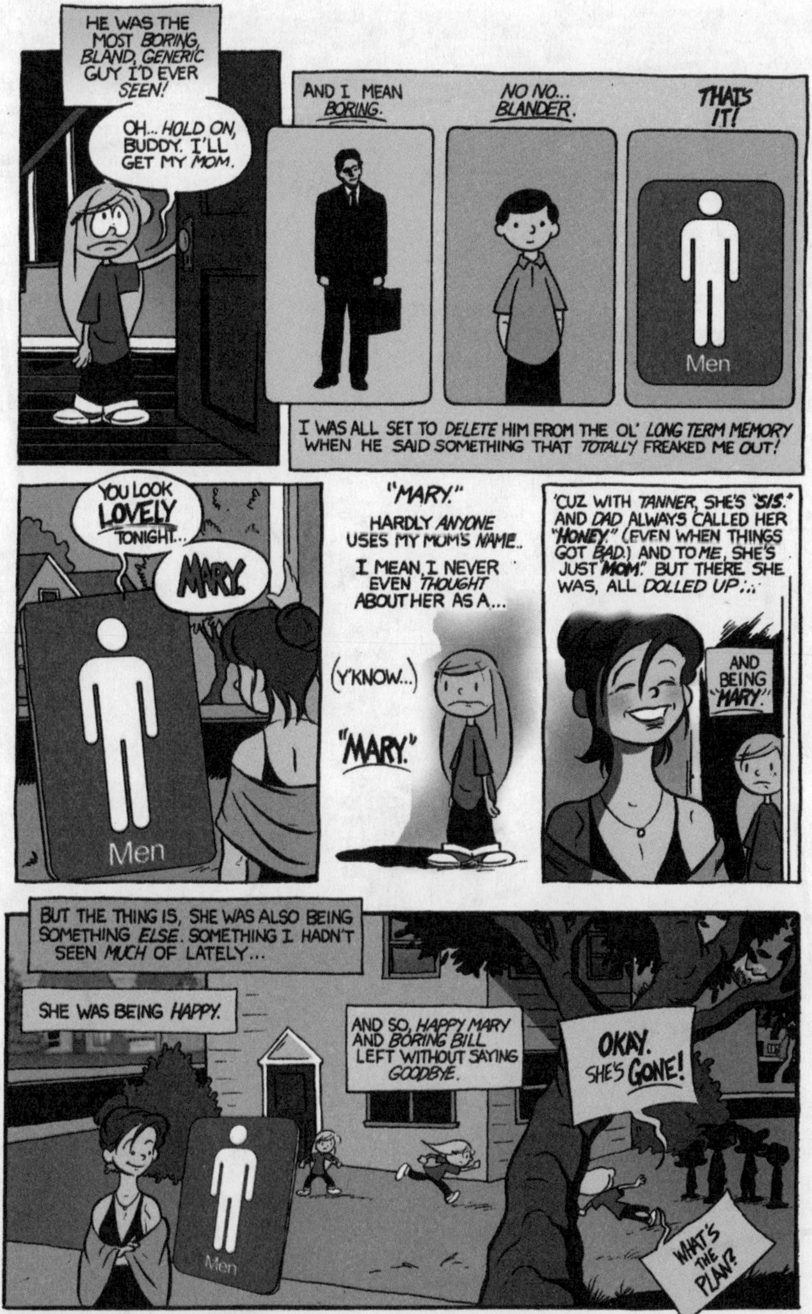
HE WAS THE MOST BORING, BLAND, GENERIC GUY I'D EVER SEEN!
OH... HOLD ON, BUDDY. I'LL GET MY MOM.
AND I MEAN BORING.
NO NO... BLANDER.
THAT'S IT!
Men
I WAS ALL SET TO DELETE HIM FROM THE OL' LONG TERM MEMORY WHEN HE SAID SOMETHING THAT TOTALLY FREAKED ME OUT!
YOU LOOK LOVELY TONIGHT...
MARY.
Men
"MARY."
HARDLY ANYONE USES MY MOM'S NAME..
I MEAN, I NEVER EVEN THOUGHT ABOUT HER AS A...
(Y'KNOW...)
"MARY."
'CUZ WITH TANNER, SHE'S "SIS." AND DAD ALWAYS CALLED HER "HONEY." (EVEN WHEN THINGS GOT BAD.) AND TO ME, SHE'S JUST "MOM." BUT THERE SHE WAS, ALL DOLLED UP...
AND BEING "MARY".
BUT THE THING IS, SHE WAS ALSO BEING SOMETHING ELSE. SOMETHING I HADN'T SEEN MUCH OF LATELY...
SHE WAS BEING HAPPY.
AND SO, HAPPY MARY AND BORING BILL LEFT WITHOUT SAYING GOODBYE.
OKAY. SHE'S GONE!
Men
WHAT'S THE PLAN?

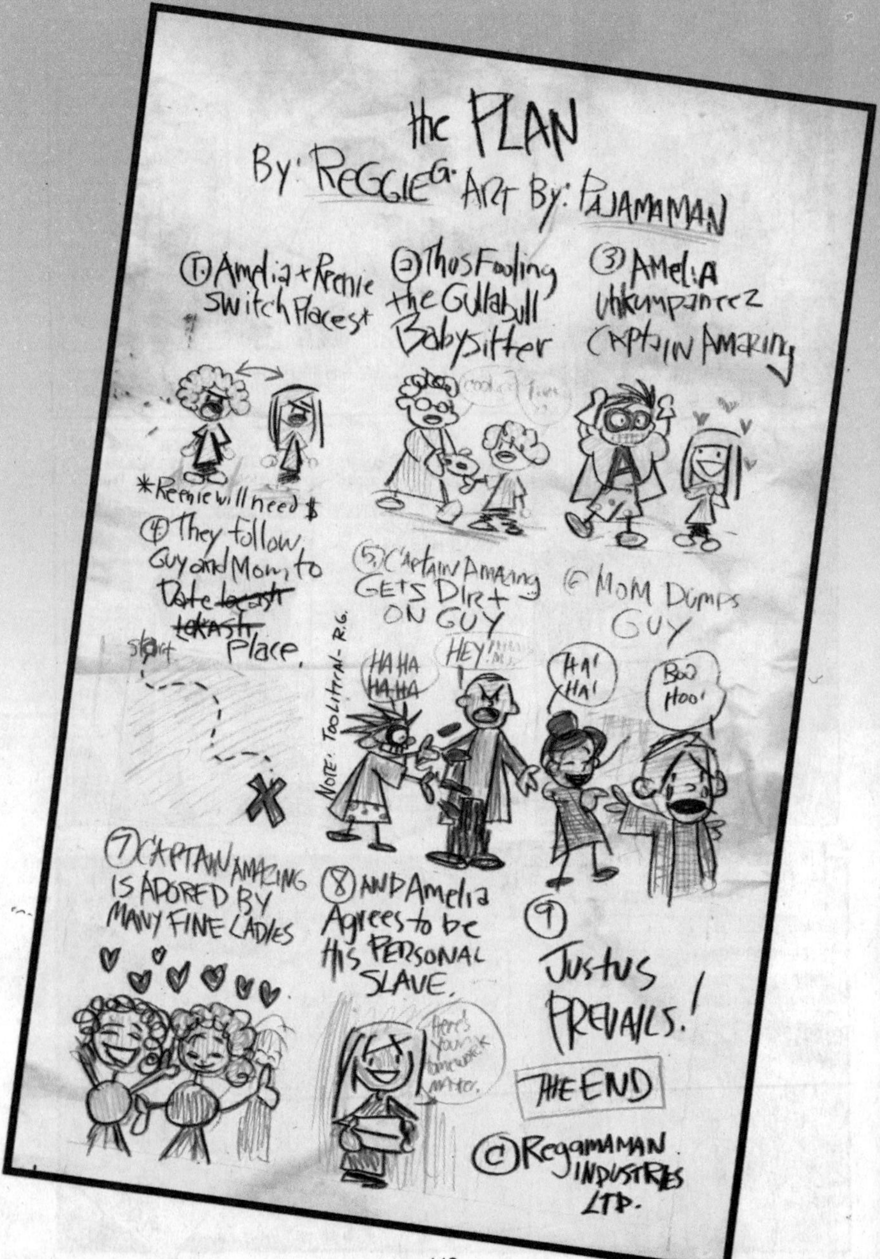
the PLAN
By: REGGIE G. Art By: PAJAMAMAN
(1) Amelia + Reenie switch Places*
(2) Thus Fooling the Gullabull Babysitter
(3) Amelia Unkumpaneez Captain Amazing
*Reenie will need $
(4) They follow Guy and Mom to Date locash lokash Place.
start
(5) Captain Amazing Gets Dirt ON GUY
NOTE: TOO LITERAL - R.G.
HA HA HA HA
HEY!
(6) MOM Dumps GUY
HA! HA!
Boo Hoo!
(7) CAPTAIN AMAZING IS ADORED BY MANY FINE LADIES
(8) AND Amelia Agrees to be His PERSONAL SLAVE.
(9) Justus PREVAILS!
THE END
© Regamaman INDUSTRIES LTD.

OKAY, SO MAYBE IT WAS A DUMB PLAN, BUT SINCE I HAD NO DESIRE TO BE "SAT" BY "KRAZY KATE," I TRADED SHIRTS WITH RHONDA'S SISTER AND SENT HER INSIDE, LEAVING ME FREE TO CAVORT WITH THE INFAMOUS CAPTAIN AMAZING.

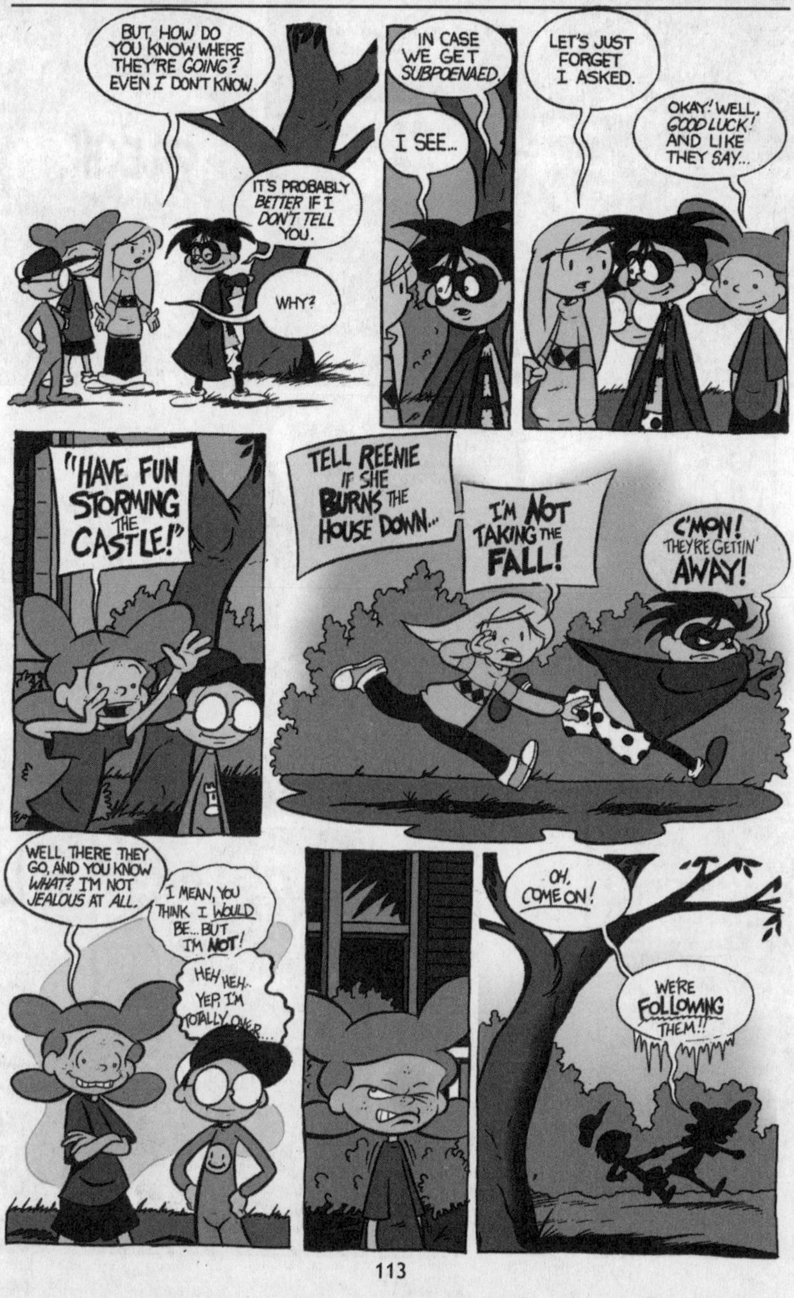

BUT, HOW DO YOU KNOW WHERE THEY'RE *GOING*? EVEN *I* DON'T KNOW.
IT'S PROBABLY *BETTER* IF I *DON'T* TELL YOU.
WHY?
IN CASE WE GET *SUBPOENAED*.
I SEE...
LET'S JUST FORGET I ASKED.
OKAY! WELL, *GOOD LUCK*! AND LIKE THEY SAY...
"HAVE FUN STORMING THE CASTLE!"
TELL REENIE IF SHE BURNS THE HOUSE DOWN...
I'M NOT TAKING THE FALL!
C'MON! THEY'RE GETTIN' AWAY!
WELL, THERE THEY GO, AND YOU KNOW *WHAT*? I'M NOT *JEALOUS* AT *ALL*.
I MEAN, YOU THINK I WOULD BE... BUT I'M NOT!
HEH HEH.. YEP, I'M TOTALLY OVER...
OH, COME ON!
WE'RE FOLLOWING THEM!!

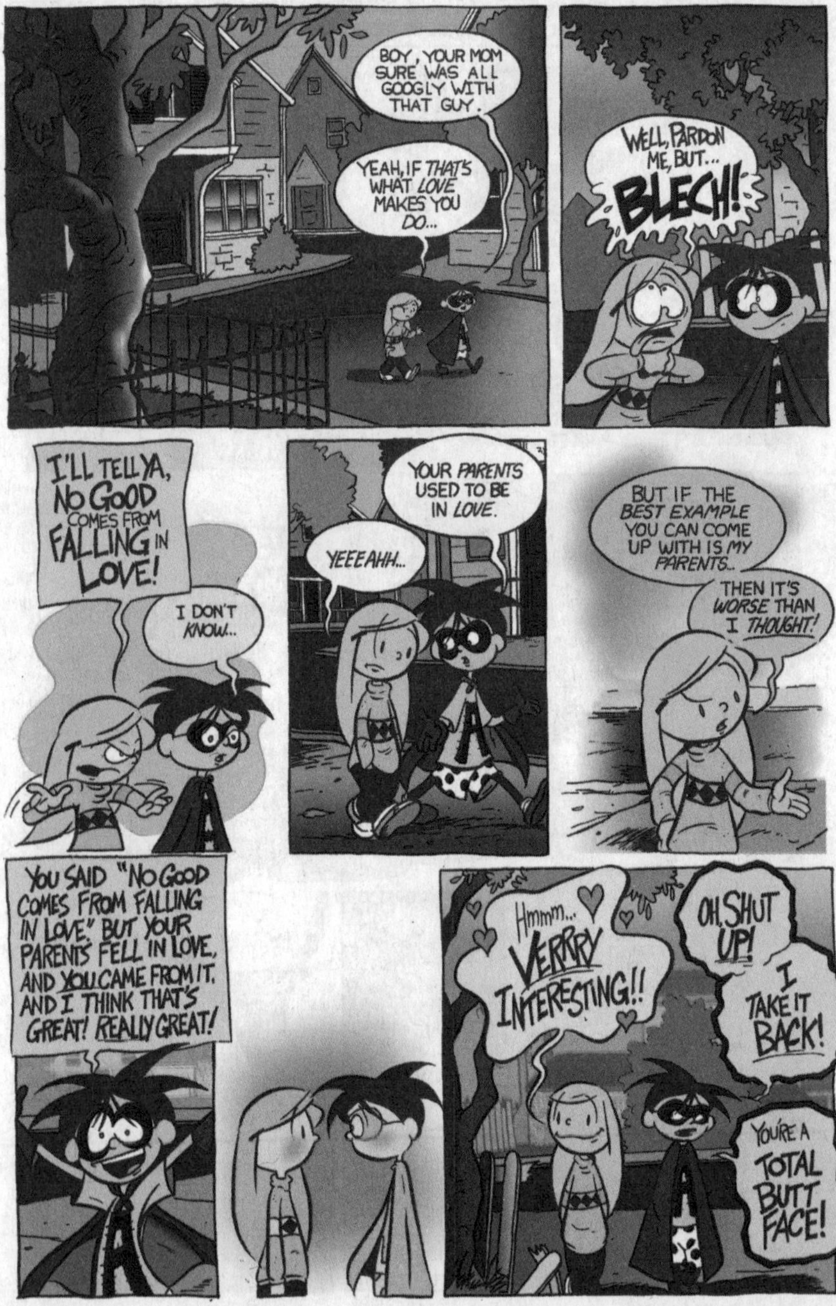

BOY, YOUR MOM SURE WAS ALL GOOGLY WITH THAT GUY.
YEAH, IF THAT'S WHAT LOVE MAKES YOU DO...
WELL, PARDON ME, BUT... BLECH!
I'LL TELL YA, NO GOOD COMES FROM FALLING IN LOVE!
I DON'T KNOW...
YOUR PARENTS USED TO BE IN LOVE.
YEEEAHH...
BUT IF THE BEST EXAMPLE YOU CAN COME UP WITH IS MY PARENTS...
THEN IT'S WORSE THAN I THOUGHT!
YOU SAID "NO GOOD COMES FROM FALLING IN LOVE," BUT YOUR PARENTS FELL IN LOVE, AND YOU CAME FROM IT. AND I THINK THAT'S GREAT! REALLY GREAT!
Hmmm... VERRRY INTERESTING!!
OH, SHUT UP!
I TAKE IT BACK!
YOU'RE A TOTAL BUTT FACE!

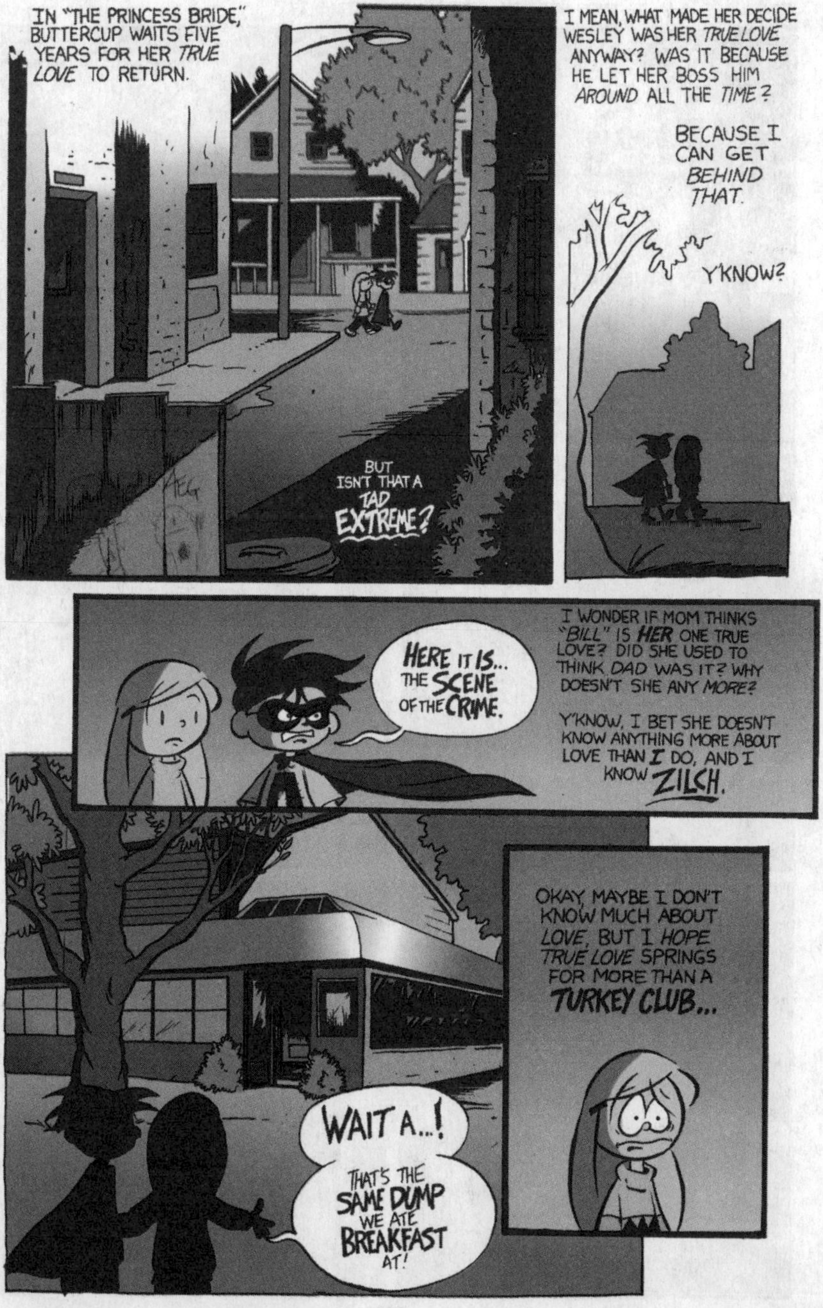
IN "THE PRINCESS BRIDE," BUTTERCUP WAITS FIVE YEARS FOR HER TRUE LOVE TO RETURN.
BUT ISN'T THAT A TAD EXTREME?
I MEAN, WHAT MADE HER DECIDE WESLEY WAS HER TRUE LOVE ANYWAY? WAS IT BECAUSE HE LET HER BOSS HIM AROUND ALL THE TIME?
BECAUSE I CAN GET BEHIND THAT.
Y'KNOW?
HERE IT IS... THE SCENE OF THE CRIME.
I WONDER IF MOM THINKS "BILL" IS HER ONE TRUE LOVE? DID SHE USED TO THINK DAD WAS IT? WHY DOESN'T SHE ANY MORE?
Y'KNOW, I BET SHE DOESN'T KNOW ANYTHING MORE ABOUT LOVE THAN I DO, AND I KNOW ZILCH.
WAIT A...!
THAT'S THE SAME DUMP WE ATE BREAKFAST AT!
OKAY, MAYBE I DON'T KNOW MUCH ABOUT LOVE, BUT I HOPE TRUE LOVE SPRINGS FOR MORE THAN A TURKEY CLUB...

OTHERWISE, WHY IS EVERYBODY TRYING SO HARD TO FIND IT?

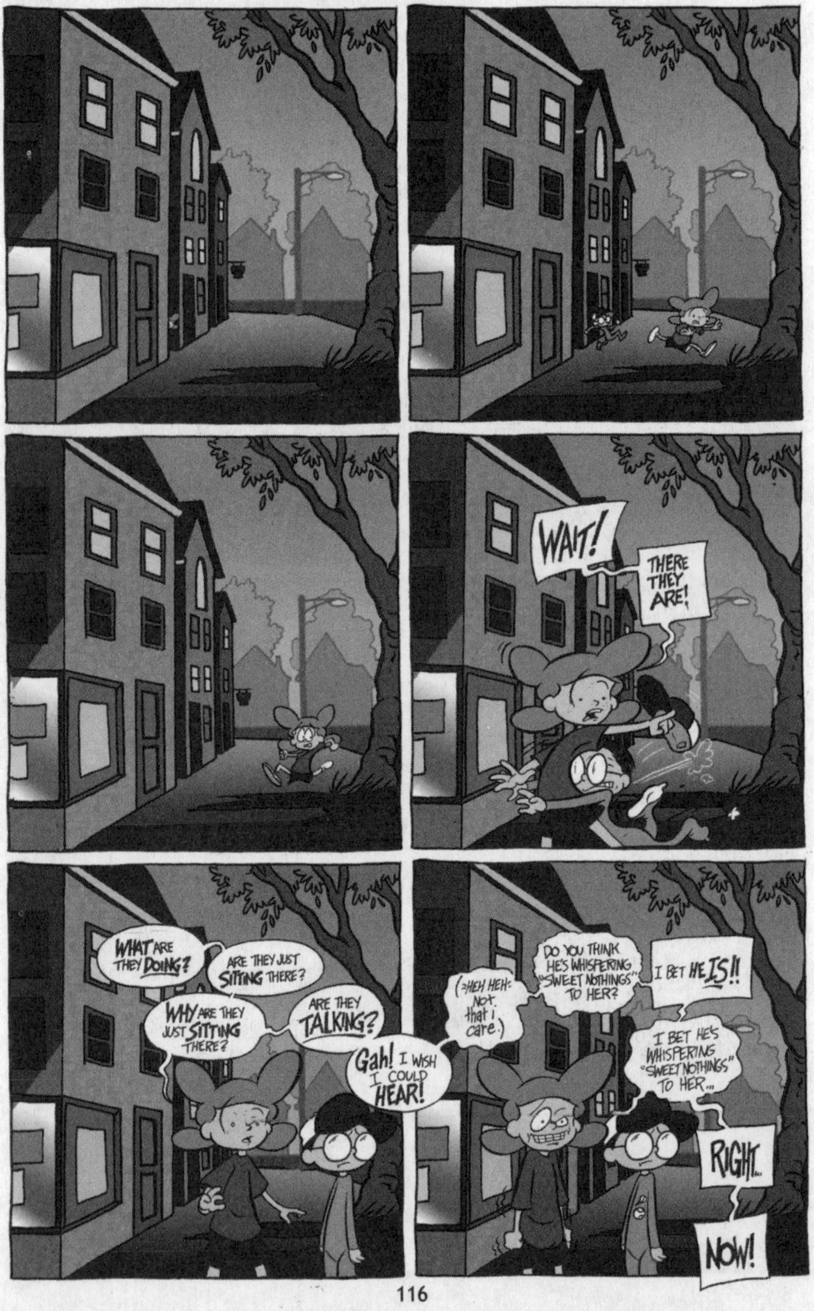
WAIT!
THERE THEY ARE!
WHAT ARE THEY DOING?
ARE THEY JUST SITTING THERE?
WHY ARE THEY JUST SITTING THERE?
ARE THEY TALKING?
Gah! I WISH I COULD HEAR!
(=HEH HEH= Not that i care.)
DO YOU THINK HE'S WHISPERING "SWEET NOTHINGS" TO HER?
I BET HE IS!!
I BET HE'S WHISPERING "SWEET NOTHINGS" TO HER...
RIGHT...
NOW!

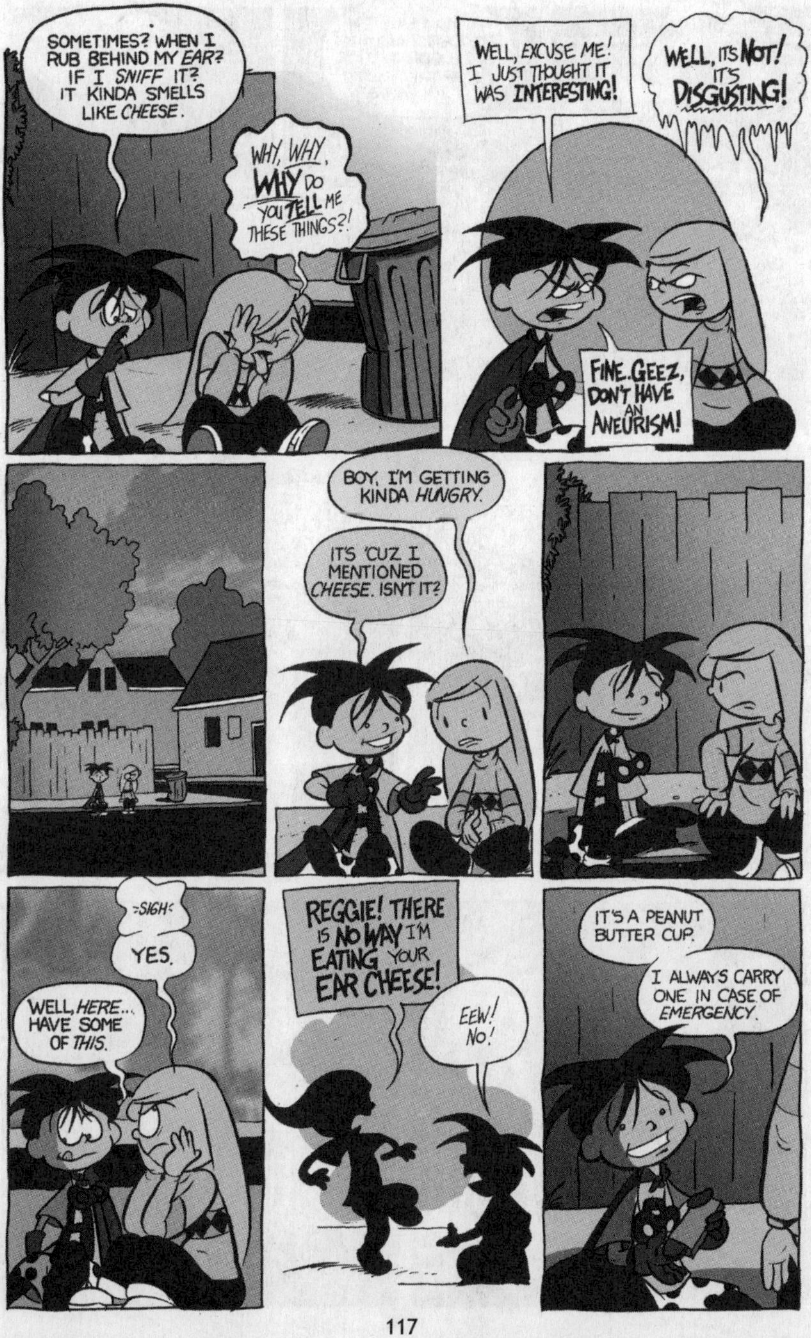
SOMETIMES? WHEN I RUB BEHIND MY EAR? IF I SNIFF IT? IT KINDA SMELLS LIKE CHEESE.
WHY, WHY, WHY DO YOU TELL ME THESE THINGS?!
WELL, EXCUSE ME! I JUST THOUGHT IT WAS INTERESTING!
WELL, IT'S NOT! IT'S DISGUSTING!
FINE. GEEZ, DON'T HAVE AN ANEURISM!
BOY, I'M GETTING KINDA HUNGRY.
IT'S 'CUZ I MENTIONED CHEESE. ISN'T IT?
=SIGH=
YES.
WELL, HERE... HAVE SOME OF THIS.
REGGIE! THERE IS NO WAY I'M EATING YOUR EAR CHEESE!
EEW! NO!
IT'S A PEANUT BUTTER CUP.
I ALWAYS CARRY ONE IN CASE OF EMERGENCY.

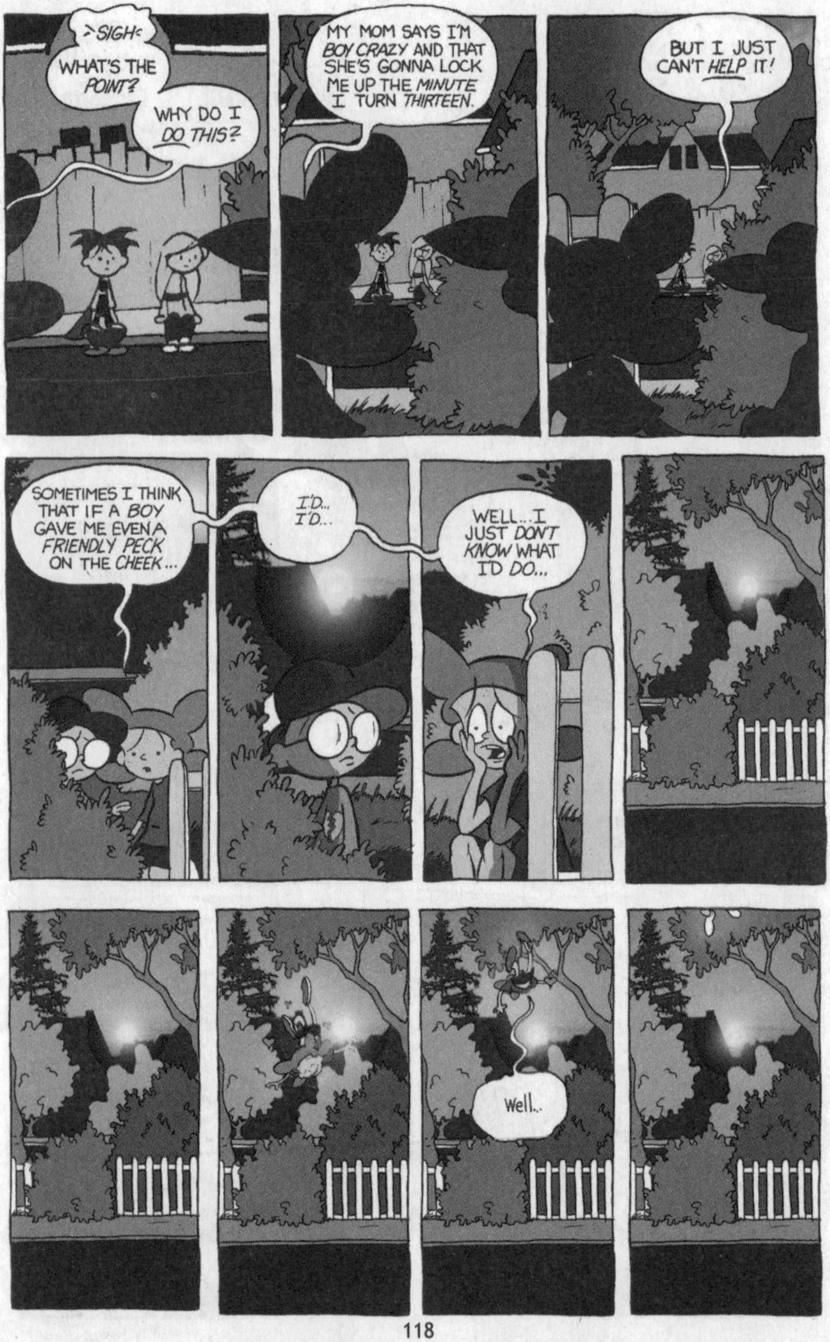
>SIGH<
WHAT'S THE POINT?
WHY DO I DO THIS?
MY MOM SAYS I'M BOY CRAZY AND THAT SHE'S GONNA LOCK ME UP THE MINUTE I TURN THIRTEEN.
BUT I JUST CAN'T HELP IT!
SOMETIMES I THINK THAT IF A BOY GAVE ME EVEN A FRIENDLY PECK ON THE CHEEK...
I'D... I'D...
WELL...I JUST DON'T KNOW WHAT I'D DO...
Well..

THAT ANSWERS THAT QUESTION.

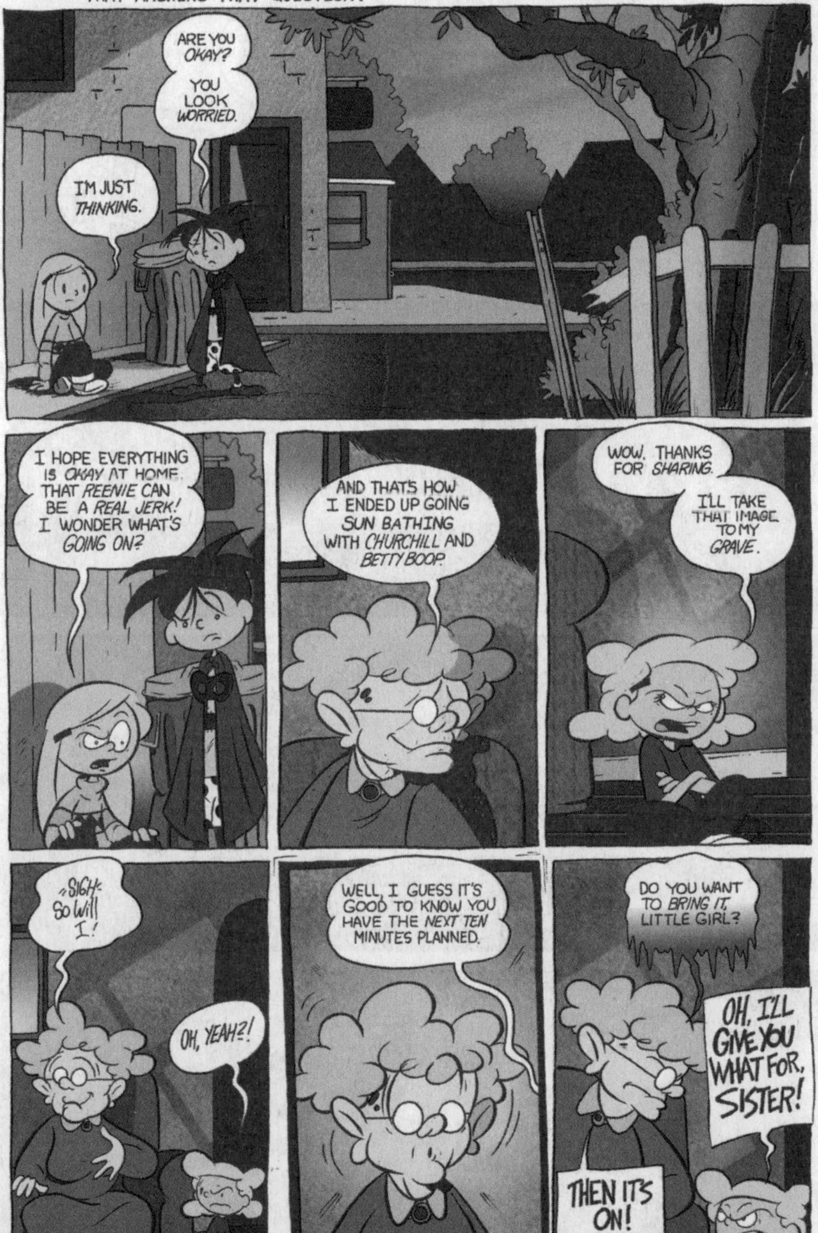
ARE YOU OKAY?
YOU LOOK WORRIED.
I'M JUST THINKING.
I HOPE EVERYTHING IS OKAY AT HOME. THAT REENIE CAN BE A REAL JERK! I WONDER WHAT'S GOING ON?
AND THAT'S HOW I ENDED UP GOING SUN BATHING WITH CHURCHILL AND BETTY BOOP.
WOW. THANKS FOR SHARING.
I'LL TAKE THAT IMAGE TO MY GRAVE.
-SIGH- So Will I!
OH, YEAH?!
WELL, I GUESS IT'S GOOD TO KNOW YOU HAVE THE NEXT TEN MINUTES PLANNED.
DO YOU WANT TO BRING IT, LITTLE GIRL?
OH, I'LL GIVE YOU WHAT FOR, SISTER!
THEN IT'S ON!

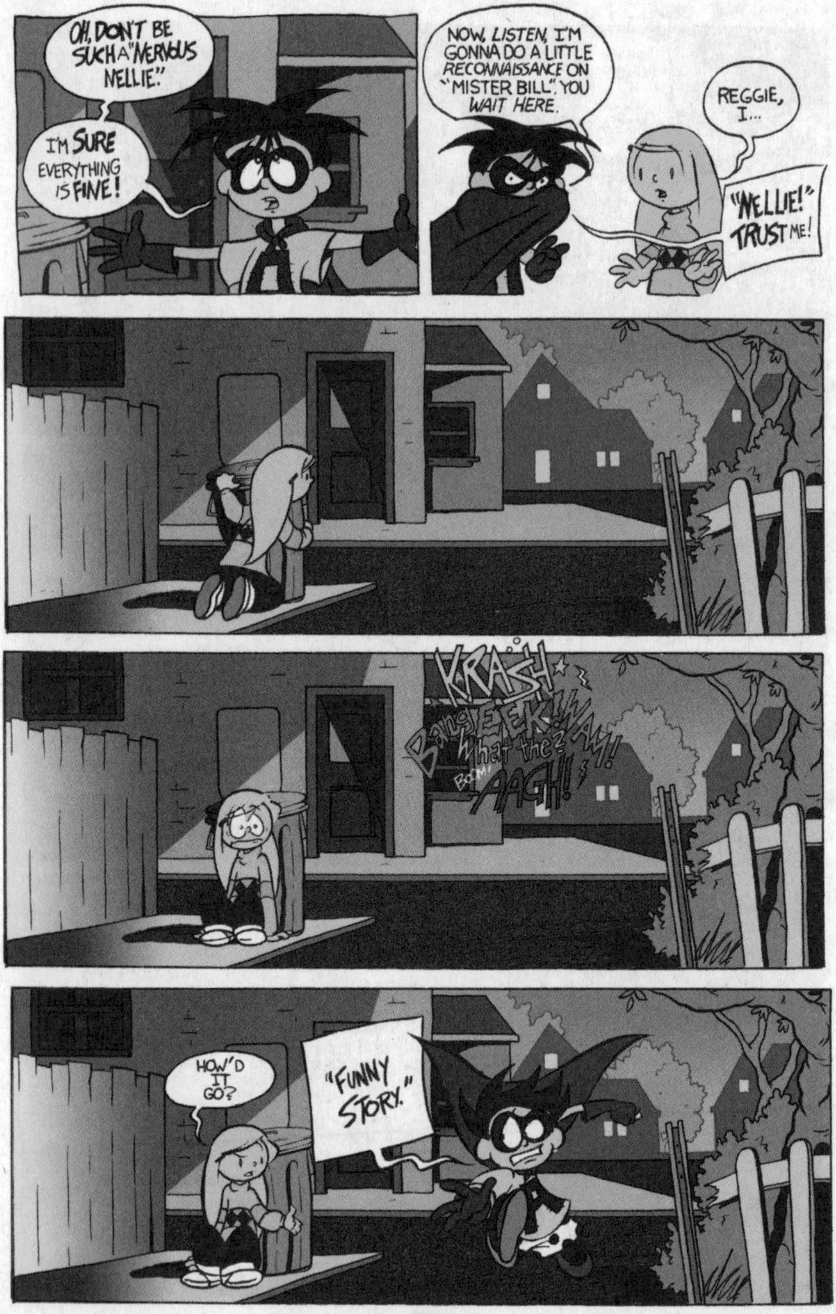
OH, DON'T BE SUCH A "NERVOUS NELLIE."
I'M SURE EVERYTHING IS FINE!
NOW, LISTEN, I'M GONNA DO A LITTLE RECONNAISSANCE ON "MISTER BILL". YOU WAIT HERE.
REGGIE, I...
"NELLIE!" TRUST ME!
KRASH
Bang
EEK!
WAM!
What the?
BOOM!
AAGH!
HOW'D IT GO?
"FUNNY STORY."

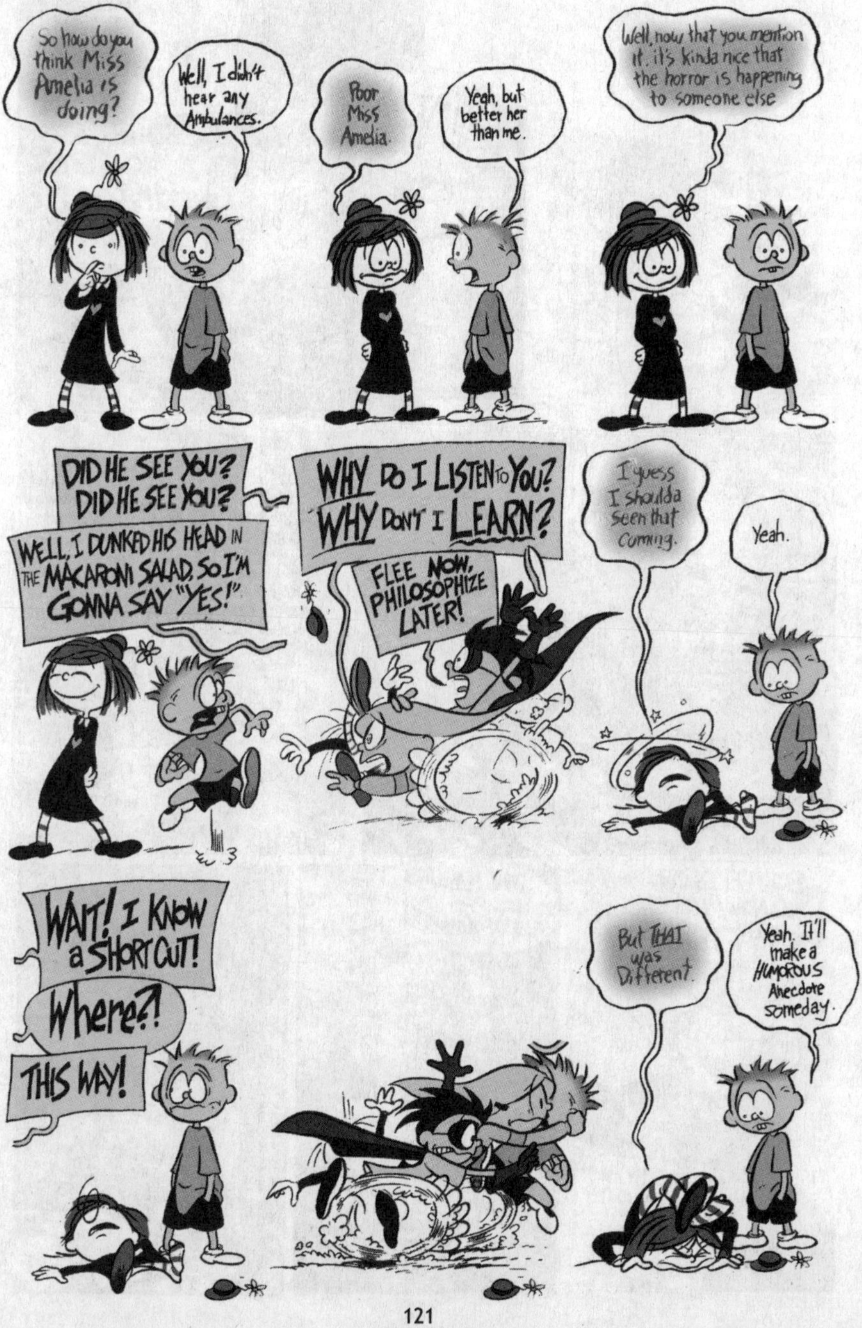
So how do you think Miss Amelia is doing?
Well, I didn't hear any Ambulances.
Poor Miss Amelia.
Yeah, but better her than me.
Well, now that you mention it, it's kinda nice that the horror is happening to someone else
DID HE SEE YOU? DID HE SEE YOU?
WELL, I DUNKED HIS HEAD IN THE MACARONI SALAD, SO I'M GONNA SAY "YES!"
WHY DO I LISTEN TO YOU? WHY DON'T I LEARN?
FLEE NOW, PHILOSOPHIZE LATER!
I guess I shoulda seen that coming.
Yeah.
WAIT! I KNOW a SHORT CUT!
Where?!
THIS WAY!
But THAT was Different.
Yeah. It'll make a HUMOROUS Anecdote someday.

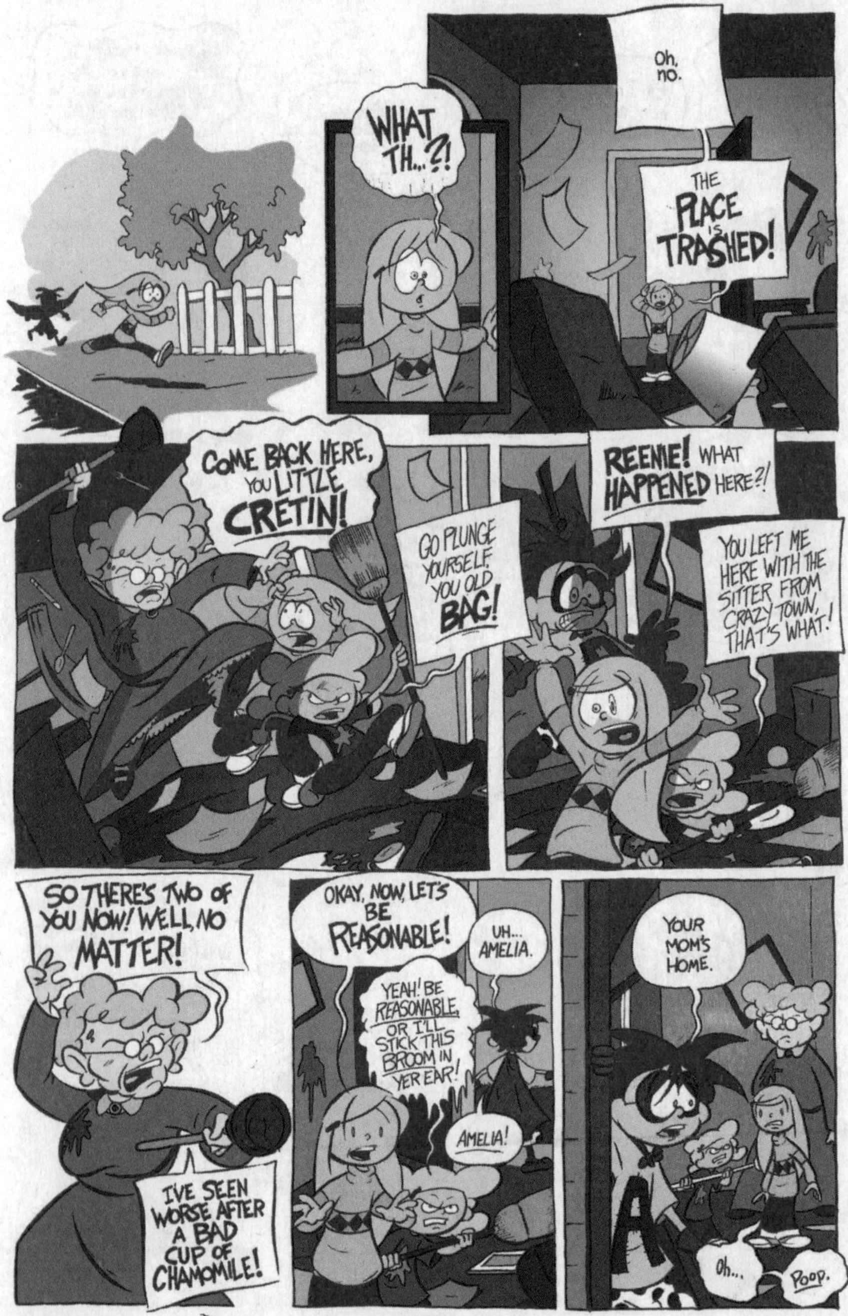
WHAT TH...?!
Oh, no.
THE PLACE is TRASHED!
COME BACK HERE, YOU LITTLE CRETIN!
GO PLUNGE YOURSELF, YOU OLD BAG!
REENIE! WHAT HAPPENED HERE?!
YOU LEFT ME HERE WITH THE SITTER FROM CRAZY TOWN, THAT'S WHAT!
SO THERE'S TWO OF YOU NOW! WELL, NO MATTER!
I'VE SEEN WORSE AFTER A BAD CUP OF CHAMOMILE!
OKAY, NOW, LET'S BE REASONABLE!
UH... AMELIA.
YEAH! BE REASONABLE OR I'LL STICK THIS BROOM IN YER EAR!
AMELIA!
YOUR MOM'S HOME.
Oh...
Poop.

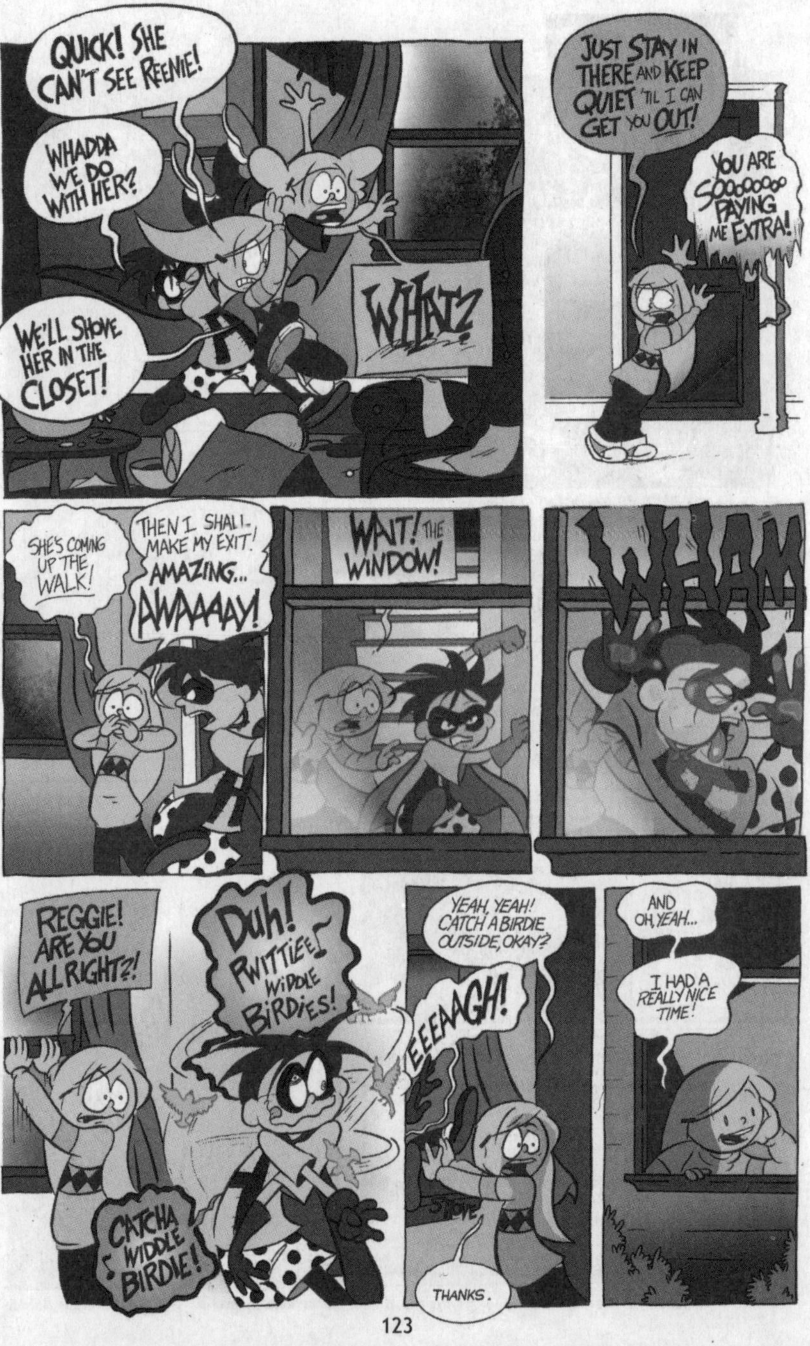
QUICK! SHE CAN'T SEE REENIE!
WHADDA WE DO WITH HER?
WE'LL SHOVE HER IN THE CLOSET!
WHAT?
JUST STAY IN THERE AND KEEP QUIET 'TIL I CAN GET YOU OUT!
YOU ARE SOOOOOOOO PAYING ME EXTRA!
SHE'S COMING UP THE WALK!
THEN I SHALL MAKE MY EXIT! AMAZING... AWAAAAY!
WAIT! THE WINDOW!
WHAM
REGGIE! ARE YOU ALL RIGHT?!
Duh! PWITTIEEE! WIDDLE BIRDIES!
CATCHA WIDDLE BIRDIE!
YEAH, YEAH! CATCH A BIRDIE OUTSIDE, OKAY?
EEEAAGH!
SHOVE
THANKS.
AND OH, YEAH...
I HAD A REALLY NICE TIME!

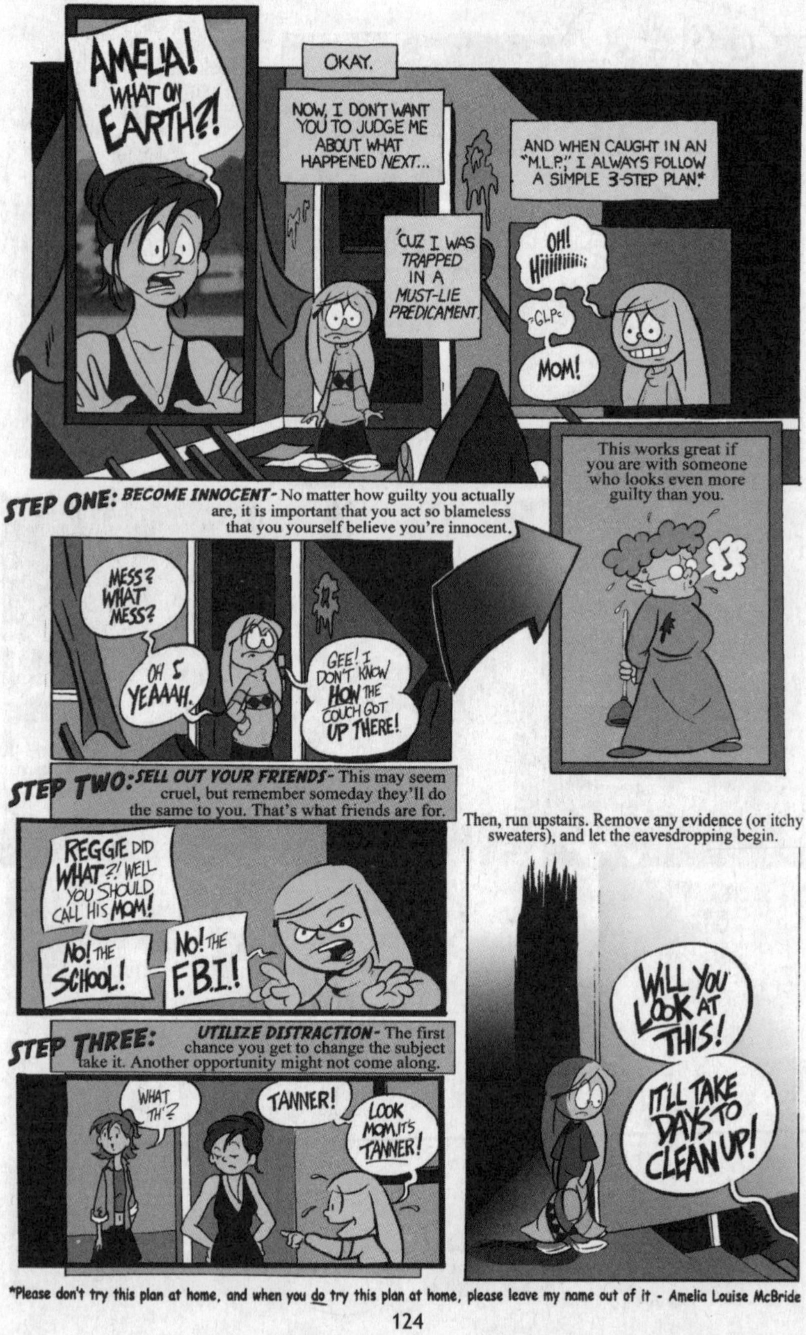
AMELIA! WHAT ON EARTH?!
OKAY.
NOW, I DON'T WANT YOU TO JUDGE ME ABOUT WHAT HAPPENED NEXT...
'CUZ I WAS TRAPPED IN A MUST-LIE PREDICAMENT.
AND WHEN CAUGHT IN AN "M.L.P.," I ALWAYS FOLLOW A SIMPLE 3-STEP PLAN.*
OH! Hiiiiiiii
GLP
MOM!
STEP ONE: BECOME INNOCENT- No matter how guilty you actually are, it is important that you act so blameless that you yourself believe you're innocent.
MESS? WHAT MESS?
OH YEAAAH.
GEE! I DON'T KNOW HOW THE COUCH GOT UP THERE!
This works great if you are with someone who looks even more guilty than you.
STEP TWO: SELL OUT YOUR FRIENDS- This may seem cruel, but remember someday they'll do the same to you. That's what friends are for.
REGGIE DID WHAT?! WELL YOU SHOULD CALL HIS MOM!
NO! THE SCHOOL!
NO! THE F.B.I.!
STEP THREE: UTILIZE DISTRACTION- The first chance you get to change the subject take it. Another opportunity might not come along.
WHAT TH'?
TANNER!
LOOK MOM, IT'S TANNER!
Then, run upstairs. Remove any evidence (or itchy sweaters), and let the eavesdropping begin.
WILL YOU LOOK AT THIS!
IT'LL TAKE DAYS TO CLEAN UP!

*Please don't try this plan at home, and when you do try this plan at home, please leave my name out of it - Amelia Louise McBride

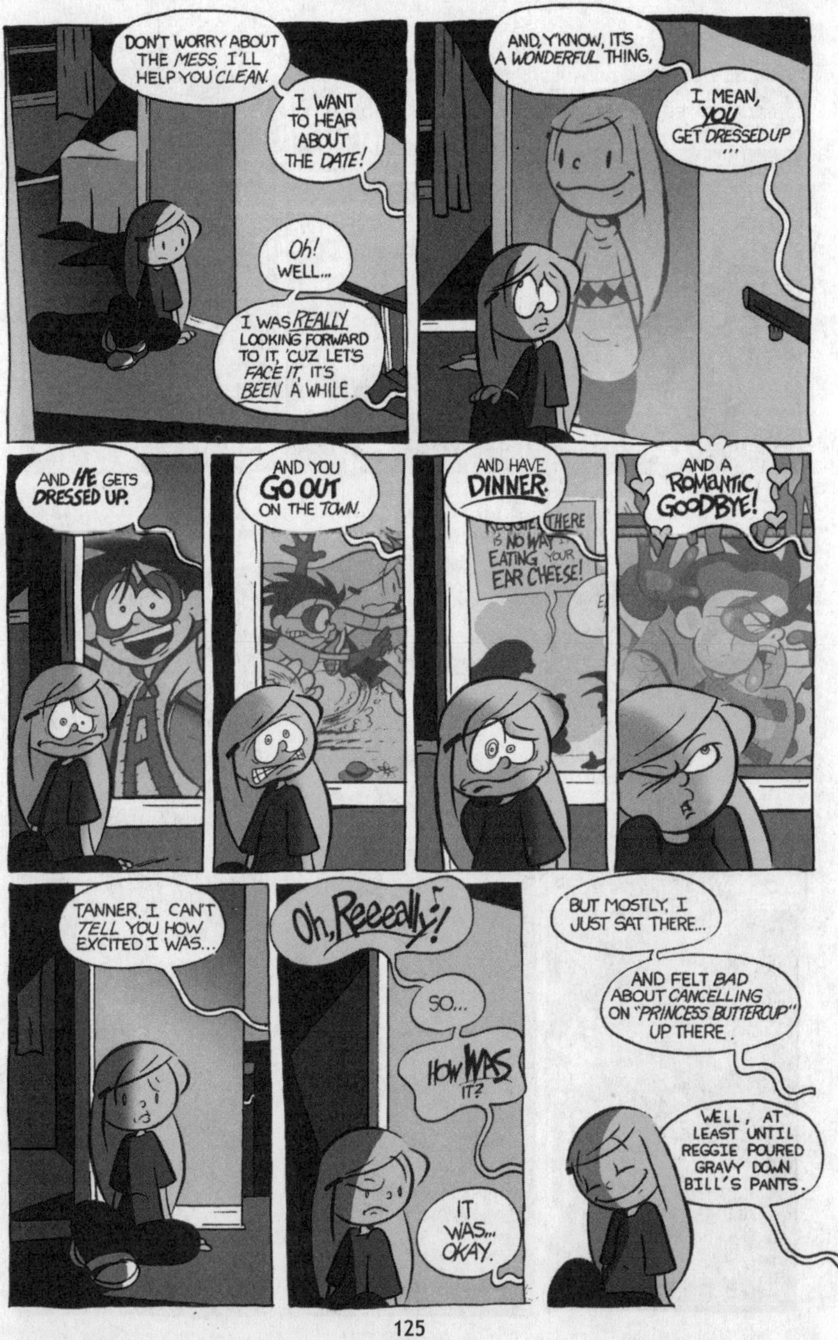
DON'T WORRY ABOUT THE MESS. I'LL HELP YOU CLEAN.
I WANT TO HEAR ABOUT THE DATE!
Oh! WELL...
I WAS REALLY LOOKING FORWARD TO IT, 'CUZ LET'S FACE IT, IT'S BEEN A WHILE.
AND, Y'KNOW, IT'S A WONDERFUL THING,
I MEAN, YOU GET DRESSED UP ...
AND HE GETS DRESSED UP.
AND YOU GO OUT ON THE TOWN.
AND HAVE DINNER.
REGGIE! THERE IS NO WAY I'M EATING YOUR EAR CHEESE!
AND A ROMANTIC GOODBYE!
TANNER, I CAN'T TELL YOU HOW EXCITED I WAS...
Oh, Reeeally!
SO...
HOW WAS IT?
IT WAS... OKAY.
BUT MOSTLY, I JUST SAT THERE...
AND FELT BAD ABOUT CANCELLING ON "PRINCESS BUTTERCUP" UP THERE.
WELL, AT LEAST UNTIL REGGIE POURED GRAVY DOWN BILL'S PANTS.

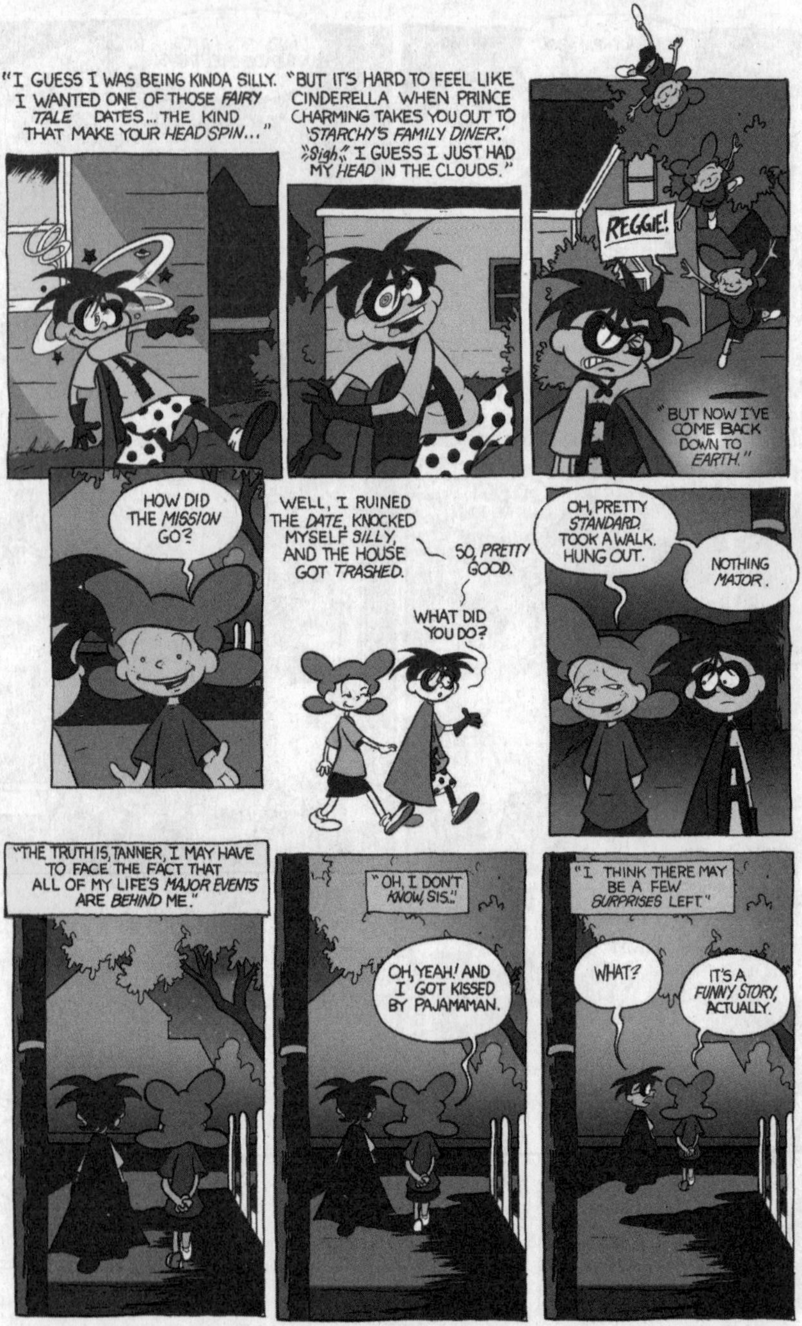
"I GUESS I WAS BEING KINDA SILLY. I WANTED ONE OF THOSE FAIRY TALE DATES... THE KIND THAT MAKE YOUR HEAD SPIN..."
"BUT IT'S HARD TO FEEL LIKE CINDERELLA WHEN PRINCE CHARMING TAKES YOU OUT TO 'STARCHY'S FAMILY DINER.' "Sigh" I GUESS I JUST HAD MY HEAD IN THE CLOUDS."
REGGIE!
"BUT NOW I'VE COME BACK DOWN TO EARTH."
HOW DID THE MISSION GO?
WELL, I RUINED THE DATE, KNOCKED MYSELF SILLY, AND THE HOUSE GOT TRASHED.
SO, PRETTY GOOD.
WHAT DID YOU DO?
OH, PRETTY STANDARD. TOOK A WALK. HUNG OUT.
NOTHING MAJOR.
"THE TRUTH IS, TANNER, I MAY HAVE TO FACE THE FACT THAT ALL OF MY LIFE'S MAJOR EVENTS ARE BEHIND ME."
"OH, I DON'T KNOW, SIS..."
OH, YEAH! AND I GOT KISSED BY PAJAMAMAN.
"I THINK THERE MAY BE A FEW SURPRISES LEFT."
WHAT?
IT'S A FUNNY STORY, ACTUALLY.

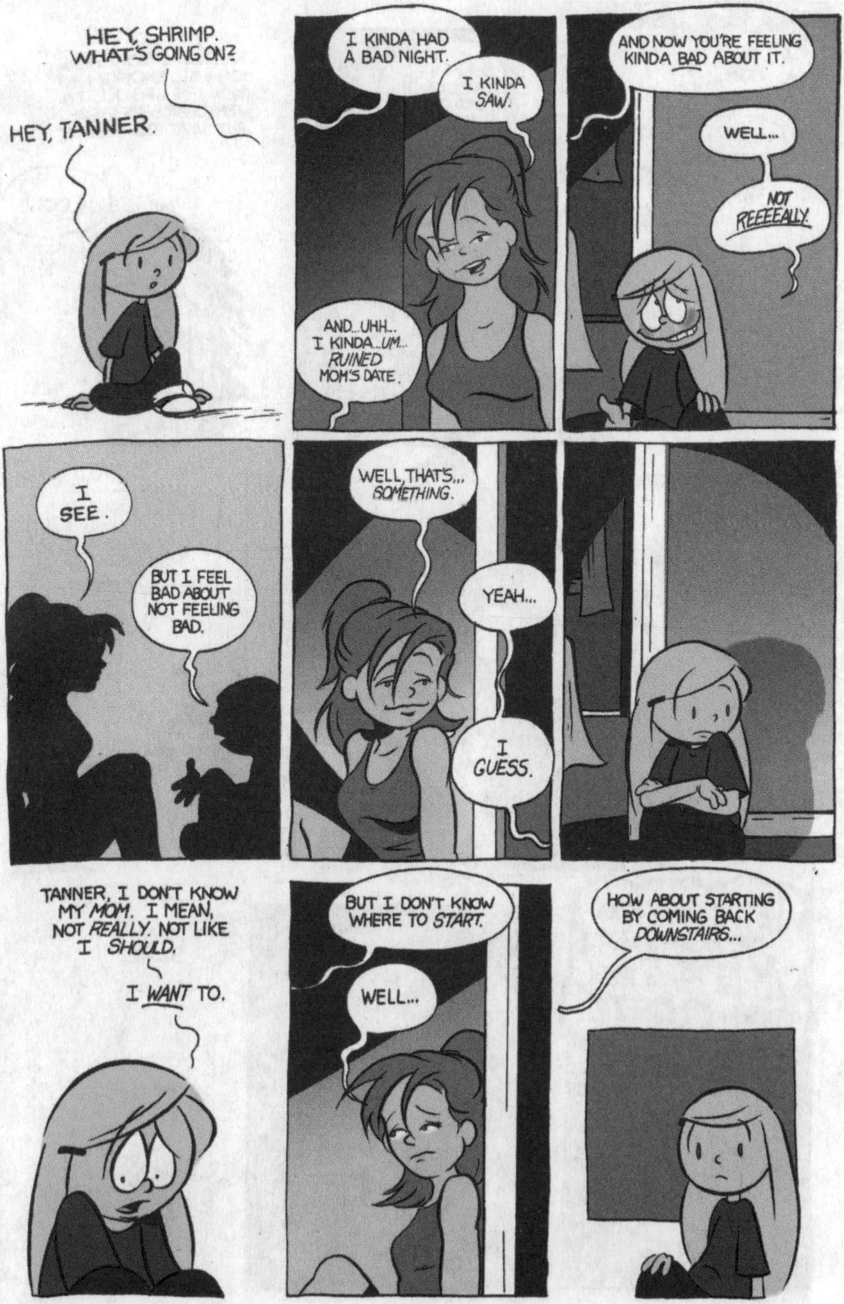
HEY, SHRIMP. WHAT'S GOING ON?
HEY, TANNER.
I KINDA HAD A BAD NIGHT.
I KINDA SAW.
AND...UHH.. I KINDA...UM... RUINED MOM'S DATE.
AND NOW YOU'RE FEELING KINDA BAD ABOUT IT.
WELL...
NOT REEEEALLY.
I SEE.
BUT I FEEL BAD ABOUT NOT FEELING BAD.
WELL, THAT'S... SOMETHING.
YEAH...
I GUESS.
TANNER, I DON'T KNOW MY MOM. I MEAN, NOT REALLY. NOT LIKE I SHOULD.
I WANT TO.
BUT I DON'T KNOW WHERE TO START.
WELL...
HOW ABOUT STARTING BY COMING BACK DOWNSTAIRS...

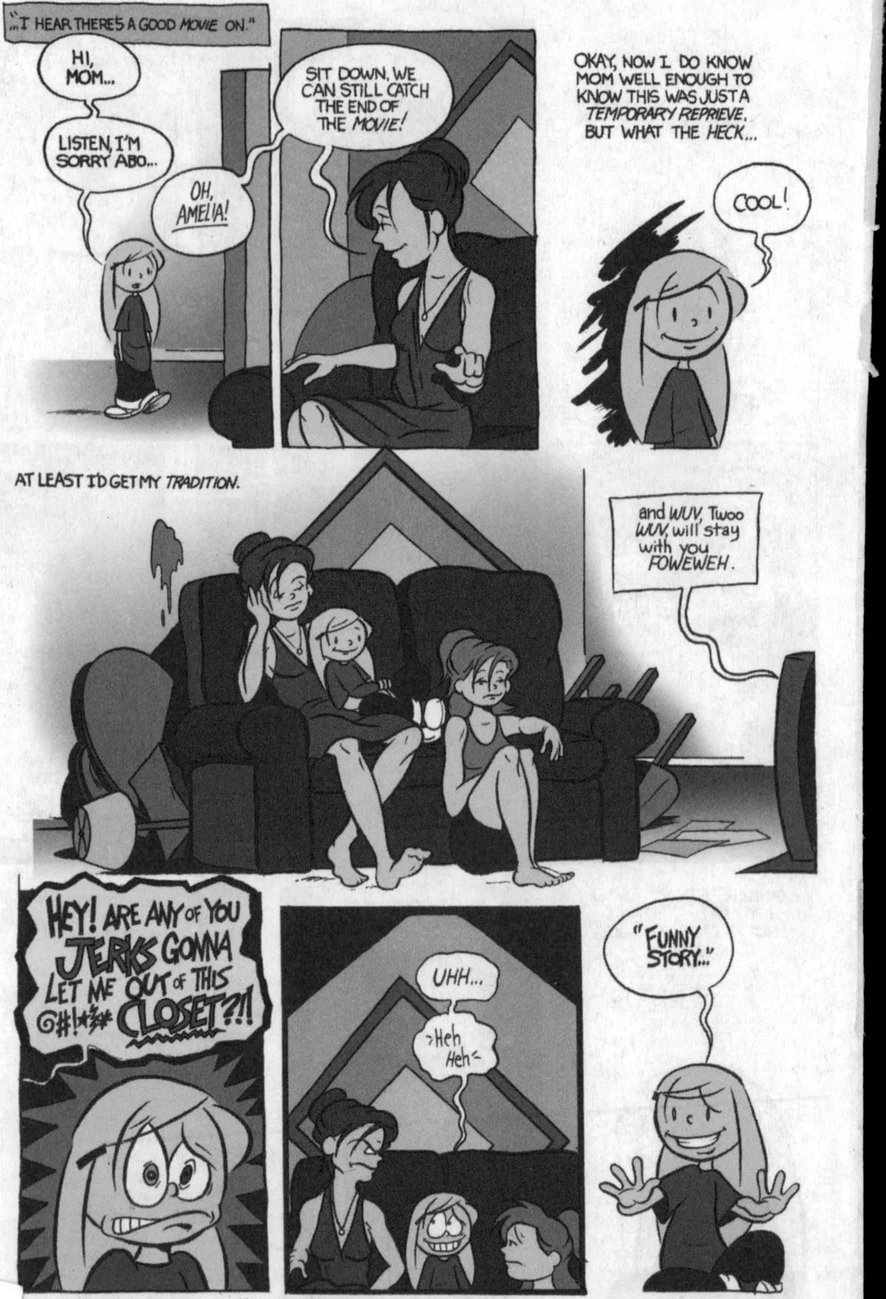
"...I HEAR THERE'S A GOOD MOVIE ON."
HI, MOM...
LISTEN, I'M SORRY ABO...
OH, AMELIA!
SIT DOWN, WE CAN STILL CATCH THE END OF THE MOVIE!
OKAY, NOW I DO KNOW MOM WELL ENOUGH TO KNOW THIS WAS JUST A TEMPORARY REPRIEVE, BUT WHAT THE HECK...
COOL!
AT LEAST I'D GET MY TRADITION.
and WUV, Twoo WUV, will stay with you FOWEWEH.
HEY! ARE ANY OF YOU JERKS GONNA LET ME OUT OF THIS @#!*%* CLOSET?!!
UHH...
Heh Heh
"FUNNY STORY..."